Surviving Object-Oriented Projects

The Agile Software Development Series

Alistair Cockburn and Jim Highsmith, Series Editors
For more information check out http://www.aw.com/cseng/

Agile software development centers on four values identified in the
Agile Alliance's Manifesto:

- Individuals and interactions over processes and tools
- Working software over comprehensive documentation
- Customer collaboration over contract negotiation
- Responding to change over following a plan

The development of Agile software requires innovation and responsiveness, based on generating and sharing knowledge within a development team and with the customer. Agile software developers draw on the strengths of customers, users, and developers, finding just enough process to balance quality and agility.

The books in **The Agile Software Development Series** focus on sharing the experiences of such Agile developers. Individual books address individual techniques (such as Use Cases), group techniques (such as collaborative decision making), and proven solutions to different problems from a variety of organizational cultures. The result is a core of Agile best practices that will enrich your experience and improve your work.

Titles in the Series:

Alistair Cockburn, *Surviving Object-Oriented Projects*, ISBN 0-201-49834-0

Alistair Cockburn, *Writing Effective Use Cases*, ISBN 0-201-70225-8

Lars Mathiassen, Jan Pries-Heje, and Ojelanki Ngwenyama, *Improving Software Organizations: From Principles to Practice*, ISBN 0-201-75820-2

Alistair Cockburn, *Agile Software Development*, ISBN 0-201-69969-9

Surviving Object-Oriented Projects

Alistair Cockburn

ADDISON–WESLEY

Boston • San Francisco • New York • Toronto • Montreal
London • Munich • Paris • Madrid
Capetown • Sydney • Tokyo • Singapore • Mexico City

Many of the designations used by manufacturers and sellers to distinguish their products are claimed as trademarks. Where those designations appear in this book, and we were aware of a trademark claim, the designations have been printed in initial capital letters or in all capitals.

The author and publisher have taken care in the preparation of this book, but make no expressed or implied warranty of any kind and assume no responsibility for errors or omissions. No liability is assumed for incidental or consequential damages in connection with or arising out of the use of the information or programs contained herein.

The publisher offers discounts on this book when ordered in quantity for special sales. For more information, please contact:

Pearson Education Corporate Sales Division
201 W. 103rd Street
Indianapolis, IN 46290
(800) 428-5331
corpsales@pearsoned.com

Visit AW on the Web: www.awl.com/cseng/

Library of Congress Cataloging-in-Publication Data
Cockburn, Alistair.
    Surviving object-oriented projects : a manager's guide / Alistair
Cockburn.
        p.   cm. – (The Addison-Wesley object technology series)
        Includes bibliographical references and index.
        ISBN 0-201-49834-0
        1. Object-oriented methods (Computer science)   2. Computer
software—Development.   I. Title   II. Series.
QA76.9.035C63   1997
        005.1'17'068--dc21   97-31805
                                                                              CIP

Executive Editor: J. Carter Shanklin
Editorial Assistant: Rachael Beavers
Project Manager: Sarah Weaver
Production Coordinator: Marilyn E. Rash
Set in Clearface and Frutiger by Octal Publishing, Inc.

Text printed on recycled and acid-free paper.

ISBN 0201498340

7 8 9 101112 MA   04 03 02 01

7th Printing   October 2001

Contents

Chapter 5 *109*

Making Corrections

Chapter 6   *153*

Advice From Hindsight

Chapter 7   *165*

Expand to Larger Projects

Foreword

Object technology is new, powerful, intriguing, and frankly, sometimes daunting. Even if trade rags shout of object ubiquity, your programmers clamor for cool object tools, and your old ways of doing things seem stale, it still is a big, big decision. Whether objects are right for your organization and project hinges on a gritty assessment of your ability to use objects and whether introducing object technology solves more problems than it creates.

One question on the minds of veteran managers is whether their prior experience rolls over to this new object development territory. Indeed, managing objects isn't all new stuff. Object management means managing people and processes, taking measured risks, and recovering from unexpected problems. To successfully employ objects, you need a clear understanding of your people, their capabilities, their roles, your development process, and the type of project you are undertaking. It also means taking seriously this business of incremental and, most likely, iterative development. The way to acquire new skills is through practice, practice, and even more practice. A one-shot development cycle doesn't give you time to recover from your mistakes.

Alistair Cockburn sheds light on incremental and iterative development processes that would benefit any development project regardless of its technology base. But object technology, which Alistair points out as being primarily a packaging technology, comes ready equipped with tools that help build neat packages—encapsulation of data and function in objects, and reuse through composition and class inheritance.

In this book, Alistair tackles the subject of managing, staffing, and building a learning organization. In so doing, he doesn't pander to object hype. He doesn't pull any punches—he is not a fan of textbook methodologies that ignore process, upper-CASE tools that perpetually show promise but don't deliver, or overly complex languages or solutions. In fact, while letting the air out of the object-hyped balloon, he does an admirable job of stating where objects work well, and more important, how to do so without having to take an all-or-nothing plunge.

I wish you many successes on your development path, and hope you not only survive but also thrive as you embark on your journey.

Rebecca J. Wirfs-Brock
October 1997

Preface

If you are thinking of starting, or have already started, an object-oriented (OO) project, and want to know what you are up against, this book will be of use to you. Organizations that have successfully made the transition to object technology claim significant time-to-market reduction. Developers say object orientation is a fun way to develop software.

There is no shortage of literature on the subject; however, the press has made so much of object technology that it is hard to sort out exaggerations and selective reporting from the actual experience one can expect. Speakers rarely seem to want to name the actual costs of making the move to objects, perhaps to avoid scaring away future newcomers.

There is, therefore, a lack of information on what sorts of unpleasant surprises await one when starting an OO project, and what to do about them. It is this lack of information that *Surviving Object-Oriented Projects: A Manager's Guide* addresses.

SCOPE

This book covers issues I have found in several dozen organizations that are doing object-oriented projects. From failed efforts, we learned specific difficulties; from successful projects, we learned how to get around the difficulties.

The early reviewers of this book unanimously said that it takes several projects to apply the lessons. They said that people on their first OO project are not sufficiently aware of the issues to detect them, are not yet open to suggestions, and cannot set aside old habits and thinking patterns. It is my hope that you can prove them wrong, that you will succeed on your first, or your second, project by paying attention to the lessons from other people's experiences.

This book is not a primer on object technology, nor is it a primer on object-oriented design techniques or of macro- or micromanagement. It is not a technical review of the literature, nor a cataloging of project types. It addresses the numerous, specific topics for which an answer cannot easily be found in the literature, or the obvious answer does not work.

The information in this book is based on personal project experiences—my own, those of people I have interviewed, and interviews I have read. Since writing the early version, I have had the chance to see these ideas applied to development of many kinds of systems, from non-object-oriented systems involving mainframes, COBOL and assembler, to client/server and web-based systems.

In this book, I identify topics, point out hazards, and name a workable strategy taken from a project that successfully cleared the hazard. The hazards and strategies are collected at the back of the book in Appendix B, Crib Sheets.

For readers interested in an introductory companion to this book, I recommend David Taylor's *Object Technology: A Manager's Guide, Second Edition* (Reading, MA: Addison Wesley, 1998). For extended investigation, I suggest Steve McConnell's *Rapid Application Development* (Microsoft Press, 1996).

AUDIENCE

Surviving Object-Oriented Projects: A Manager's Guide is intended for the busy professional. Here is a reading strategy for four types of possible readers:

1. *The executive scanning for impact to the organization.* Read the Preface and the first two chapters. These take you through concepts, project histories, expectations, and costs. If you are interested in the next level of depth, skim the setup issues involving project selection and staffing, and the chapters on large projects. At that point, you may wish to give the book to the project manager.

2. *The manager before starting on a project.* Read Chapters 1, 2, 3, and 5 of the book. These cover expectations, project setup, and incremental and iterative development. Then look through the list of strat-

egies (Appendix A) and hazards (in Appendix B) at the back of the book to get a sense of the total set of issues.

3. *The manager on a project.* The primary audience for this book is the manager, working with the technical lead, on a project. Some issues are technical enough to require terms of object technology. You, the project manager, may find that the technical lead will bring these problems to your attention or will help you work through them.

   Skim the entire book to get the nature and location of topics. When working on the project, look up particular topics as they occur. The chapters are organized in roughly the order topics usually show up and need to be dealt with. Reread Chapter 5 about making corrections before each increment.

4. *The project's technical leader.* Use the book to help your manager understand certain issues, such as organizing teams, developing iteratively, and resisting unproductive tools and activities. I have added technical depth in a few areas where a project hazard lurks and there is no simpler way to carry through on the discussion.

   Among these are: simplistic modeling of the business (sometimes passing under the name of "analysis"), overstaffing at the beginning of a project, and false productivity measures. For some issues, it is up to you, the technical leader, to work with the arguments in the book to convince other developers and the management team to adopt a sensible direction.

I have included an extended section on C++ because it is my carefully considered opinion that C++ represents an additional hazard to the survival of a project. If you favor using C++, read through this section and deal with the issues to ensure your project's success.

ORGANIZATION

The book has eight chapters and two appendices, roughly matching the chronology of encounter with the issues.

- Chapter 1 summarizes and introduces sucess and failure factors, and defines terms you will have to become familiar with.
- Chapter 2 is a reality check. What expectations do you have about object technology, and how should you adjust those expectations? The chapter contains stories about a dozen projects, which are referred to throughout the book.

- Chapter 3 deals with selecting and setting up a project. This is the best place to work on survival, even if survival means walking away from the project. It covers all the standard issues of staffing, training, tool selection, methodology, legacy systems, and the like.

- Chapter 4 covers some basic issues you will encounter when running the project: methodology, estimates, plans, milestones, measurements—and design.

- Chapter 5 deals with the inevitable corrections you will have to make. I start by citing my favorite project, which started dismally and then was turned around. From this project, we can learn a great deal about fine-tuning. You will have much tuning to do; do not feel bad about making changes during a project.

- Chapter 6 is written as a reflection on the first five chapters. You can pretend that you have just finished your project and are giving advice to another person who is about to start a project. What would you highlight for him or her? Here is where you can get hindsight in advance.

- Chapter 7 addresses organizations that have safely made it to the point (or declared themselves at the point) of committing large numbers of their staff to using object technology. There are new costs and new dangers lying in wait for those who move on to larger projects.

- Chapter 8 is another reality check in which I compare the contents of the book to a real project. It opens the topic of organizational culture in overall software success.

- Appendix A is a collection of 12 success strategies presented in a medical diagnosis metaphor.

- Appendix B is a summary—a "crib sheet"—to copy and tape to the wall as your daily reminder about the basics of an object-oriented project. A condensed version is printed on a card at the back of the book.

Throughout the book, the topics cross-reference each other extensively. To keep the reading uncluttered, the links to other pages are noted in the margin with a page number, as shown here.

chapter 1, 1

Your project's survival depends on developing your insights and reflexes. To help you develop them, I use material taken primarily from first- and second-hand experiences, my own and those of the many people I have interviewed. I devote space to a few published papers, which were carefully done and provide insights. They are noted in footnotes or in further reading sections in some of the chapters.

PLACE IN THE CRYSTAL *BOOK COLLECTION*

The *Crystal* collection highlights lightweight, human-powered development of software. Crystal works from two basic principles:

◆ Software development is a cooperative game of group invention and communication. Software development improves as we improve people's personal skills and improve the team's collaboration effectiveness.
◆ Different projects have different needs. Systems have different characteristics, and are built by teams of differing sizes, containing people having differing values and priorities. It cannot be possible to describe the one, best way of producing software.

The foundation book for the collection is *Software Development as Cooperative Game*. It works out the ideas of software development as a cooperative game, of methodology as a coordination culture, and of methodology families (categorized in colors: clear, yellow, orange, red, and so on). It separates different aspects of methodologies: roles, techniques, activities, work products, standards, and so on.

Some books discuss a single technique or role on the project, and some discuss team issues. *Surviving Object-Oriented Projects* is one of the latter. It presents some of the projects that helped me see the primacy of people in developing software, and includes ideas for working with people on a team. It contains a brief description of a *Crystal/Orange* methodology, aimed at IT projects of 25-50 people. It goes through the issues that affect many projects, issues ranging from selection of technology to staffing to scheduling strategies. As with all the *Crystal* collection, this book is self-contained in the topics it addresses.

Acknowledgments

I thank the nontechnical people around me: Kieran, Sean, Cameron, Deanna. I now know why so many authors thank their families. Thanks also to the people at Beans & Brew, who provided good coffee, a good atmosphere, and good conversation.

As Plato said:

> Only if the various principles—names, definitions, intimations and perceptions—are laboriously tested and rubbed one against the other in a reconciliatory tone, without ill will during the discussion, only then will insight and reason radiate forth in each case, and achieve what is for man the highest possible force. . . .

This book received much benefit from the testing of principles and the "rubbing together" of ideas in conciliatory tone and without ill will. For that I thank the following individuals:

- ◆ Bruce Anderson, IBM Object Technology Practice
- ◆ Carol Burt, President, 2AB, Inc.
- ◆ Dave Collins, Outback Software, Ltd.
- ◆ Anton Eliens, Vrije Universiteit (Amsterdam)
- ◆ Adele Goldberg, Neometron
- ◆ David Gotterbarn, East Tennessee State University

---

[1]From Plato's 7th letter, cited in translation from Göranzon, B., Florin, M., *Dialogue and Technology: Art and Knowledge*, p. 46 (London: Springer-Verlag), 1991.

- Brian Henderson-Sellers, Swinburne University of Technology
- Jeremy Raw, Independent Consultant (Durham, NC)
- Arthur J. Riel, Vangaurd Training, Inc.
- Cecilia Shuster, Independent Consultant
- Dave Thomas, IBM (formerly of OTI)
- Daniel Tkach, IBM Consulting Group
- Rebecca Wirfs-Brock, Wirfs-Brock Associates
- The editors at Addison-Wesley

for helping to improve the book. I am indebted to Sam Adams for the terms *big-M* and *little-m* methodology, and to Dick Antalek and Wayne Stevens who taught me the most about big-M methodologies. Marilyn Rash at Addison Wesley Longman helped save my sanity during the production of this book.

I also want to thank the authors of the Eyewitness Accounts for taking time to contribute their knowledge about object-oriented projects:

- Jim Coplien, Bell Labs
- Ward Cunningham, Cunningham & Cunningham
- C.D., Independent Consultant
- Harvie S. (Sam) Griffith, Jr., President, Object Methods Software
- Luke Hohmann, SmartPatents
- Glenn House, formerly of Mentor Graphics
- K.L., Independent Consultant
- Jon Marshall, ParcPlace-Digitalk
- Tom Morgan, Brooklyn Union Gas
- Jeremy Raw, Independent Consultant

K.L. and C.D. asked that I not use their names, in order not to discomfit any companies.

All these people were kind enough to contribute their experience to this book. They may not agree with everything I write, but we all share the wish to help you succeed on your project.

Figure List

Chapter 1

Success and Failure

From success you can learn how to succeed.

Object orientation (OO) is a technology and a mind-set: a technology of software packaging and a mind-set for thinking about programming. The following points affect you:

1. It is a technology *new* to your organization. Many of the survival issues have nothing to do with object technology, but come simply from introducing a new technology.
2. Its practitioners expect to *use* modern software development techniques. Iterative development, user-based requirements, and organization for reuse will be brought forward during this project. Although object technology does not depend on them, OO practitioners put them up as primary issues.
3. It *requires* as well as *enables* increased communication between groups.

The two goals of object technology are *minimizing* the impact of changes and *creating* a sound model of a business. The consequence of the first is increased communication needs within the development team. The benefit of the second is an increased ability of the development team to communicate with users and executives. The two forces call for a different kind of software developer, one comfortable with abstractions, uncertainty, and communication. This change in the developer's personality profile creates a new force on the project.

It is only fair that I state my bias. I have practiced and researched object technology since 1980. I consider it an improvement in software technology; better in some ways though not in all. It is also fun! Still, I require that it "pay its own way" with increased software robustness and developer productivity. I do not hesitate to criticize the technology in places where it gives one difficulty.

Object orientation offers the following attractions: encapsulation of design decisions, reducing the damage of requirement changes; improved communication between the programmers and the users or business executives, resulting in more effective application structure and improved developer morale; additional emphasis on and mechanisms for reuse, a diabolically difficult topic.

These benefits come with a cost, the greatest of which is training. Experience indicates that new OO programmers may take nine months to fully earn their salary again. Multiply that by the hundreds or thousands of programmers that some companies will have to train, and the cost is staggering. Some executives will look at this cost and immediately say, "Not acceptable." Seeing the costs and not the benefits, they decide to wait until the object wave has passed. This book is not for them. They will read it and (rightly) claim, "I told you it was expensive and hazard-prone." Others will decide to launch a pilot project and watch what happens. Still others will rewrite a terminally ill legacy application. A final group will bet their companies on it.

If you are going to run a pilot project, make sure it is big enough to be significant, and then try to gain some useful information from it. If you are rewriting a significant application, you need the project to survive to completion, as quickly as possible, with your staff getting trained en route. If you are going to bet your company on object technology, you need to know what to expect, and to get some ideas for dealing with the training.

Here, then, are four critical success factors—four "simple" steps for creating a surviving, even thriving, project:

1. Use incremental scheduling and staging.
2. Find and fix failing ideas.
3. Develop a habit of delivering.
4. Develop a good sponsor, project manager, and technical leader.

Simple does not mean easy. Simple often implies difficult, because simple things must be repeated daily or may require changing your work habits, which is the most difficult thing to do. The book reiterates these four key success factors throughout.

I have also identified the following two key failure indicators:

1. The absence of incremental development.
2. The use of C++ in a commercial information systems (IS) department.

For the absence of incremental development, the argument is simple. If your project plan does not include a place to recover from an initial error, you are unlikely to recover. Most of the projects I have visited have made mistakes, and the key to success was to have a way to recover from them.

Chapter 3 on selecting technology includes C++, Smalltalk, Java, and OO COBOL. Although each presents a hazard due to various misconceptions, C++ has been the cause of enough troubles that it merits extra attention. Even C++ experts agree that one should take certain precautions. The chapter also provides additional information, which has been checked by specialized consultants, where C++ is concerned.

managing C++, 53

At this juncture, I offer a metaphor for having a project survive, even thrive. It is based upon an old Japanese story about three physician brothers. The youngest brother, a court physician, was widely renowned, but he deprecated his fame, saying, "I am by far the worst of the three physicians, for I am forced to wait until the sickness is visible, and then must resort to puncturing veins and spreading salves. My older brother is better, for he can detect sickness at onset and make minute changes that keep it from developing. My eldest brother is best, for he sees the spirit of sickness and removes it before it takes shape. He acts so early that he is not even known as a physician."

In the spirit of this metaphor, I distinguish the interventions needed for a project. Adequate interventions are done in time to solve the problem. Better interventions are early and small, when the "spirit of sickness" appears. The best are acute, advanced observations fed into a balanced risk-reduction program, thus not looking at all like interventions. But these present a difficulty to the external observer and chronicler, for the best-run projects show the least outward signs of course corrections; everything looks easy. Therefore, I have selected as a study project one that went wrong at the beginning, and then was put right. The lessons for us all are how the project was put right again (Chapter 5).

a study project, 109

Success is better than failure. Although you can learn some lessons from failure, from success you learn how to succeed. I wish you success and the learning that comes from it.

BASIC CONCEPTS

Although this book is not a primer on object technology, we need some common definitions of its vocabulary. The following are the main terms you should become familiar with: object technology in general, class, object, inheritance, encapsulation, polymorphism, framework, and incremental and iterative development. I illustrate them through a simple example of a salary system:

> Kim, Pat, and Chris are employees.
>
> Kim works part-time, paid on an hourly basis.
>
> Pat is full-time, paid on an hourly basis.
>
> Chris is full-time, paid on a salaried basis.

Object Technology

Object technology is fundamentally a technology of program packaging. It gives the designer a new set of packages from which to work: data-only, data-and-function, or function-only packages, in a full continuum. The new packaging lets designers build models containing both the data and the functions associated with the things modeled. Giving the data behavior allows designers to work as though the software packages are actually the items modeled. They can re-create the problem domain's structure and put that structure directly onto the computer. This is good news. The packaging also lets designers put those software elements that are likely to change together. This reduces the cost and trajectory of changes. That is the best news.

If program packaging is what is fundamentally different, then only the program packaging aspects of project management should fundamentally change. This is what I find on projects and what you will see in this book. Object technology changes project management much less than it changes the thinking of the designers and the maintainability of the software, all of which is good news to you, the project manager.

User involvement, incremental and iterative development, risk reduction, and reuse are not fundamental elements of object technology; you should already be doing those. It just happens that OO people insist on them. Those topics are in this book because they still are not widely practiced and they affect your project's success.

Class

A *class* is the collection of subroutines packaged together, along with a description of the data included with them. It is a description of a certain class of objects from which individual instances may be created. This combination of subroutines and data provides the continuum just referred to and is the first of the packaging improvements of object technology. In the `salary` example, there might be a class called `Hourly-Employee`, which would define that the rate of pay and the hours worked need to be tracked separately for each employee. In other words, each `HourlyEmployee` instance has two data slots, one for `rateOfPay` and one for `hoursWorked`. The class would contain the functions needed to compute the wages based on the hours worked and rate of pay. A common way of drawing such a class is shown in Figure 1-1, with the class name on top, the data slots next, and the function last.

Object

Officially, *object* means an instance of a class, but it is often also used to mean the class description itself. Thus, you might hear designers talk at one moment of the "object model," meaning the class descriptions, then at the next moment of an "account object," meaning an instance of the `Account` class. The context usually makes their intentions clear. When it becomes important to separate the two, they do so. I follow that convention in this book to familiarize you with the terms as they probably will be used on a project. A common way of drawing an object instance is as a donut (see Figure 1-2), with the functions on the outside, protecting the data on the inside. Different modeling languages use various ways of drawing object instances. On your project you will use whichever drawing style is given by the modeling language you select.

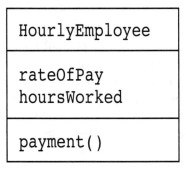

Figure 1-1 *Sample diagram of a class*

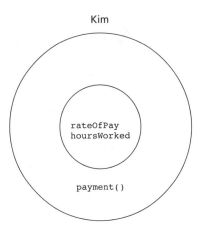

Figure 1-2 *Sample diagram of an object instance*

Inheritance

Inheritance is a programming mechanism that lets the common part of selected classes be shared. The common part is made a class in its own right, and is called a *superclass* of the selected classes. Each selected class is called a *subclass* of the superclass. The selected class is linked to the superclass to indicate that the superclass is really part of the selected class's definition. Selecting common parts to put into a superclass is one of the key decisions in creating a robust OO system and thus is not a trivial decision.

Inheritance is the second packaging advance in object technology, after classes. It allows a programmer to extend an existing program just by adding a new subclass, taking advantage of all the thought and labor that went into the superclass. It allows the designer to program *just the differences* between two systems.

Figures 1-3 and 1-4 show three possible ways to organize the classes in the `salary` example, using the Unified Modeling Language (UML) notation. None of the three designs is "right" or "wrong"; they work well under different circumstances. In any real system, every box will be filled with the data and functions that make each employee type different, differences that I omit for this little example. Each superclass defines some information for its subclasses, and the subclasses therefore do not repeat that information. That is what I mean by programming just the differences.

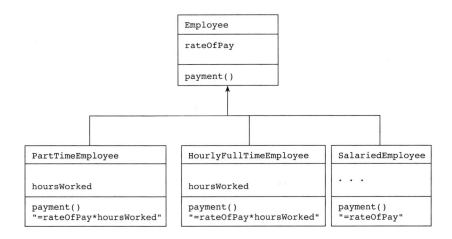

Figure 1-3 *One possible way to organize the* `salary` *example classes*

Encapsulation

Encapsulation refers to putting program elements related to one topic in one place, and creating a set of functions to access and operate on that topic. Although encapsulation can be accomplished without object technology, it is one of OO's essential characteristics. The most powerful thing you can encapsulate is a *design decision*. Encapsulating a design decision means putting the data and functions related to that decision into one place, thereby creating a set of functions to access and operate on that topic. A perfect example of encapsulation and its value is given in Tom Morgan's Eyewitness Account in Chapter 2.

Tom Morgan's EWA, 28

In the three possible inheritance structures for the `salary` example, each class and superclass is designed to hold—that is, encapsulate—all the critical information pertaining to that topic. Thus, the Employee class should hold whatever information, decisions, data, and functions that are common to all employees, no matter what their payment structure. The assumptions are that all employees have a `rateOfPay` and get paid. The designers will select between the three designs based on what best fits the encapsulation needed on the project. If they predict heavy use of the notion of `HourlyEmployee`, then that class is a good one to create. Future changes to the way hourly employees are treated can all be handled by modifying just this one class, which is the smallest trajectory of change possible.

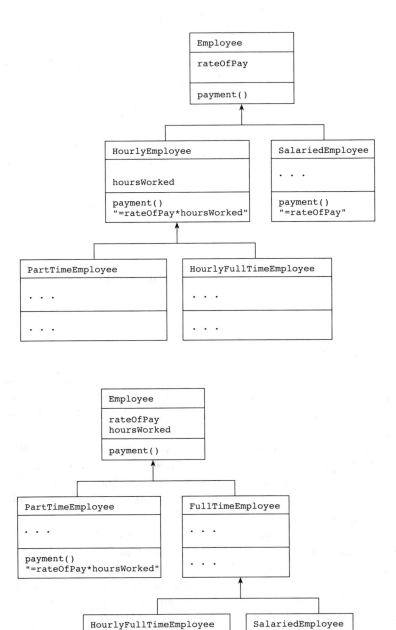

Figure 1-4 *Two other valid ways to organize the* salary *example classes*

Polymorphism

Polymorphism refers to the ability of a function name to provide different detailed behavior depending on the particular type of object being held at that moment. In the `salary` example, the function `payment( )` is polymorphic: The calculation of the payment is different for each class even though the intention is the same. Whether you ask for Kim's payment, Chris's payment, or Pat's payment, you mean the same thing even though the rules of calculation differ. Although we do not use that term, polymorphism is common in spoken language. We say "answer the phone," "answer the door," "answer the letter," and "answer the question." We are not at all confused that answering the door is a different activity from answering a phone, letter, or question—a common intention links them.

In programming, polymorphism allows continual extension of the design. As new classes are added, they might add a new behavior to an existing function name. If done well, this is another way of programming only the difference. Polymorphism always adds to the testing effort, because every new polymorphic function must be tested against all previous uses of that name.

Framework

A *framework* is a collection of objects, classes, or subsystems that provides most or all of a needed function and can be tailored to different situations. A framework is designed so that selected situations are particularly easy to address.

An OO framework takes advantage of classes, inheritance, and polymorphism. The trick in designing a framework is to guess which new situations should be most easily supported. For different proposed future needs, different classes and superclasses are best. It is the guesswork about the future needs that makes framework design difficult, costly, and revision-prone. However, once a suitable framework is available, development costs drop dramatically, since only a simple tailoring activity is needed. Because a system's architecture relies on numerous frameworks, designing frameworks for other developers' use is a primary activity of the lead designers.

In Chapter 2, which discusses benefits, I mention responsiveness to evolutionary changes as the greatest benefit of object technology. This responsiveness is directly due to classes, inheritance, polymorphism, and framework design.

responsiveness to change, 23

Incremental and Iterative Development

Incremental and iterative development are two distinct scheduling and staging strategies. Both involve doing analysis and design more than once during the project, and possibly gathering requirements more than once. *Incremental* development involves completing parts of the system at different times and at different rates; it does not imply revising any part of the system already completed. The aim is to improve the quality of the process by fixing errors in knowledge about the software development process.

Iterative development involves reworking a part of the system to improve the quality of the system. The user interface and the infrastructure of a system are two parts of software systems that benefit the most from the improvement. The user interface is improved to better serve the users, and the infrastructure is improved to simplify the evolution of the system.

Incremental development is easier to adopt than iterative development, and more crucial to the success of the project; it is easier to use because the schedule can be thought out in advance and linearized. Iterative development requires initial guesswork, constant observation, and flexibility in execution; I suggest that you use incremental development, and in the increments learn how to manage iterative development (see Chapter 5).

increments and iterations, 117

Chapter 2

Project Expectations

Plan to survive or bail out early.

Are you investigating object technology because your maintenance costs are too high? Do your competitors claim to be getting benefits from objects? Do you have a program development backlog? Has your boss just ordered you to start using objects? Whatever the reason, you know that the move to OO will cost you.

What are you willing to pay? What do you expect to get back? When do you expect to realize a payback? This chapter addresses what you could be looking for, what you should really expect to receive, what you probably should expect to pay, and what you may be overlooking.

PROJECT HISTORIES

This section summarizes 11 projects; I was able to interview each project leader, and gathered project data and reflections on what went wrong and what went right. Each summary offers an insight into a failure or a strategy for success. I have seen these issues repeated on other projects. For discretion and because some information is proprietary, I name only Object Technology International, Brooklyn Union Gas, and Mentor Graphics; the other projects have been given nicknames to make them easier to refer to throughout this book.

Each project story starts with a project profile card, indicating the project name or nickname, the key topic I associate with it, the size and experience of the staff, historic details about the evolution of the project, and some additional comments based on an overall evaluation of the project.

Alfred: *Success with Changing Requirements*

Project	Project Alfred
Key topic	Project setup
Project staffing	Small (5–10)
Project type	Investigative
Staff experience	New to OO
Duration	Six months

Project Alfred was set up to take a look at object technology. It included one super-programmer from the internal staff, two regular developers, a user-interface developer, and a business expert with no programming experience. It was managed by an experienced project manager familiar with incremental and iterative development. The only person with any OO experience was a part-time OO expert, who acted as trainer and design guide.

The first increment was set for six months. The business model was built and programmed first, prior to any user interface; the user interface was attached at the end of the increment. Just prior to the completion of the six-month increment, the sponsoring executive told the design team that acceptance of the technology would depend on this test:

> There is a new requirement we have wanted to add for a long time, but have not because it will take four months and 10 people to make the software and the database changes. You will be given from Friday morning until Monday morning to make that addition.

Six people worked through the regular working hours on Friday. Four people worked until late afternoon on Saturday, at which time the addition was done, including changes to the database. The team showed it to the executive on Monday, demonstrating their ability to react to change.

The primary insight to draw from this project is the way the project executive set up a test bed for the technology, staffed it carefully, and then gave the technology a test. This is a good example of an investigative

project purpose, 36   project (see Chapter 3).

Brooklyn Union Gas: *Success Through Attentiveness*

Project	Brooklyn Union Gas
Key topic	Risk management
Project staffing	Large (100+ people)
Project type	Legacy rewrite
Staff experience	New to OO
Duration	Several years

In 1986, Brooklyn Union Gas (B.U.G.) was programming in PL/I using mainframes, IBM 3270 terminals, and a relational database. The company needed to rewrite its billing system. After evaluating structured development techniques, management concluded that it would take too long to finish the system using those techniques. They decided it would be worth the added risk to develop the system in the early years of the next-generation programming technology rather than in the waning years of the existing programming technology.

Not much was known about the long-term consequences of certain design decisions. They decided, in particular, that the inheritance hierarchy would be an area of risk, that they would not be able to change it easily once they put it onto their database. Therefore, B.U.G. designed the hierarchy for simplicity and stability rather than for maximum reuse. They selected and followed simple, conservative standards. For key risky and important areas, such as the OO dispatch mechanisms, they allowed for several revisions. Through these and other policies, they created an object-oriented dialect of PL/I, delivered the system, and demonstrated improved system evolution over time.

They demonstrated that object orientation could be managed on any platform, in any language. Having visited dozens of projects, I also feel it shows the quality of their management and development teams. This project contains numerous lessons for keeping any project alive:

- Thoughtful planning (see Chapter 4)
- Using increments and iterations (see Chapter 5)
- Using previous experience (see section later in this chapter)
- Setting and following simple standards (see Chapter 4)
- Using the best parts of previous methodology (see Chapter 4)

Tom Morgan's EWA, 28 Tom Morgan's Eyewitness Account appears later in this chapter; a more detailed report about the B.U.G. project was published in 1993.[1]

Ingrid: *Success in Migrating to C++*

Project	Project Ingrid
Key topic	Recovering from mistakes
Project staffing	Medium (20–40)
Project type	Production
Staff experience	Beginners
Duration	Two years

The managers who started Project Ingrid decided to use C++ for the wrong, but obvious, reasons that they wanted to use objects and had staff trained in C. The 25 programmers assigned to the project had no experience with OO programming. The company did not hire consultants or invest in training, believing that good programmers would be able to learn this new language on their own.

Recognizing the risk they were taking, the project manager led a successful campaign to deviate from the corporate-standard, waterfall-based scheduling and staging strategy. He obtained permission to use an incremental, not iterative, strategy, in which not even the requirements would be written all at one time, but only for the next segment of the project.

At the end of the first increment, the team was faced with a disaster. They were behind the schedule, the design was not good, and morale was down. At this point, the project managers replaced 24 of the 25 programmers, changed the management structure, introduced training, and then redid the first increment as part of the second increment. They delivered the first and second increments together, albeit behind the new schedule.

After additional process and management changes, the team instituted an internal self-tutoring process. By this time, they were comfortable and skilled with objects, and made their third and fourth increments without difficulty. The project manager said they were able to take increasing advantage of internal similarities, achieving internal reuse that allowed them to beat their scheduled delivery times.

---

[1]Davis, J., and Morgan, T., Object-oriented Development at Brooklyn Union Gas, *IEEE Software* (January 1993): 67–74.

I consider this to be the ideal study project because it illustrates the theme of this book. Project Ingrid started with some mistakes, but the team corrected them in time. The key insights to draw from this project are the team's willingness to change everything in order to succeed, and their use of increments to give them the breathing space they needed to make those changes.

a study project, 109

technology, 47

increments and iterations, 77

Manfred: *Failure in Prototyping*

Project	Project Manfred
Key topic	Iterations
Project staffing	Medium (10–20)
Project type	Production
Staff experience	New to OO
Duration	One year

Project Manfred was scheduled to use Smalltalk on a new and critical production system. It was staffed by experienced C programmers who had no experience with OO programming. As in Project Ingrid, they did not hire consultants or invest in training, assuming that good programmers would be able to learn this new language on their own. The team leaders decided that since Smalltalk had such a good development environment, their design method would be to build and revise prototypes. After the final prototype was accepted, they would reprogram the entire system in production-quality code.

When they put the first prototype out for evaluation, they were told it was far too slow. "That is all right," the programmers said. "It is just a prototype. Tell us what you want." The reply was, "We want it to run faster." The story was the same with the second and the third prototypes. By this time, higher-level management was getting nervous because it appeared that the team either was not taking feedback seriously or that Smalltalk would be too slow for the production system. The design team kept saying that it was OK for the prototype to be slow because it was not engineered for production.

Ultimately, however, the team was told to make the prototype run at production speed or the project would be canceled. They were able to make some performance improvements within the given timeframe, but not enough to meet the production-speed requirements. The project was canceled, at great cost.

The first of a trio of mistakes on this project was to confuse prototype and production software. It is a familiar syndrome ("The prototype looks good; when can we ship it?") to which I have not seen a successful counterstrategy other than not to build a nonproduction prototype. My suggestion is to call it a "requirements model," and to throw it away as soon as possible so that a production-quality version can be started.

take the time to design, 104

The second mistake was that the designers believed that prototypes could replace design (see Chapter 4 and K.L.'s Eyewitness Account). I have seen the same mistake made on a 200-person project as well as on 10-person and 1-person projects.

increments and iterations, 117

The third mistake I call "prototypitis," which is discussed in Chapter 5; it is made by not controlling the amount and degree of iterations.

Mentor Graphics: *Trouble Migrating to* C++

Project	Mentor Graphics
Key topic	Corporate conversion project
Project staffing	Large (about 600)
Project type	Production
Staff experience	New to OO
Duration	Several years

Mentor Graphics once dominated a segment of the computer-assisted design (CAD) marketplace. It was a seasoned and aggressive C programming shop. In the early 1990s, the management committed to converting the firm to a C++ shop with the release of version 8.0 of its software.

That release nearly sank the company. Delayed beyond a reasonable marketing time, it soon became clear that the hardware Mentor Graphics' customers were running on would have to be upgraded to run the new software. (Glenn House, formerly vice president at Mentor Graphics, was involved in release 8.0, and contributed the Eyewitness Account in Chapter 7 about the experience.)

Glenn House's EWA, 172

In a very short period of time, the firm lost a great deal of its market share. Since then, the company has recovered and has learned how to use C++. At the time, however, the executives put much of the blame on C++.

Clearly, having C programmers does not automatically mean succeeding with C++ (see Chapter 3). The second immediate lesson is that moving an entire company to OO is not as simple as issuing a decree and selecting a compiler (see Chapter 7).

technology, 47

larger projects, 165

Object Technology International: *Success in Productivity and Speed*

Project	Object Technology International
Key topic	Productivity
Project staffing	Small to medium
Project type	Production
Staff experience	Expert
Duration	Several months

Object Technology International (OTI) has been doing business since the late 1980s contracting to deliver hard real-time systems in Smalltalk, "on time or you pay nothing." The company's president, Dave Thomas, relates that at the time they started, no one would contract with them unless their project was dangerously late and a company was desperate.

Using experienced developers and a custom development environment, OTI met every project deadline and performance requirement over a 10-year period. Thomas said he allots nine months for every new hire to fully earn his or her salary. Running a small company, he recognizes both the cost and the value of education.

Regarding the methodology OTI follows, Thomas said they hire good people and give them good tools to help them get their work done. Around 1993 these included code-generation and program-measurement tools, but not graphical modeling tools. Eventually, one of them, Envy/Developer, was made available to the market as a versioning and configuration management system for Smalltalk.

The insights to draw from OTI include that the team developed their own, organization-specific methodology (see Chapter 4), which covered projects to turn down and which tools to use. They also acknowledged their limitations and the limitations of the current technology (see Chapter 3). Finally, they were able to demonstrate that Smalltalk could be used successfully for hard real-time systems with tight performance constraints, including waveform generation on an oscilloscope.

methodology, 77

technology, 47

Reginald: *Failure with Changing Rules*

Project	Project Reginald
Key topic	Project setup
Project staffing	Small
Project type	Production
Staff experience	New to OO
Duration	One year

Initially, Project Reginald was staffed by two programmers who were given the assignment of investigating object technology. They were asked to report back after six months as to whether it was viable for the group. Both were experienced C programmers, investigating C++, and were given access to training and industry consultants. The task was to learn computer communications and protocol development.

As the project became more important to the division, the staff grew to three programming teams in two countries, connected by satellite links. Over the course of a year, the scope kept changing, and at the end of the year, the project manager was removed and the project folded for lack of results.

In the debriefing, we tried to determine just what went wrong. It appeared that the language was not to blame, but rather the deliverables-heavy methodology used, the distances separating the groups, and the changes in the project's scope. The project was not restarted and reoriented to a new goal as the ground rules changed. The two original lead designers thought they were working on a low-key, small, investigative project to find out what C++ could be used for. Suddenly, it became an important production project, and they became team leaders. They never *project purpose, 36* made the shift (see Chapter 3).

Stanley: *Too Much Cutting Edge*

Project	Project Stanley
Key topic	Cutting-edge technology
Project staffing	Large (100–200)
Project type	Production
Staff experience	New to OO
Duration	Several years

The company running Project Stanley was not in the computer industry and did not have an experienced software team. The project sponsor simply fell in love with object technology, and declared the company was going to embark on a large project, a modern project, "another Brooklyn Union Gas." The requirements document was a collection of all the latest ideas, and included newer notions every few months.

Over time, the proposed system evolved to one requiring numerous, fully decentralized, peer-to-peer servers running distributed Smalltalk. At the time, there were no Smalltalk distribution frameworks, and CORBA had not yet been developed. The project restarted several times over several years, and at the time of this writing, it still has not been deployed.

Several lessons are clear. One is not to change requirements so frequently, which I hardly need to comment on. Second is not to plan on using new technology for a time-critical project if the technology is not available or in your group's experience (see Chapter 3). Although it appears rather obvious in this lopsided story, overambitious technology plans cause many project failures.

technology, 47

Tracy: *Failure Through Naiveté*

Project	Project Tracy
Key topic	User involvement, methodology
Project staffing	Medium (10–20)
Project type	Production
Staff experience	New to OO
Duration	One year

Project Tracy was run by an experienced software development group, with experienced developers learning object technology. They read the literature and came away with two impressions: get users involved, and model the real world.

They started with the assumption that object technology was "just another programming language," which could be learned by their programmers. This meant, in particular, that they did not get special training.

The group tried to involve users in the system specification and design review, but got only lukewarm support, because they had access to only whichever users happened to be free at any moment. They therefore had a continually shifting user group, with varying views, opinions, and skills. Thus, there was no continuity in the discussions with the users, and the more experienced users never found the time to come to the meetings.

They were under the impression that if they just "modeled the world," they could turn the model directly into their classes. In the postmortem, they decided their modeling was naive, and that even a decent model of the world might not result in a good software design.

The mainframe and workstation groups were physically separated, with the mainframe group being the larger of the two. The two groups did not communicate well, making it hard to alter the overall architecture. Although both groups claimed they were doing their jobs properly, the total system did not function smoothly. Eventually, they changed the team structure so that people were assigned to total, cross-platform functions as well as to subsystems.

Jon Marshall's EWA, 138

The insights here are: Get real user involvement (see Jon Marshall's Eyewitness Account in Chapter 5), do not be naive about business model-

the domain model, 140

ing (see Chapter 5), assign a person to every form of deliverable, use cases

methodology, 77

and classes in particular (see Chapter 4).

Udall: *Success by Restarting Smaller*

Project	Project Udall
Key topic	Attitude, architecture
Project staffing	Medium
Project type	Production
Staff experience	Mixed
Duration	Two years

Project Udall was a medium-sized project that found itself in trouble when developers started milling around without a cohesive architecture for them to work around. A few of them convinced their management that the only way to make progress was to start over, with a smaller team. To that end, they put the dozen or so developers on hold until they could be useful. Then the smaller team worked over several months to create an architecture, and they defined subsystems for further development. When a good team leader was found and brought up to speed, a few developers were invited to work with that person on the subsystem. Those not considered valuable by the team leaders were simply not invited on any team. Eventually, the system shipped and was considered a success.

The success of this project reportedly hinged around the team members being able to put the project plan into reverse, to admit that they had overstaffed and proceeded along a false direction. Fortunately, system delivery was considered more important than pride in the initial project plan and more important than optimizing use of salaries (a reference to developers sitting idle). The other insight from the project is the value of designing the architecture first, with a small group of people, followed by development of subsystems by small teams (see Chapter 5).

your project increments, 129

Winifred: *Inattentive But Persistent*

Project	Project Winifred
Key topic	Incremental development
Project staffing	Medium (20–40 people)
Project type	Legacy system rewrite
Staff experience	New to OO, with mentors
Duration	Two years

Project Winifred involved rewriting a legacy mainframe system, replacing it with a three-tier, client/server mainframe system. It used Smalltalk on the workstation, C on a relational database server, COBOL on the mainframe. The project started off with an OO-experienced executive, an OO-experienced lead designer for the workstation portions, an experienced mainframe designer for the mainframe portions, and an experienced project manager. In addition, they had access to OO experts, training, and tools; they had funding, management support, and an incremental development strategy. The project had two goals: deliver the new system, and train a dozen newcomers to object technology.

The project immediately encountered morale problems. Communication within and across the teams did not work, and the OO consultants lectured instead of listening. The requirements phase was done all at one time, taking nearly four months. During this time, no architecture or design activity took place, and the group began to tire. Job assignments were not clear, and technical leaders, each of whom had his or her own style, were replaced frequently. The morale and communication problems lasted for half of the project.

Most of the programming was done by novices working under experts, who were overwhelmed by the task of programming and teaching concurrently. Initially, the staff was teamed according to delivered function. With no ownership of the classes' design, they became collect-alls of different people's ideas, and no one dared touch them.

The first increment barely shipped, and did so with a weak internal architecture and minimal functionality. On the second increment, the expert staff was changed, new teams were set up, and a greater emphasis was given to the internal architecture. The second increment shipped successfully and with the first coherent architecture. Over subsequent increments, the architecture evolved and the team became confident about delivering the system on time and with function.

To deal with continually shifting requirements, an iterative process was set up within each increment, requiring two fully functional viewings by the user community to settle final requirements. At all times, management support was good, money was available for equipment, and there was an accessible and fairly stable user group.

The project manager, when asked what she thought of the claims of maintenance and productivity made for object technology, answered that the Smalltalk group consistently made changes faster than she was accustomed to seeing, that there was no way the mainframe COBOL group or the short-staffed database group could keep up with the iteration cycle being used on the workstation. As a result, they changed the rules for iterations so that the Smalltalk group had three iterations per increment, and the others each received a draft specification followed by a final specification.

legacy issues, 72

The first insight to draw from project Winifred is not to forget the simple lessons of previous experience: the importance of job assignments, lines of communication, ownership of deliverables (see Chapter 3). The second is that the unwavering support of upper management can provide constant encouragement and freedom to maneuver during periods of low morale. The third is to use incremental development (see Chapter 5), which gave this team a chance to identify their weak areas, reorganize teams, and develop the architecture. It gave the team increased confidence and morale. By the third iteration, they knew they could, and they knew how to, produce a system every three months. This knowledge gave them the freedom to experiment a bit, even under time pressure.

*increments and
iterations, 117*

user involvement, 134

*Project Winifred
revisited, 188*

The fourth insight is that this team managed to keep their users involved consistently (see Chapter 5). Project Winifred is analyzed in Chapter 5.

How many of the successes and failures just described were due to object technology and how many to the absence of normal software engineering practices? The first goal of this book is to remind you to apply the principles you are familiar with from your non-OO projects. For some readers, the shift to objects will provide a first opportunity to put these suggestions to use.

Learn how some cleared the chasm and became productive.

POSSIBLE BENEFITS OF OBJECT TECHNOLOGY

You may have heard of some of the possible benefits of object technology. The following 11 sections describe my ordering of the benefits based on interviews with project leaders, discussions with consultants and experts, and reading project reports. They are listed according to each one's probable contribution, with the most likely and most rewarding ones first.

Responsiveness to Variations on a Theme

Object-oriented software excels when your next program differs only slightly from your previous one. OO design orients itself toward this situation. Properly designed classes and frameworks let you add new features just by describing the differences between the new and old systems.

If your company competes on time to produce variations on themes (as with sales promotions, financial instruments, insurance policies, and so on), then object technology is naturally suited to your situation.

Responsiveness to Change

Major and unpleasant changes can often be made relatively easily to an object-oriented system, due to *encapsulation*, as discussed in Chapter 1. Encapsulating design decisions into classes helps to localize design changes in software. Part of the OO design procedure is to identify probable changes and to localize them. Again, refer to the Eyewitness Account by Tom Morgan later in this chapter for an example of encapsulation in action.

encapsulation, 7

Tom Morgan's EWA, 28

Consistent attention to encapsulation of design decisions pays off when unexpected and significant requirements changes are encountered. These might be to change the hardware platform, a server or its function, or the nature of the user interface. I make the distinction between such significant requirements changes and maintenance and evolution because of the difference in frequency, effort, and cost savings.

Time-to-Market

If one factor is pushing you toward object technology, it is probably time-to-market. Most systems contain internal similarities—parts of the system that are similar to each other rather than to other products. Using incremental development, the development team can capitalize on the first two benefits of object technology—encapsulation and variation on themes—to take advantage of the internal similarities.

The first release of the incremental development staging corresponds to an initial product, in which the basic classes and frameworks are created. Subsequent releases evolve and extend the classes and frameworks, taking advantage of the internal similarity. Your time-to-market benefit will vary depending on the amount of internal and external similarity you can exploit.

Communication Between Developers, Users, and Executives

Object technology lets developers work in users' and executives' vocabulary. Normally, there are two translations involved in creating a program: when the developer translates a user's or executive's statements into the programming language, and when the developer tries to convert the program's structure back to something the user can use at the user interface. Both are error-prone and costly. Simplifying the translations reduces cost and effort, both of communicating ideas and of developing systems.

It is the packaging technology that lets the developer put the user's vocabulary directly onto the computer. Thus, instead of arguing about data structures on the disk, developers—as Tom Morgan said about the B.U.G. experience—argued "about whether the fault was in the gas meter or the gas line." Although that may sound rather odd as a benefit, organizations that have made the transition to objects successfully have repeatedly cited improved communications as one of the most significant benefits (see Ward Cunningham's Eyewitness Account in Chapter 4).

Ward Cunningham's
EWA, 94

Maintainability

Your situation may be that your current code is old, weakly structured, and difficult to modify, and you hope that the new OO code will be so well structured that it will be easy to maintain. The good news is the ability to encapsulate design decisions, as explained in the preceding Responsiveness to Change section. Use of encapsulation will improve maintainability.

There are, however, new risks of creating poor software structure. If many classes are used to carry out each system function, it becomes difficult to understand how the system works. Each new person will have a hard time learning how the system works and may make mistakes in correctly deciding which classes to change. Thus, OO design does not automatically confer maintainability; it only provides the capability for it.

Reuse

Perhaps you expect to reap massive gains on subsequent projects through reuse. Reuse in object technology is "business as usual"—with a bit of good news. Object orientation provides additional reuse mechanisms: classes, inheritance, polymorphism, and frameworks. They allow you to reuse both smaller and larger parts of the program, and to develop by "programming the difference" from what you already have.

The bad news is that reuse really depends on human constraints. These are, first, the willingness of your developers to suppress their egos long enough to look for and use someone else's solution; and second, the willingness of your managers to allocate time and money to finding reuseable components. Reuse within a project is fairly easy; across projects, it is fairly hard; and across an organization, it is exceedingly difficult. Object technology on its own cannot mitigate the human factors.

One last piece of good news is that infrastructure frameworks, which are expensive to develop, do not confer much competitive advantage to a business system. As a result, there is a growing market and a growing number of providers for them. These frameworks provide cost-effective reuse for difficult parts of the system.

Productivity

Perhaps you have a productivity crisis and are hoping that an OO system will increase everyone's productivity so much that you can work through your backlog. While I would confidently put my money on a team of experienced OO programmers against any other programmers in the world, that sentiment contains two important criteria: experience and programming.

Remember, only a fraction of the total development time is spent in programming. Requirements gathering, requirements analysis, system test, rollout, installation, and training times are roughly the same. The programming time will be reduced only if you are using experienced programmers with over 12 months of active OO programming behind them. But the odds are that your staff will be using the project to learn, and so will be less productive. Therefore, restrain your expectations about productivity gains.

Window-Based User Interfaces

Object-oriented programming confers no benefit to the user's perception of quality looking at the user interface. The same interface can be programmed in any of many languages, and the user will not care. In fact, the OO, direct-manipulation interfaces up through the mid-1990s were almost all written in non-OO languages! The point is, do not feel motivated to move to object-oriented programming just to get an "OO-looking" user interface.

That said, there may be some benefit to programming the user interface using objects. In the early 1990s, development of window-based software was so labor-intensive and variable that OO programming was one of the few ways to manage it. User-interface generators made simple interfaces easier to create, and lowered the attraction of learning OO programming. So-called drag-and-drop interfaces made them harder to create again, and are more naturally suited to structuring the code with objects.

This seesaw between making user-interface programming more difficult, then coming out with tools to simplify it, may be expected to continue. The justification for introducing object technology just to simplify user-interface development must be made in the context of available tools.

Morale

It is unlikely that you will introduce objects just to increase the morale of your developers, but you can consider it a pleasant side-benefit. Most programmers find the programming environment so advanced compared to what they are used to that their task of programming will become more enjoyable. They will be encouraged further because they are using the newest, latest technology, which is important to people working in a technology-sensitive field.

people, 42
As covered in Chapter 3 on staffing, a few of them will not enjoy it. There are two groups of people likely to have difficulty with the new technology: those who are expert in another language and cannot handle the stress of becoming beginners again, and those who have developed a dependence on a strict waterfall, "give me the requirements, go away, and let me program," process. Most of the staff will enjoy the move; some will not.

Automated Code Generation

Some tool vendors advertise that your programs will be automatically generated from the domain model, since objects are the same medium of description in both analysis and programming. In practice, on a recent project, we estimated the amount of code amenable to automatic generation to be a disappointing 5 to 15 percent. This code came from structural aspects of the business domain classes and from the user-interface classes. The behavioral parts of those classes still had to be written by hand, as did all of the links between the user interface and all of the infrastructure. These comprised the bulk of the code and the majority of the difficult software design.

The bottom line? Do not look to regain your initial costs simply by pushing a button and having systems generate from analysis models.

Software Process

Many organizations have difficulty getting different groups of developers to work together in a socially responsible and predictable way; they are still personality-driven. Object technology will not fix that. If there is one place I would not recommend injecting object technology, it is into an organization that is late on a project and is suffering from software process problems.

The reason is that object development requires more, rather than less, communication. One project team described their experience as "living out of each others' pockets." Object technology emphasizes minimizing the impact of change, even if that means increasing personal and interprogram communication.

Therefore, do not look to object technology to fix your software process. Use it, perhaps, as an incentive to rebuild or build a more controlled software process.

Work toward responsiveness to variations on a theme.

The following Eyewitness Account illustrates using encapsulation to reduce the cost of system evolution. Its writer, Tom Morgan, was one of the architects on the B.U.G. OO project during the late 1980s.　　　*B.U.G., 13*

◆ **OO Design, Encapsulation, and System Evolution**   *Tom Morgan, Brooklyn Union Gas*

Some weeks prior to the planned installation date of the system, we were running large-scale systems tests. The tests involved approximately 50 people, running through test scenarios at a rate that would be representative of the system's use during its first days of operation. As a matter of prudence, we involved some neutral second-party observers to be certain that we weren't deluding ourselves as to the results. One of the observers was a skilled CICS expert.

During the tests, we discovered a significant memory leak in "work-in-progress management" for the system; it caused the CICS region to use up all available memory in an enormous address space within an hour or two.

In a typical CICS transaction system, support for work-in-progress is spread throughout the application code. The CICS expert dutifully reported to the project manager that the fault observed would require several months to resolve.

We had the error fixed by the next morning. The reason, of course, was the tendency to use single implementations in OO systems [see Chapter 1, Encapsulation]. Work-in-progress management, like most things in the application, was implemented as a behavior of one object, and the implementation was shared by all consumers of the behavior. A single recompilation of a method resolved the memory leak, system-wide.

Case material contributed by Tom Morgan, used with permission.

Morgan's account is fairly representative. A "showstopper" alteration can be taken in stride because the issue resides in one and only one software module, encapsulating the design decisions and reducing the trajectory of change.

COSTS

So those are the benefits. Now, what are you willing to pay? Probably you are expecting to pay for one to two weeks of training in a new programming language, and perhaps an investment in some new CASE tools. And you are looking for ways to minimize both.

Are You Underestimating?

With that in mind, the following seven sections discuss factors you may be underestimating.

Time to Get New Developers Productive

The length of time it takes to get a new developer productive in OO varies. Replace your original idea of 2 weeks with 8 to 10 months.

Immaturity of the OO Industry

Even though objects were invented several decades ago, they are entering the commercial IS marketplace slowly. Certain things considered standard in the IS world are still missing; typical examples are money and transaction classes and version management of the modeling and programming tools.

Hazards of C++

C++ is one of a set of languages occupying a position at the strategic crossroads of objects and C. The others are Objective-C, SOM, C@+, and Java. C++ won those language wars, perhaps because of its backward compatibility and attention to performance, but it is a difficult and complicated language. For some reason, C++ still gets recommended for large-scale IS use, even when the language complexities are not handled well by the staff.

One experienced development leader, after wrestling with C++ on several medium-sized projects for a year, finally gave up, saying, "I don't believe it is possible to deliver a project in C++. . . . You ought to write a book warning people . . . but they won't believe you any more than I did."

I disagree that it is not possible to deliver a project in C++. There are success stories, and places where the language is appropriate, but the challenges of the language should be taken very seriously (see Chapter 3). *managing C++, 53* In contrast, Java is now attracting attention for its relative simplicity and portability.

The Difficulty of Reuse

It is difficult to achieve reuse among your developers. You need to scale down your expectations, scale up your education program, and put checks into place. "Reuse" is too simple a word for the concept—it should be unpronounceably difficult, to give the sense of how hard it is to achieve.

Establishing a Software Process

Getting developers to follow a process is difficult. Putting a process into place fails for two reasons: The process is probably wrong, and the programmers won't be able to (or just won't) follow it. Expect people to take detours.

Business Modeling versus Software Design

There is a significant difference between business modeling and software design. Despite much wishful thinking, it is still not the case that an "accurate" business model makes a "good" software design. Converting a clear business model to a good software design requires thought and creativity. The software design must address the additional constraints of modifiability and performance.

It is important to recognize that once you have an initial, clear, business model, you still have to undertake the creation of a good software design. If your designers do their work well, the final design not only will be an accurate model of the business, but it will also run fast enough and be able to localize changes. Quite possibly, it will look different from the original business model.

The Cost of CASE Modeling Tools

automated code generation, 27

Modeling the domain is only a small portion of the total design effort (see Benefits section). CASE tool vendors and researchers are very optimistic about the capabilities of their "pet" tools, but history is not on their side. You should plan on getting only minor code generation from an object-modeling tool.

Probable Costs

The following are some fairly realistic costs to expect in terms of time and money:

- *Training*. Spend 3 to 6 weeks of classroom training per developer.
- *Experience*. Spend 6 to 9 months waiting for each developer to start earning his or her salary again while getting the "hang" of thinking in terms of OO trade-offs.
- *Tools*. Ignore your current investment in CASE tools for software development. Forcing a tool to do things it was not built to do will eventually turn it into just a drawing tool at very high cost. Buy the right tool.
- *Consultants*. Good consultants are expensive and fully booked. For that reason, there is a market for "experts" with only 6 to 9 months of experience. Nonetheless, you need access to experience. That will cost you, either in making the mistakes and learning from them yourself, or hiring someone who can steer you away from them or help to correct them. You spend the same amount of money either way, but the latter takes less time.

There. The bad news is all out on the table so that you can assess it. How are you doing? Are you ready to develop an organization that makes steady gains over several years?

Budget $200,000, plus $6,000, and six months per person.

NONOBJECT ISSUES CHECKLISTS

Actual project management is largely independent of object technology. Gathering and understanding requirements do not depend on the technology. Testing, documentation, and deployment still need to be done. Twenty or more people working together need a project framework with a communication infrastructure.

Use your current way of working as a baseline. The lists that follow specify items that do not depend on object technology. The first one lists activities that always take time. The second list itemizes the tools and processes of object technology.

STANDARD PROJECT ACTIVITIES

- Interview users and project sponsors to determine project requirements.
- Research and document the existing system, listing all the interfaces that must be matched in the new system.
- Train the developers and managers.
- Analyze user wishes and requirements.
- Argue over differences of opinion and miscommunications.
- Create technical infrastructures for the operating system, the network, error messages, the user interface.
- Deploy a prototype and reevaluate requirements after the feedback session.
- Create test cases.
- Integrate the work of different groups.
- Document.
- Make last-minute changes, just before delivery, as all the pieces are put together.
- Formulate last-minute insights about the system as they become apparent.
- Release an alpha and a beta version of the product, and correct both as needed.
- Prepare training materials.

TOOLS AND PROCESSES

- *Technical needs*—versioning, configuration management tools, LAN connections, e-mail, and the like
- *Diversity of skills*—COBOL programmers, C programmers, network experts, database designers

- *Process needs*—the form of deliverables exchanges; the form of interaction between the groups
- *Social needs*—team leaders, documenters, testers, team interrelationships

project teams, 136

These two lists should give you confidence in your ability to manage an object-oriented project, building on your non-OO background. Some differences have to be taken into account, particularly team structures, as Chapter 5 discusses. However, much of what makes OO appear difficult is bringing reuse, increments, and iterations to the fore, plus the mythology that has grown around object orientation.

Object systems still have to "talk" to a legacy, non-OO mainframe system. This is not something that should break your project; it is a matter of designing an interface. Make sure you have a system architect who is familiar with both workstations and mainframes. If you do not have such an architect, or you have many architects at odds with each other, then you do have a survival hazard to fix, quickly.

Consider restructuring your COBOL system prior to replacing it with an object-oriented system. Very powerful COBOL analysis and structure tools and services are available, making the task practical. As a result of the restructuring, you will find it easier to document the interfaces to the COBOL system and to separate modules for replacement. You may even reduce the size of the object-oriented revision, which will save you money.

Your architect may recommend that the mainframe non-OO code be developed in a different way from before. Several mainframe experts have told me that an effective server design is "object-centered," meaning the server is organized around the structure of the data requests coming from the workstations. The data access requests mirror the structure of the classes, because the classes are generating the requests. Interestingly, this design recommendation did not originate with the OO developers, but with mainframe experts.

Unfortunately, mainframe and workstation developers do not speak the same language and are unlikely to negotiate well with each other. The architect or technical lead must be able to sensibly settle disputes over the assignment of responsibilities.

Use your previous experience to avoid the most common traps.

Chapter 3

Selecting and Setting Up an OO Project

Select for time-to-market.

Your first OO project: not too big, not too small, not too important, not too unimportant. What does this mean? The project should either deliver value directly or show you how the company will react to object technology. It must fit the history, temperament, and capabilities of the company.

Consider two extremes, each faulty. On one extreme is a small, test project with just two people. Such a project will be fine for those two people; it will improve their résumés. But it is unlikely to show whether the company ought to use object technology because it will not characterize your situation. People are unlikely to pay attention to the results. On the other extreme is a company-critical project as a first project. It can be done, but the risks are high, so you must take special precautions.

Your first OO project should be selected to reveal how the technology will be used and what problems you will encounter. It should be important enough to be noticed, but not so critical that the risks are deadly. Because all rules have exceptions, here are four complementary guidelines:

1. A project designed to get as much done as possible quickly should consist of two people, to avoid the communications difficulties that accompany OO projects.
2. A project to investigate the technology should have at least four people on it to reveal some of the communications issues that accompany OO projects.

3. A project to decide whether to shift the entire company to object technology must be serious enough that completion, or failure to complete, is a significant event to the company. Otherwise, its success or failure will be inconclusive.

4. A project, the failure of which would be disastrous, needs special precautions and backup measures. It should not be allowed to fail because of neglect, poor management, or insufficient funds. That would be a triple blow: the failure of the project, the failure of the management involved, and a failure to master the technology.

The best first step is to set up the project well. The next sections go over topics you should address before you get underway: selection of a suitable project and establishing its purpose; selection of staff, language, and tools; evaluation of the need for training and advice; and legacy issues.

PROJECT SUITABILITY

Judging by the project histories I have collected, project success is not linked to "suitability to object technology." OO projects that did not appear naturally suited to object technology have been successful (see the

B.U.G., 13

Brooklyn Union Gas story in Chapter 2), and "naturally suitable" projects have failed from obviously poor management. Yet it is still useful to characterize whether a project is naturally suited to object technology. I consider a project more naturally suited to OO if the following apply:

♦ The system will be extended by variations on a theme.
♦ Objects obviously give a significantly simplified program structure.
♦ The design relies on memory-management features of the OO language.

Suitability becomes relevant in answering the far more important question: How soon will the new technology pay for itself? A simplified program structure reduces the cost of maintenance. OO mechanisms allow variations on a theme to be added by programming just the differences, which creates a dramatic cost savings.

Variations on a Theme

Certain types of programs grow internally in similar ways. The simplest example is a drawing program: All the shapes need to be created, sized, moved, and colored, although each is done in a slightly different way

polymorphism, 9

(think of polymorphism—see Chapter 1). The program evolves by programming the simple shapes first. Over time, you add the more compli-cated shapes, taking advantage of the existing program parts.

Rapid variation provides a critical competitive edge. For example, rap-idly varied sales promotions and rapid response to competitors' promo-tions make promotion modeling a natural for object technology. Finance companies compete on creation and variation of financial instruments. Insurance companies compete on slight variations in target population, insurables, benefits, payments, and so on. If you can identify critical themes in your business that vary rapidly, you have found the place where object technology can pay for itself the quickest.

Simplified Program Structure

Almost every program can benefit to some extent from being packaged around classes. Simulation of physical systems is an obvious candidate. In a traffic simulation, it makes sense to have program elements centered around cars, roads, lights, and the like.

User-interface programs of all sorts benefit from attaching program logic to the objects on the screen. Pert charts, computer-aided design (CAD) programs, graphical displays of train schedules, and routing pro-grams are examples.

Sometimes the data being used within the program is very diverse: Multimedia programs manipulate text, voice, shapes, and video streams; geological systems manipulate seismic data, pressure readings, and spec-trographic data. These programs are a natural fit with object technology because it is most convenient to co-locate all the program parts that manipulate a particular data type.

Repeatedly, people report that their OO programs better localize design decisions, making it easier for the program to evolve (see Tom Morgan's Eyewitness Account in Chapter 2). Is this, perhaps, because they *Tom Morgan's EWA, 28* were able to design the system from scratch, with the benefit of hindsight and advancements in the software field? My experience is that few IS developers are trained in encapsulation. Many students have commented during object-oriented training that encapsulation considerations are new to them. They need classroom training, plus the enforcement from the OO language, to change their design habits.

Memory Management Features

Occasionally you will encounter a program that can take dramatic advan-tage of one particular language mechanism. One project I encountered was to implement a communications protocol; it paid for the use of C++ simply by its ability to handle data buffers. A message arriving at a network point gets put into a buffer and passed across different protocol layers. Allocating, handling, and freeing those buffers is both prone to error and hard to fix. The project leader said that the constructors and destructors of C++ simplified programming enough to pay for the entire move to object technology. Although it is unusual, you may recognize when you are in such a situation.

What Is Not Suited?

It is hard to answer, "What is not suited to object technology?" Recall that object technology is fundamentally a program-packaging technology that permits a continuum of function-only and function-plus-data packages. It is therefore not inappropriate to any particular type of system. Objects have been used in oscilloscopes, payroll systems, CAD systems, user interfaces, and banking and insurance systems.

The question really is, "When is it not *worth the cost* to retrain your development staff in OO?" This is easier to answer. If your system serves its purpose, keep using it and avoid the training costs and general agony of shifting to a new technology. The average *CRUD* (create/retrieve/update/delete) application, which reads and writes data to a database, is nicely served by current application generators. Some CRUD systems are being rewritten in objects, but many organizations choose not to make the shift just for this kind of application.

If your current way of building software is causing you difficulties, try to find a project with one of the natural affinities to object technology, as just described. Aim to offset the training costs with a gain in time-to-market or maintainability.

Make sure the system is worth the cost of training the people.

PROJECT PURPOSE

The sections that follow describe these four broadly different types of projects:

1. *SWAT*—Accomplish something relatively small but particularly difficult.
2. *Investigative*—Report on the technology.
3. *Production*—Produce a new or replace a legacy production system.
4. *Full-Commit*—Move the entire organization over to objects.

Each has a different set of ground rules, and each requires a different set of staff skills. One of the survival recommendations is: Be clear and consistent about the purpose of the project.

SWAT

SWAT, a term used by the police force, stands for Special Weapons and Training. It is an appropriate term for some software projects, because the purpose of a SWAT project is to get as much done as quickly as possible. Typically, this method is used on a small, difficult task. To approach such a project, take the following steps:

1. Relax other restrictions on the project.
2. Create the project with a clear and simple set of requirements.
3. Use a small, high-powered team, and give them whatever tools and training they need ("special weapons and training").
4. Free the team from phase deliverables and most of the intermediate documentation deliverables that accompany larger projects.
5. Let the team get their primary job done as quickly as possible.

The people you choose for a SWAT team should be able to "think outside the box." They need this kind of ability, or you would not need them for this project. Use two, three, or at the most, four people, sitting in close proximity to each other to avoid additional communication hazards.

Review Project Reginald (see Chapter 2) for a potential pitfall, that of adding more people as soon as the original team's work looks promising. A larger team has different needs and should be set up appropriately. If you wish to make the shift, declare the first project at an end, and set up for a Production project.

Project Reginald, 18

production, 40

Investigative

Suppose you wish to find out how well suited object technology is for your organization. The purpose of the investigative project is to detect the problems you may encounter, and to learn a way of working around them. Be sure to design and instrument the project to give you that information or you will not be any further ahead at the end of the project.

First, unless you are a small company, assign at least four people to the project. If you assign just two designers to learn object technology, you run the risk that they get trained, update their résumés, have fun, and produce a graphical prototype. What should you decide on the basis of this? Your development manager needs answers to the following questions, which your project setup team should take care to address:

1. How long will it take to train the average person in the department? How many people need to be trained? To what extent does the field staff need to be retrained to use the newer products?
2. How do we manage development of the project? Same as before or different? How do we control versions and share development information between groups?
3. What new tools do we have to buy? How many of the old tools can we use?
4. How do we test the new system?
5. What are the maintenance characteristics? When a change request comes in, how much improvement is there in turnaround time?

The project team should consist of four to seven people so that the communication issues show up. In contrast to a SWAT project, which should have only a few people to minimize communication needs, the investigative project needs enough people to encounter these communication issues. Experience indicates that OO development requires more person-to-person communication than structured programming (see Chapter 2). You want to discover how to synchronize the teams' versions of the software and documents, and to let them experience their interdependencies.

software process, 27

Staff the project with a business expert, one or two of your better programmers, two or three of your standard development staff, and an object technology mentor.

The business expert will turn your exercise into an investment. The team will design business objects right away, and the business expert will be the only person on the team who can properly describe the interdependence of various rules, attributes, and other elements of the business. Without this person, the rest of the team will design something that possibly will be quite good, but will not accommodate needed variations. The business expert will become accomplished at object modeling and will act as the team's ultimate information source.

Ward Cunningham's EWA, 94

The good programmer will ensure that the program gets written. A good systems or C programmer with a lot of programming experience will do well. She or he will be able to adapt quickly to the needs of object technology. This person may also write small tools, interfaces, or algorithms, or establish the team's programming style.

The two or three standard developers act as a test of the technology on the people who are going to have to adopt it wholesale. They will show where the technology is hard, easy, different, or the same. You will probably want to choose some of your better developers, both to increase the chance of success and because they will become team leaders on the next project. If their expertise and capability are too different from the rest of the company, the project will produce unreliable information.

The OO mentor's role is to provide a safe journey through this first project. The mentor must be comfortable with one or more ways of developing a system and be able to communicate with the team, to put them relatively at ease. She or he is responsible for safe design habits, and because her or his design habits and programming style are likely to be copied throughout the organization, they are important. The mentor need not be full-time, although half-time or more might be needed.

The charter of the project must include tests to identify the issues that will affect success in deploying the technology to the organization. These are some questions that may arise:

◆ Do we know how to estimate a project? plan the project? test the system?
◆ How much training and education is needed?
◆ What is the transaction throughput?
◆ What is maintenance like?

You might even decide that the team's first assignment should be to articulate the proper questions. A project topic that is a reasonable precursor of what will be asked of the development department needs to be selected.

Allow 6 to 10 months for the project. Six months is the minimum amount of time to give people to learn about the technology. Ten months is the most time that should be allowed for such an experiment.

Have the executive running the experiment prepare two project statements, the first to give to the group at the beginning to help them to learn the technology and to come to terms with the development process. When that time is up, the second project statement should be revealed. It should be a typical change request that affects the user interface, program logic, and database. The stopwatch runs from the time the second project statement is shown to the group until they deliver complete results. That is the way maintenance improvement claims can be judged.

At this point, review the successful, if aggressive, program adopted by Project Alfred (see Chapter 2). A small company may need to adjust the setup of its Investigative project. It may not have four to seven people to put on an experiment. Such a small company should use the SWAT approach to evaluate and learn the technology for the company. The SWAT team must explore various avenues of development rapidly and come up with recommendations for the rest of the group. Not only should this SWAT team consist of good designers, they also need to be articulate

Project Alfred, 12

in passing on their recommendations, and accurate in their estimation of the company's capabilities. The team will set the company's programming standards and be the chief educators.

Production

A Production project puts a real system into use. It is not an experiment; it must succeed, but it should not break the company if it is late. Whether it is a new system or a replacement for an existing legacy application, there probably will be a considerable number of interprogram interfaces to track. I assume here that the project involves both object and nonobject technology, and describe the legacy application version of the Production project. The only difference is the presence of additional experts on the legacy system.

Your project will probably select itself. It is usually clear which application needs replacing or creating, provides noticeable benefit to users, or does not endanger the company. One common hazard is that the users get so excited by the first glimpse of the new system that they overwhelm the development department with new demands.

The Production project will use a mix of people from the department because it is too large to staff with "superstars." The staff should be made up of experts on the existing system, standard developers who will get trained, and some object technology experts. The experts on the existing system will speed up knowledge transfer about how that system works or how the new system needs to fit in. They know the interfaces and can provide insurance against forgetting necessary functions.

You may decide to hire an external team of specialists to do the bulk of the work. This can be very effective: They are more expensive per day, but they work faster. I assume, however, that you will use your present developers to make use of and train your existing staff.

training: Day Care strategy, 232

As explained in detail in the Day Care strategy in Appendix A, create two categories of teams. Put the expert developers into *Progress* teams to do most of the development work. Keep them as free as possible from distractions—teaching, in particular. Assign one or two of the experts to training the novices in *Training* teams. You may let the Progress teams do 90 to 95 percent of the system development, and assign the Training teams only 5 to 10 percent of the development work. The idea is to let the novices learn by doing, give them a dedicated teacher, give them time to deliver useful function, and keep them out of the way of the expert developers. You may find that the Progress team works 10 or 20 times faster than the Training team. Base the project schedule on the Progress team, not the total number of bodies. As the novices become adept with the technology, let them migrate to the Progress teams.

This strategy is in stark contrast to the more common one, which is to build mixed teams with three or four novices and one expert. The idea of mixed teams is to keep the student-to-teacher ratio low. The result that shows up repeatedly is that the expert does not have time either to design or to teach, and does not have a peer discussion partner. Thus, progress and quality both suffer. In the meantime, the novices do not have a full-time teacher, so they do not develop good design habits. Forming Progress and Training teams makes it possible to tackle the two issues separately.

Full-Commit

A Full-Commit project needs your best manager and technical leader, a group of really good programmers, a team of standard developers, and one or two full-time object experts. Because the project will have a large number of developers pulling in different directions due to differing philosophies, your technical leader must be respected and persuasive to be able to align them in whatever technical direction gets selected.

Your really good programmers will learn the nuances of OO design quickly and become development leaders; the standard developers are simply your regular staff. The one or two full-time object experts will provide the training, the standards, and expertise to the rest of the organization. They will work with the technical leader to establish the organization's techniques, standards for design, coding, testing, training, and so on. The object experts will help establish and disseminate your organization's new methodology. Plan on using them for one to two years.

The Full-Commit effort should start with one or more projects that are important to your organization, but that, if delayed, will not bankrupt it. Not every company has this luxury, of course. Use incremental development to give yourself space for course corrections, and trust your best manager to pay close attention to the health of the projects.

Other Project Categories

Although I classified projects by size and purpose in this chapter, other classifications are possible. Information Systems (IS) groups and their projects differ from scientific/engineering groups and their projects. Real-time projects differ from end-user application projects, and so on. Their differences show up in technology selection and methodology rather than in setup. Whether you are in an IS or an engineering department, creating an application or a real-time program, you may choose a SWAT project, investigate, or you may move the whole organization.

How bold should the project be? Should you choose a safe topic, or one on the edge of possibility? Your organization will probably do on this project much as it did on its previous project. If your group is used to large projects or new technology, then a major step into object technology may be within the team's comfort zone. If, on the other hand, your organization is used to making small changes, then you will probably choose a safe topic. Brooklyn Union Gas launched a 150-person, mission-critical project as its first venture into object technology, partly because the organization was used to large-scale projects (see Chapter 2). If you select an unusually aggressive project, be sure to include an extra risk factor just for the shift in the boldness. To counter this risk, add someone to the project who has experience with bolder projects. This theme is picked up again later in the Technology section of this chapter.

B.U.G., 13

the cutting edge, 66

Ultimately, the size and boldness of the project will be determined by the expertise of the people you can bring in at various times and costs. The next section discusses this.

Let the charter and staff fit the purpose.

PEOPLE

The three most significant people on your project are the executive sponsor, project manager, and technical leader. The absence of any one of them can cause almost any project to fail. The *executive sponsor* is responsible for getting the project the "nutrition" and support it needs. The *project manager* is responsible for the quality of communication between the teams. The *technical leader* is responsible for ensuring that a design is used that both satisfies requirements and can be built by the team.

Some other people who may influence the success or failure of any OO project are the technical staff and the users. You also will want to consider how personality types could affect the overall outcome of the project.

Executive Sponsor

The executive sponsor is a critical success factor, according to many project leaders I speak with. In many cases, the sponsoring executive is not in the project developer's immediate line of command. Sometimes, the sponsoring executive is in the user community (see, for example, K.L.'s Eyewitness Account in Chapter 5). The point is, find that support-ing executive, wherever he or she might be.

K.L.'s EWA, 106

Do not, however, invent all sorts of productivity gains for object tech-nology in your effort to gain executive sponsorship. You are unlikely to achieve such gains on your first project unless you are deliberate in get-ting highly experienced OO developers to execute your project, and false productivity claims may instead put you in an awkward position during the project.

Try not to make any claims for the technology that cannot be demon-strated on your project. Instead, examine your organization's situation and understand where it is suffering. If you can identify one or more of the probable benefits of object technology that will help with that, then it will be reasonable for your executives to consider the technology.

Support for object technology comes from one of three places:

1. *The executive team*. They know where they are troubled, and have looked at a number of options. They may be ready to try object tech-nology as the next logical alternative.
2. *The users*. The user community often funds or affects funding. They may have seen OO projects done with close user interaction, perhaps even designed by users.
3. *The programmers*. They may have gotten the latest C compiler, which happens to be C++, so there is no way to stop them from working with objects. Perhaps the organization is dominated by the program-mers, and when they decide to try object technology, the manage-ment follows.

Whichever of these is your source of support, try to get the agreement of someone who will support you when you get stuck and need to make changes in your proposed project. You will have peace of mind if you know your sponsor is behind you at some potentially embarrassing moment in the project (see Project Winifred in Chapter 2).

Project Winifred, 21

Project Manager

All projects rely on management skills. The project manager must be able to judge the expertise present, how and when to improve it, and how to scale back the project if the expertise is not sufficient. A good project manager, even one with no OO experience, will be able to adjust for the few different considerations that object orientation creates. If I had to choose between a good manager with no OO background and an OO-experienced but inept manager, it would be no contest; I would choose the good manager. The project manager's lack of OO experience can be filled by the technical lead; but the absence of management skills cannot be covered by anyone else. The project managers I interviewed were unanimous that objects change the project manager's life relatively little, while changing the developers' lives significantly.

Technical Lead

If your project manager has no prior OO experience, make sure you have a technical lead with good communication skills. The technical lead can let the project manager know when the project's needs are unique to objects. (This book should also help.) If your project manager is not comfortable with "object-speak," and the technical lead is not helpful and communicative, then you have a problem that needs to be fixed.

The qualities and skills of your technical lead are related to the type of project you are undertaking: SWAT, Investigative, Production, or Full-Commit. SWAT and Investigative do not require that the technical lead have OO experience, but Production and Full-Commit do.

Technical Staff

Technical staff includes your experts, your regular staff, and the mentors. It is important to distinguish between experts and mentors. The responsibility of the design expert is to make sure the system gets built, and to a sufficient standard of quality. His or her key characteristic is technical proficiency, with communication skills secondary. The responsibility of the mentor is to improve the staff's ability with objects. The mentor must know how to practice safe design and teach it. His or her key characteristic is the ability to communicate clearly, with technical proficiency necessary but secondary.

More object projects are starting up than there are experts to lead them, and even large consulting houses are having difficulty finding experienced OO developers. This means two things to you. The first is that after you train novices for a year, they may quit and become self-declared experts. The second is that the expert you hire may be someone else's former one-year novice.

The protection against the novice–expert is simply to check their references and experience. I advocate that programmers carry portfolios with samples of their programming and design work. These samples can tell your interview team more about a programmer's thought processes than hours of talking. If a programmer does not have one, consider asking her or him to do some small task as a sample even if you have to pay to get it done. After all, you are thinking of paying $100,000 for this person over some time period.

To prevent people from quitting, you will have to examine the way you educate and use staff. The market value of your designers goes up as you train them, so either pay them more to keep them, or take a certain attrition rate into account as part of your project's survival. Remember, it costs at least half a year's salary to introduce a new employee to the organization. I suggest paying the good ones enough to stay with you.

Users

Put "real users" on your requirements and design teams. Many intermediaries incorrectly claim to know how the users work and what they want. Read Jon Marshall's Eyewitness Account (see Chapter 5) for an example of how differently people think compared to how others think they think. In that project, in Project Winifred (see Chapter 2), and in the Smalltalk projects in K.L.'s Eyewitness Account (see Chapter 4), success involved letting the user community create the system, and in one case, actually design part of it. On Project Manfred (see Chapter 2), by contrast, one of the team's criticisms was that they had a changing stream of users who were only superficially involved in the process. User Involvement, in Chapter 5, reviews the topic of links between developers and users.

Jon Marshall's EWA, 138

K.L.'s EWA, 106

user involvement, 134

Consider assigning an experienced and articulate user to the project full-time. This person will become familiar with the capabilities of the programming technology, and will carry that knowledge back to the users. Experienced users will pay for themselves over and over again by checking assumptions and smoothing the transition to the new system.

At the very least, have a few users available periodically, several hours each week, to discuss ideas and to make their work understood. Some projects gain an understanding of the users' priorities and obstacles by having a few designers work within the user community for a few days and by videotaping the process. A rare and farsighted project will hire someone to work with, videotape, and study the users at work for several weeks to identify where the process breaks down. These projects find the places where the most good can be done, instead of where just some good can be done. The bottom line is, everything you do to involve users strengthens your project.

Personality Types

Is there one personality type that is better suited to object technology than all others? This question is relevant to your project because it appears the answer may be yes. That answer does not come from any detailed study but from informal conversations I have had with other designers, consultants, and trainers. What could cause this? Here is an argument built from plausibility, backed by personal observation.

The ideal object designer/programmer thinks abstractly, deals well with uncertainty, and communicates reasonably, in contrast to the quiet, detail-oriented programmer stereotype. Good designers rely on the ability to look at things in the world, at words and concepts, and to extract from them properties that they share, that can be named, and that can be classified into a hierarchy. An object called a *strategy* is by no means easy to think up, and yet it becomes one of the most powerful elements in the system. What are the properties that all your user-interface screens have in common? The quality of the answer depends on the ability to identify commonalities and imagine various futures. Thus, the quality of OO design hinges on abstract thinking.

iterations, 123

Most OO projects are run according to an iterative scheduling process, often with aggressive changes across iterations (see Chapter 5). This means the requirements, the internal design, and the user interface may be in flux throughout much of the project. Programmers used to working from fixed specs may not feel comfortable in this environment. It is actually not object technology, but the iterative process that causes this discomfort.

Finally, there is an additional communications burden that comes with object technology. Because of the intensive use of interfaces, the designer is not going to be able to sit alone in a cubicle and crank out code from a spec. The design of the interface is crucial to the success of the class, and must be examined by other designers.

Although I am describing the ideal designer, most of the good object designers I know fit into this category. Also, I gave their characteristics in priority order. Abstract thinking is most important, dealing with uncertainty is second, and communication skill is the most dispensable. What happens to the people who do not fit this profile? The following true story illustrates. Note in this story that program designers benefit from being abstract thinkers, but requirements analysts need to be thorough.

> Kim and Megan were teammates, responsible for the requirements and preliminary design of the business classes. Kim was particularly detail-oriented. She was proficient when it came time to go over the requirements document to see whether we had researched all the system interfaces, whether our

drawings were consistent, and whether we had neglected any issue we had agreed to cover. She was also excellent at working out our schedule. But we could not engage her in a conversation about the general nature of legal agreements or policies. After months of coaching, her designs still looked either like the screen specification or the description of the relational tables, and her code still looked like COBOL. She badly wanted to do object design, but she was not getting there.

Megan, on the other hand, had no patience for paper-and-pencil work, but she was quick to sort out the differences between insurance policies and general contracts. However, she repeatedly overlooked requirements and interfaces, and was sloppy in her specifications.

Over the course of the project, we let Megan take on the internal design role. We could not afford to have her overlook critical interfaces and we could make use of her subtle appreciation for the differences between classes. So she was told the requirements, and spent her time designing classes and, eventually, frameworks.

Kim became indispensable on the requirements team. She made sure that all issues were covered with the users or the executives, that all interfaces were defined, that the schedule was updated, and that the design documentation was in order. Periodically, she asked to design some business classes, which we permitted since major flaws in her designs would be caught and corrected. The advantage to us was that she stayed highly motivated and paid her way fully in her other work.

The ideal OO designer thinks abstractly, deals with uncertainty, communicates with colleagues.

TECHNOLOGY

Selecting technology for your project could occupy several books. This chapter covers four topics: how you make your selections; programming language; tools, including CASE tools; and the cutting edge of technology.

The Selection Process

Your selection of technology and tools profoundly affects your chances of survival, so observe how your team makes technology decisions. Usually, a decision is made because one person is persuasive or stubborn; the team already knows a similar technology; it is considered a safe, popular, or standard choice; or because a group of people decide it is the rational choice. I wish I could say that one of these is the best way to proceed. I have watched projects get in and out of trouble with all of them, so it is worth spending some time going over their strengths and weaknesses. Try to switch to a different method if you run into trouble with a weakness of your usual method.

One Person Is Persuasive or Stubborn

Many organizations have one person who is particularly persuasive or stubborn. It is not clear whether this person is wrong for being stubborn or right for being persuasive, or vice versa. Here are two short stories to illustrate. As usual, I have chosen to keep the project participants anonymous.

> Project Amber was the initial, small, and successful project conducted prior to moving a department of 50 to 60 mainframe COBOL programmers to objects as part of a corporate initiative. Only two people had done any workstation development, and that was in C. One of them had just received the new C++ compiler. Not surprisingly, he advocated that the pilot project be done in C++. Because he was the most advanced workstation programmer in the organization, the others, of course, listened to his advice. A consultant was asked to check the project setup, and recommended Smalltalk over C++, based on basic considerations, as in this book. He stressed the difficulty of moving COBOL programmers to C++. The decision took several weeks to make, since the two initial programmers were faced with learning an entirely new language. They finally decided to run the initial project in Smalltalk. They got training, mentoring, and so on, as would be hoped. A few months later, they were happy with the decision. The initial project was successful and the organization continued to use Smalltalk.

Project Amber illustrates a case of the key person being open to discussion. This probably also helped the group to accept the advice that made their project eventually successful. One is not always so fortunate.

> Deedee was a very small company, with only three programmers. Management added a fourth person, who refused to program in any language but Forth even though he was the only person there who knew it. He did the company's next projects in Forth. When he eventually left the company, it suddenly had legacy programs in a language no one knew.

Sometimes the person being stubborn is right, but sometimes he or she is wrong and is just being stubborn. It is hard to tell whether someone is wrong or is really two steps ahead of everyone else. In such a dilemma, what can you do? Get additional advice and take a rational decision-making approach. If the person in question still differs from the rest of the group, decide whether you can run the project without that person. Some systems are shipped with obvious design flaws, because without that stubborn person, the system simply would not have shipped. The managers evidently decided that a slightly flawed, shipped system is better than one that does not ship at all.

The Team Knows a Similar Technology

I used to believe people who said: "We have to use C++ because we already know C." Or, "We have to use this CASE tool because we already have it in house." Eventually, I learned, and I hope you learn sooner rather than later, that *retraining in object-think swamps all other costs.*

I have learned that it is faster to teach C programmers Smalltalk than it is to teach C programmers C++. Thinking in objects is easier in Smalltalk, the language is smaller, and the environment is more forgiving (refer to Project Amber, just described). You can, of course, build systems in either language. Each has it strengths, and projects have succeeded and failed in both languages. There are reasons and times to select C++, but they do not include "We already know C." More on C++ later in this chapter.

managing C++, 53

The same is true of CASE tools. Many projects have tried to take advantage of their organizations' investment in nonobject-oriented, upper-CASE tools, but they consistently find that they cannot express the OO functions they really want to. The tool is reduced to an expensive drawing package (see also Upper-CASE Tools later in this chapter).

upper-CASE tools, 61

If the team wishes to choose a technology because they know something similar, they should check to find out to what extent that similarity actually transfers to good advantage.

The Technology Is Safe, Popular, or Standard

Here is the story of a company I'll call Franco.

> Franco's research department developed a sophisticated system in CLOS. When it came time to market the system, someone said it should not be shipped in that language because CLOS was not standard or popular, and that the system should be reprogrammed in C++ since the production department "already knew C and would be moving to C++—they couldn't be expected to maintain the system in CLOS." The problem, of course, was that the researchers did not know C++, and had little interest in rewriting their system in a lower-level language. Franco's efforts to bring the system to market came to a standstill.

What might Franco have done? Because the system was ready in CLOS, my recommendation would have been to market it as it was. Users usually do not care what language a system is written in, and the CLOS version could have established the market for the sophisticated system.

I have seen organizations select technology on the basis of the number of copies of a book sold, or a company's sales volumes. Nothing in object technology is yet so standard that this argument should be the driver. Instead, you should *select the technology that gets you market.*

Minimize the constraints you put on your decision-making process so that you can allow each alternative to show how it will benefit or hurt your organization in reaching its goal. Where performance is an issue, "fastest possible" is not an acceptable goal. Figure out *how fast* it must be and measure against that threshold.

The Technology Is the Rational Choice

Much of the time, a rational selection process works well. One rational process is to discuss openly and then get a consensus. Consensus means that even people who would prefer another choice agree to be satisfied with, and even defend, the agreed-on choice.

A second rational process is to create a selection matrix in the following way:

1. List the characteristics you want to consider down the left side of a piece of paper, and the choices along the top.
2. Mark each cell with a tick mark if that choice has that characteristic.
3. Evaluate the matrix to decide the winning choice.

Some people put a weighting factor on each characteristic, then evaluate by multiplying each mark by the weighting factors and adding up the numbers in the columns. The highest score wins. There are two problems with using weights. One is that if the weights are close in value, a set of secondary factors might combine to outweigh the primary factors.

A second difficulty with weighting schemes is that the weights really are the personal preferences of the people putting the matrix together. I have found it easy to predict the outcome of a weighted selection process simply by discovering the preferences of the dominant people in the exercise.

The primary goal in working with the matrix is to discover the dominant factor in making your selection. Often, there is just one dominant factor that overshadows all others. On rare occasions there may be two. To illustrate, I offer the following conversation I had with my wife, which brought the point home to me.

> SHE: "We can buy any car you like, as long as it is as reliable as a Toyota."
>
> I: "This one has more trunk space, more legroom in the backseat, and you told me you liked the ride in the passenger seat."
>
> SHE: "That is fine. As long as it is as reliable as a Toyota."
>
> I: "This other one has faster pickup and better gas mileage."
>
> SHE: "That is fine. As long as it is as reliable as a Toyota."

You can guess which car we bought. Once reliability was settled as the deciding factor, nothing else mattered. At first I thought the car situation was an anomaly, but I have seen similar scenes repeated as organizations select technology.

Portability was the factor that drove organizations to consistently select C++, until Java. In its early days, C++ used a preprocessor that produced ANSI standard C, which could be run on workstations, servers, and mainframes. In contrast, there was one Smalltalk for UNIX, another for Windows, a third for OS/2, and none for mainframes. No combination of other factors could replace portability. For AT&T, backward compatibility with millions of lines of installed C-code was a dominant factor. No number of subtle advantages of Smalltalk, CLOS, Eiffel, Object Pascal, and other languages could outweigh that one consideration.

Ease of learning and *maintainability* leads to the selection of Smalltalk. These factors tend to show up in IS organizations, so Smalltalk is often recommended for IS applications. Ease of learning and maintainability do not show up as the dominant factors in scientific and engineering organizations.

Programming power sometimes leads to the selection of CLOS. That is why Project Franco researchers used CLOS originally. The Franco management team incorrectly decided that language popularity was the dominant factor for their product.

Use a selection matrix to help discover the dominant factor(s). Go through the exercise of attaching weights and filling in the matrix. As you evaluate the matrix, watch carefully to see whether minor characteristics add together to give you the "wrong" answer. You will know the wrong answer because it will not have some characteristic you simply must have. Strengthen that characteristic so that the minor ones cannot overpower it. Repeat the process. After a few passes, you will have isolated one or two characteristics that overshadow the rest. At this point, think carefully about your values and needs, and make a final choice.

Choose a technology that gets you to your goal,
not one that is popular.

Programming Languages

Every programming language brings with it a set of hazards. The hazards often come from preconceptions about the language, which may obscure the experience you will have. In this section, I discuss three languages—Smalltalk, C++, and OO COBOL—in some detail, and Java more peripherally due to the shortage of completed Java projects from which to draw conclusions. From these discussions, you may be able to anticipate hazards for other languages.

When preparing to make your language decision, assume that knowing your current language will not reduce the training time. Ask, "What damage might this language cause on the project?" and assess the answers to that question.

Managing Smalltalk

THE MISCONCEPTION: "SMALLTALK IS SMALL". It sounds small. It even says small in its name! Yes, the language definition itself is small, but anyone learning the class library will tell you it is not a small system. Smalltalk comes with a library of several hundred classes, with several thousand methods; it has been evolving continually for over 20 years, and includes a vast array of useful components.

The large class library is actually an asset; the alternative would be for your developers to design some of those classes on your project's time (see Chapter 5). Still, it is disconcerting to be faced with the size of the system if you think it will be small.

*polyBloodyHard
Reuse, 146*

When you use Smalltalk, the primary hazard to deal with is performance. Some people worry about the absence of compile-time type-checking in Smalltalk, but I have not seen a project impacted by the absence of compile-time type-checking. On the other hand, I have seen projects damaged for poor performance and lack of design (dealt with in Chapter 4).

*take the time to
design, 104*

PAY ATTENTION TO PERFORMANCE BUDGETS. Smalltalk is often criticized for being too slow for production systems. Object Technology International demonstrated that Smalltalk need not be slow by delivering a number of hard real-time systems written in Smalltalk, one of which was an oscilloscope.

On one project, accusations about the Smalltalk performance alternated with those about database performance. It turned out that neither was the primary cause of performance delays; rather, it was the overhead of many small requests going to the database. When the team modified the design to create as few requests as possible, each asking for the maximum database processing, performance improved by several orders of magnitude.

Nonetheless, many projects have given up on Smalltalk after being disappointed with the performance of their system. Therefore, manage the performance issue carefully. Work in the following way:

1. Allocate time in your project plan for performance improvements.
2. Buy a performance measuring tool and use it.
3. Establish maximum acceptable delays for your functions.
4. Make your system function correctly before going to the next step.

5. Make your system function fast enough by doing the following:

   - Measure the delay of your function. If it is acceptable, move on.
   - Do not overoptimize the performance. You may, of course, change the performance requirements.
   - Assuming performance is not acceptable, find the bottleneck. It is usually in one or two small areas. Improve the performance of as few places as possible. Do not overoptimize the performance of any area that is not a bottleneck.
   - To improve the performance of a bottleneck, change the data structures or the algorithms used. Do not use a different language unless there is a compelling argument for doing so.
   - Once the system's function is adequate, stop optimizing.

With this procedure, you will be able to write your system in Smalltalk, and still get acceptable performance.

DESIGN AND CODING STANDARDS. Buy some books to help you establish best practices and good habits for your group and then use them. These are the titles I recommend as the starter set: *Design Patterns*, E. Gamma, R. Helm, R. Johnson, and J. Vlissides (Addison-Wesley, 1994); *Smalltalk with Style*, S. Skublics, E. Klimas, and D. Thomas (Prentice-Hall, 1996); and *Smalltalk Best Practice Patterns*, K. Beck (Prentice Hall PTR, 1997).

Smalltalk is not small.

Managing C++

THE MISCONCEPTION: "C++ IS LIKE C". It has C in its name. It is advertised as "a better C." But, C is a small language, whereas C++ is a big language, much harder to learn and to use. Even its standards committee is trying to stop adding features because it is getting so big. That is just the language; the class library is or will become as large as the Smalltalk class library. So C++ is not really like C.

When you use C++, you must deal with three hazards. The first is the *complexity of the language itself*, the second is the *restrictions the language places on the design*, the third is the *impact of the language on the design process*. More specifically:

- It requires designers to introduce complexity into the design.
- It requires significant recompilation when a class changes.
- It requires programmers to keep track of the heap.

The first issue is design complexity. The rules of visibility and type-checking oblige designers to work some fairly complicated schemes into their design. Examination of the books recommended at the end of this section, plus a little further investigation, will give you an idea of the level of sophistication and subtlety needed to construct a good design. That complexity is not part of the your problem domain, it is the complexity added by the rules of the language. `Header files`, `virtual`, `public`, `protected`, `private`, `friend`, `const`, `casts`, `templates`, `multiple inheritance`, `constructors`, `destructors`, `reference counting`, and `run-time type indicators` are all topics your designers have to master and keep in mind while designing. Your maintenance team also will have to master these topics, and then, as the system evolves, understand how the original application designers were using them.

The second issue is static type-checking using classes as types, and recompilation. The spirit of object orientation is to *reduce the impact of change*. In C++, however, function calls are compiled in a fragile way. When the definition of a function's class is changed, even if the function itself isn't, all classes in the entire system that call the function get recompiled. This goes against OO's intention of reducing the impact of change, and it introduces long recompilation periods into your project development. Recompilations of 8 or 12 hours are common. Both the fragility of the system and the time consumed by recompilations add hazards to a project.

memory management features, 35

The third issue is absence of automatic garbage collection. Explicit control of memory is sometimes needed (protocol and real-time systems; see earlier in this chapter). Most projects, however, need to build the system as quickly as possible; anything else distracts. Keeping track of objects on the heap distracts, in an energy-consuming way. Automatic garbage collection algorithms have progressed enough by now so that having manual garbage collection should be a thing of the past.

I consider C++ the most significant technical hazard to the survival of your project and do so without apologies. Still, I expect many of you to decide to use C++ anyway, even after reading this chapter. So here I have the following three goals:

1. To get you to consider another language.
2. To guide you past the obvious hazards, should you decide to use it anyway.

getting advice, 67

3. To get you to hire someone who can get you past the rest of the hazards.

Project Amber, 48

CONSIDER USING ANOTHER LANGUAGE. If you are lucky, as the Project Amber one was, you will find another language that will work for you. If you are observant, you will be able to detect whether your organization can pass the tests for succeeding with C++. If you decide to use C++ and you are not suited to it, acknowledge that as soon as possible and start over. A number of large projects were delayed but then succeeded when they switched from C++ to Smalltalk after the first year of work. A year of lost time is still less than losing the project altogether.

WHY DOES C++ EXIST AT ALL? C++ was designed, quite deliberately, to occupy a design point different from Smalltalk. Where Smalltalk was slow, C++ was designed to be maximally fast ("pay as you go" is the phrase). Where Smalltalk was incompatible with C, C++ was designed to be compatible. Where Smalltalk had no static type-checking, C++ was designed to have compile-time type-checking. Where Smalltalk hid garbage collection in the run-time system, C++ gave it to the programmer and required no run-time system. These all represent valid language design trade-offs.

C++ sits at the crossroads of object orientation and C, a crossroads that is so important that more than five language systems compete for pole position: Objective-C, C++, C@+, SOM, Java, and some proprietary variations. At the time of this writing, C++ leads that competition, probably because its dominant factors are performance and backward compatibility. The following are guidelines to keep in mind as you evaluate whether your organization should use C++:

- Consider using C++ if your staff consists of engineering or systems programming people. Do not consider C++ if you are an IS organization and your staff has a COBOL background. This difference in background matters more than the project nature or size. People with engineering backgrounds are more accustomed to the subtle interactions between the language features they will find in C++.
- Consider using C++ if you are doing a low-level, real-time system.
- Consider using C++ if you have a severe backward compatibility issue.
- Consider using C++ if your key developers will quit if faced with having to use Smalltalk. Also, consider hiring new key developers.

CREATE SUBSETS OF AND STANDARDIZE THE LANGUAGE. The first step in managing C++ is to develop a standard usage of the language, and have people *use it*. Having a standard approved set of C++ locutions means that everyone who joins the project can read and understand the code. It means that designers will not spend time worrying about or discovering new ways to do simple things. It gives consistency to the system, and saves time.

Creating a standard usage is difficult, and getting people to use it is even more difficult. Use the ideas that follow to guide your effort.

Find an expert to set up the language standards. This person must be technically strong, a bona fide C++ expert who understands the strengths and weaknesses of the language features as they apply to *object-oriented* development. She or he must also be personally convincing and strong enough to be respected and to persuade others on intricate matters of programming. If you are just starting with C++, and do not wish to hire outside help, send your most experienced and most trusted programmer to C++ school, with the assignment to get this information.

Check out one of the current books on C++ idioms. More appear all the time; some good ones to start with are listed at the end of this C++ section. Numerous organizations have gone to the trouble of sifting through the language to set up conventions, so why not use this information to get a head start? If you find you can base the standards entirely on a book, all the better.

Develop standards that call for a simple and object-oriented use of the language. The best OO C++ programs have the general appearance of:

```
object.message;
object.message;
object.message;
```

and so on. Note the absence of language-specific clutter. These programs are efficient *and* easy to read. This is, of course, an embarrassment to the language specialists who wish to make use of every nuance C++ provides; they will not be able to brag about all the language features they used. Your challenge is to create a development culture in which efficiency and readability are valued.

Get your group to use the standards. First, get the standards accepted by the technical leaders. Most seasoned lead designers have their personal preferences about using the language, but are willing to set some of them aside in order to get a common design/coding discipline. Some negotiation may be necessary.

Second, hold a half-day internal class or meeting to go over the standards that have been developed. Do not underestimate the value of this meeting. I have seen good standards ignored because such a meeting was not held. The primary purposes of the meeting are to show each programmer that every other programmer is there, to hear all the questions and answers from each person, and to build a culture and establish that the standards are real. The people present will ask very specific questions. Some questions will uncover flaws in or legitimate exceptions to the standards. Other questions will show personal fears that the standards do not have enough power or sophistication to handle some situation. A good answer will allay those fears. A secondary value to the meeting is to save time by answering all the questions at one time, instead of repeating the answers individually over the months that follow.

Establish design and code reviews. You should have these anyway. You particularly need them if you are trying to keep to a subset of C++. If the technical leaders are behind the standards, getting people to accept them is relatively easy, but reminding everyone to use them is still necessary, and design/code reviews serve that purpose.

Allocate time in the schedule for periodic restructurings of the class hierarchy. This will be necessary no matter which language you use. When you use C++, it just will take a little longer to do all the editing and recompiling.

If you follow the preceding suggestions, you will be on your way to managing C++. Jeremy Raw's Eyewitness Account tells more about this.

DESIGN AND CODING STANDARDS. I recommend the following books to help you get started on establishing best practices and good habits for your group: *Effective C++: 50 Specific Ways to Improve Your Programs and Designs*, S. Meyers (Addison-Wesley, 1992); Koenig, A., Moo, B., *Accelerated C++: Practical Programming by Example* (Reading: MA, Addison-Wesley, 2000); *Design Patterns*, E. Gamma, R. Helm, R. Johnson, and J. Vlissides (Addison-Wesley, 1994); and *Object-Oriented Design Heuristics*, A. Riel (Addison-Wesley, 1996).

If you can't avoid C++, find someone knowledgeable enough to set and ensure simple standards.

◆ **Disciplined Use of C++** *Jeremy Raw, Independent Consultant*

The most successful big C++ project I've been involved in clearly revealed the strengths and limitations of C++. It was undertaken by a design and coding team of seven people, four of whom were very experienced in either C++ or object-oriented design; the rest were experienced in C programming. The application was to be delivered on a workstation platform on which all the participants had some experience. C++ was chosen as a matter of convenience, since some of the project goals demanded a certain level of "unique" functionality.

The primary pitfall for this project revolved around finding a disciplined, OO way to use the language, despite many temptations to take shortcuts. We adopted strict coding standards at the beginning, some of them obvious and some of them arbitrary. They included:

◆ No "downcasting," other than to specifically designed classes
◆ No visible use of C types in implementations of our project-specific types
◆ No pointers to members
◆ No multiple inheritance
◆ No friend functions
◆ No public data members

We also took the position that implicit type conversions among our own types (other than those planned from derived to base classes) would be frowned on.

Despite a warning from one experienced programmer, the client expected the project to be built with Microsoft Foundation Classes (MFC). We quickly determined they should be framed as an implementation detail and that the system object model would be developed in complete isolation from MFC. This was for portability and to make sure our goals were not crimped by incompatible characteristics in MFC's object model.

Our initial coding standards held up quite well. We had planned to use a variant of Hungarian notation (special prefixes on names), but found in practice that the most useful information to code into a name was its scope or "where it came from"—clearly marking out global names, parameters, local names, and class members. The fact that this was a different scheme from that used in MFC also worked to our advantage since it became very clear what was "ours" and what was "theirs."

We also found that the pressure to "code in C" was extremely intense, particularly as we worked close to MFC code. There was a lot of internal resistance in the group at first to throwing away working code, even after it was shown to be incompatible with the model we were aiming for. We also had trouble retreating to analysis and design once we had started building the application in earnest, although the project's initial shortcomings rapidly convinced us that we would have no choice.

Ironically, as we relaxed about "making it good from the beginning" [see Chapter 5, Managing Precision, Accuracy, and Scale], we had an easier time concentrating on the design, disengaging egos, and improving the structure of the object model and the application itself.

The project as a whole was a generally positive experience for everyone involved. We concluded that if we had it all to do again, we would have made an even bigger point of not implementing anything in final form until there was no alternative, adhering to one programmer's motto: "Easy to write, easy to read."

Case material contributed by Jeremy Raw, used with permission.

Managing OO COBOL

THE MISCONCEPTION: "OO COBOL IS LIKE COBOL". Your people will either write paragraphs that are object-oriented or write just COBOL. Selecting OO COBOL will not make your COBOL designers suddenly able to create good objects. The designers of OO COBOL learned from Smalltalk, C++, and the early CORBA work, so as an OO language, it is sound. At the time of this writing, however, there is not yet much project experience with it. What might we expect as project hazards to fix for this language?

The hazard has to do with expectations. It would seem reasonable to think that if your developers know COBOL, they should be able to learn OO COBOL, and if they do not master OO COBOL, they can still work in COBOL. But this thinking overlooks that object-oriented design is the design of modules, it is not the writing of the code. If your designers do not master OO thinking, then their design will not be object-oriented, and it will not help if your programmers have mastered the new language syntax. An OO COBOL design is either objects or just COBOL.

The second possible faulty expectation is to think that by the time your designer has been trained in object thinking, a COBOL-like writing style will be the most efficient. Recall, retraining in object-think swamps all other costs.

Smalltalk is so simple that the entire language can be taught in an afternoon and mastered the next day. What eats up learning time are: (1) OO concepts, (2) design principles, and (3) the contents of the class library. OO COBOL has those costs, plus the cost of learning how and when to do things differently in OO versus standard COBOL. At the time of this writing, Smalltalk is becoming the legitimate successor to COBOL for object-oriented applications on the workstation. It is now available on the mainframe.

The third hazard has to do with the class library. Smalltalk's class library has been growing for several decades, and the library for C++ for over 10 years. The OO COBOL class libraries are in their infancy. You may be faced with spending money to develop software that you should, in principle, be able to buy.

USING OO COBOL. When, then, should you consider OO COBOL? Suppose there is a large amount of COBOL work being done on the mainframe, and your lead developers want to experiment with object-oriented structure on the mainframe. OO COBOL allows them a reversible path. They can apply some object-structuring techniques in a few places, and stay compatible with the rest of the team. For other appropriate times, we shall have to wait and see.

An OO COBOL design is either objects, or just COBOL.

Managing Java

Java is the newest arrival at the crossroads of C and object orientation. What you lose in the move to Java is exactly what C++ chose to optimize: backward compatibility with C, no need for a run-time system, and control over performance (pay-as-you-go performance features). What you gain with Java is less design complexity, greater design stability, and increased portability. With both C++ and Java, you leverage your programmers' experience in C, and your developers still have to learn object design principles and the class library.

Although more complex than C, Java is considerably simpler than C++, and avoids the key problems I associate with C++: language complexity; a fragile, static type structure based on classes as types; and no automatic garbage collection.

Java is a smaller language because it gives up compatibility with C in favor of being completely object-oriented. It uses dynamic type-checking, and allows inheritance of interfaces, as opposed to forcing one to inherit interfaces plus all the implementation details. This feature simplifies some of the complexity C++ designers face when using multiple inheritance. Finally, it provides automatic garbage collection, which eliminates a major area of concern for developers. It is a fully OO language that comes with a run-time package, as does Smalltalk.

Java is most often targeted at internet and intranet applications because the run-time portability pays most quickly for the cost of moving to this new language. Java, of course, is a general-purpose language, and may be used for any sort of application.

Although Java is evolving quickly, it will for a time suffer from immature class libraries and development environments. Smalltalk has a 20-year head start, and C++ has a 10-year head start.

All the general Smalltalk and C++ advice given earlier applies to your Java project: Take the time to design, set standards, and follow the standards. Given the use of a run-time system, you can expect performance problems from Java for some time to come, so this advice from Smalltalk also holds: Develop time budgets, get the program to work correctly, and improve the design *where needed* until the performance goals are met.

The Sam Griffith Eyewitness Account (on pages 62 and 63) describes using Java in 1996 through 1997.

Java is easier than C++, but still young.

Tools

Does your choice of tools affect your survival? Yes, if you do not know exactly what you need them for. If you buy a tool believing that it will somehow guide your people in their thinking, then you have added risk to your project.

Know what each person is going to produce (see the discussion of tools in Chapter 4). Once you know that, you can buy, mix, and adapt all sorts of tools to your needs. As Humpty Dumpty said to Alice in Lewis Carroll's *Alice Through the Looking Glass*, "The question is, which is to be master—that's all." Do not buy the latest CASE tool, work through all the diagrams it supports, and hope that the software will somehow pop out—it will not. Most of the later design work cannot be generated from prior information, but requires new information and careful thought. Recheck your expectations about tools.

methodology, 77

In over a dozen project debriefings, I asked the teams for their tool priorities. They were consistent in naming

- Versioning and configuration management
- Communication
- Performance monitoring

The common characteristic of these most highly valued tools is that people cannot or will not perform these tasks manually. In general, tools considered useful record and track work, or analyze it to give your people insights as to what they did. Recording–tracking tools include text and drawing editors, group communications tools, versioning systems, project-tracking systems, and code-packaging systems. Analyzing tools include run-time performance monitors, code-consistency testers, compilers, linkers, and metrics-gathering tools.

You can build some good, small tools on your project, a small code generator to create accessor functions and declaration files from simpler specifications being one example. Such tools are fairly easy to write, and save hours of keystrokes. You might write a small metrics-gathering tool to monitor code complexity for design reviews. Most projects have people both capable of writing and delighted to write such small tools.

Upper-CASE Tools

By upper-CASE tools, I mean those tools that let the team draw diagrams of the object model, and that claim to generate code, check consistency, or reverse-engineer existing code. They deserve a special mention as they can create extra work for an already busy team, draining valuable energy from the project. The extra work may push the team into a depression caused by a sense of bureaucratic overload.

◆ **Using Java**   *Sam Griffith, Objects Methods Software*

Interactive Web Systems worked on a project to build a wireless network configuration engineering support tool. The tool was supposed to support a very progressive GUI, and replace a system that ran on a mainframe. The engineers enter data about a module they need to configure and the system munges on the data, figures out what equipment is needed, and where to place it in the module, draws a picture of the module, and then lets the user rearrange the equipment in that module using drag-and-drop.

Why did we use Java?
We used Java because our client wanted their applications to run over their intranet, and because Java support in internet browsers is strong and getting stronger. We did look at using Sun Microsystems' Safe-TCL, which is available for Macs, PCs, and UNIX boxes. However, it requires a plug-in and is also a relatively obscure language to PC programmers.

One of the things we had to do was to educate the client on the current state of Java and its support of various platforms. They had heard all the hype and none of the downsides. The client was a little disappointed in the current state of things, but optimistic that the situation would improve by rollout time.

Java versus C++
Java is definitely an easier language to program in than C++, with many fewer "gotchas." One look at the book *C++ FAQS* and a potential C++ programmer may be scared to death or ready to become a new member of the sadomasochistic community. :–) With Java there is no need to know the many different ways that const may be interpreted based on its position in the source: const before a function, const before a function argument, const after the function, and so on. Java also makes memory management a nonissue. It has a nice feature that it borrowed from Objective-C called interfaces, which are used in place of C++'s multiple inheritance. Interfaces allow programmers to easily codify exactly what must be implemented and allow the compile-time and run-time systems to verify support of a particular set of messages. The run-time verification is what C++ doesn't have.

Java versus Smalltalk
Java is not as mature or as portable as Smalltalk. Java tries to be platform-independent, but the GUI libraries are its downfall. This is

---

minimum CASE tool requirements, 65

This subject is politically sensitive. Every year, tool vendors claim they have made dramatic tool improvements, eliminating the problems from previous tools. Then, some executives feel they must run the project with the latest computer-based tools. The record of the upper-CASE tool industry is poor enough, however, that I recommend extreme sobriety in judging these tools. Later in this chapter, I give specific suggestions about needed improvements to tools.

Over a period of four years in the early and mid-1990s, I debriefed numerous projects on several continents, both inside and outside IBM. I always asked about upper-CASE tools. I often got an embarrassed headshake: They had not thought enough of them to give them serious consideration. A few projects related how they had investigated and taken classes evidenced by the team at Marimba (four of the original Java team members) feeling obliged to create their own GUI library. Using only the very basic low-level classes that the AWT provides, they have created a rich GUI library that is much better and more extensive than the AWT that comes with Java. It should be noted that Microsoft is doing the same thing with a new class library they are creating. Other things that Smalltalk has that can make problem solving and programming easier include Blocks (Closures for Lisp fans), programmer-definable control structures, keyword message syntax; and everything, including numbers, is an object. The Smalltalk environment is also light-years ahead of Java's. In Smalltalk, one can extend the environment just by adding code and saving the image. I can't do that with any of the Java development environments. Most Java development environments are written in some other language.

Our results

We dealt with Java's GUI issues by using the Bongo GUI toolkits from Marimba and Symantec's Cafe development environment. Cafe gave our team an environment that is modeled after Smalltalk, and Bongo gave us a decent GUI class library. Our client easily accepted that Marimba charges a fee for using its technology. The Marimba tools had other advantages, such as ease of distribution, that far outweighed the fees in the client's eyes.

Our team consisted of several former Smalltalk programmers. Out of that group one team also had extensive experience in Objective-C, C++, CLOS, Object Pascal, and several other OO languages. The team found that learning Java was easy. It was the immaturity of the GUI libraries and development tools that they were most frustrated with. Our team has not found one development environment in which we can debug reliably, so we constantly fall back to the old standard of printing our state to the console.

Despite the immaturity of Java and the associated tools, the team came away with an overall good feeling. Yes, we are living on the bleeding edge, but we do get quick turnaround on editing, compiling, and debugging; it's not quite as fast as Smalltalk or Lisp environments, but much better than any C++, Pascal, or other statically compiled environment. Our turnaround time even beats Visual Basic.

Hey, Java's the future, so why fight it? Plus, it's easier than C++!

Case material contributed by Sam Griffith, formerly of Interactive Web Systems, used with permission of author.

in various tools. After examination, they decided that the tools detracted from the project, rather than adding value. Tom Morgan of the B.U.G. project said he had concluded that drawing notations do not scale up to large projects. All of B.U.G.'s critical work was done in text, and they easily built very effective cross-referencing and consistency-checking tools. In more recent work, I asked the same questions and got similar answers. Although there have been improvements with respect to reverse-engineering and code generation, they are small improvements when compared to the total purchase, training, and time cost of the tools.

B.U.G., 13

Exactly what should you want from your object modeling tool? The following subsections describe three of the possible answers.

DRAWINGS. You will want to discuss the object model in open meetings, with managers, testers, database designers, domain experts, user representatives, object designers, and others. It is not practical to bring the Smalltalk browser or C++ listings to the meeting and expect the different parties to make decisions by looking at the text. A drawing of the classes, their relationships, responsibilities, and attributes facilitates the conversation, and helps to draw out questions.

Do you need a CASE tool for this? Many people use a drawing package, one specially designed for diagramming or drawing designs. A CASE tool costs more and is usually harder to use. As Dave Thomas of OTI repeatedly says, "Why should I turn my best OO designers into draftsmen?" Whichever tool you use for drawings, understand what you get for your money.

CONSISTENCY. Some CASE tools track changes to class, relationship, and function names so that changing the name on one part of the drawing changes it on all parts. Some tools will alert you when a class grows past a certain size. Again, take a look at how easy it is to enter and change the drawing. I provide a test for this issue shortly.

CODE GENERATION. On a recent, fairly large IS application, my colleagues and I estimated that perhaps 5 percent of the total system code could have been generated from the business object model. That was primarily names of data items and simple accessor functions for them. In the case of C++, there is enough boilerplate header material to be written that a tool's assistance is quite handy.

The problem comes when you must add some computation that cannot be generated automatically. At that moment, the drawing of the object model, which moments before was an asset, becomes a liability—a burden of double maintenance. From then on, your team will have to maintain both the drawing and the final code. I have yet to interview an industry project that successfully managed double maintenance. On one project, I set up selected resynchronization points between the drawing and the code by designated individuals. Before I left the project, the drawings were already out of date compared with the code, and were not put right again.

The double-maintenance problem is diabolical, because multiple design documents are almost impossible to keep in sync, and there is no known way around them, yet. Double maintenance pertains to non-CASE material as well, such as simple drawings. The only difference is that drawing editors do not claim to solve it.

Every year I hear about a tool that is "about to come out that will take care of your concerns." A year later, the tool proves hard to use, causes as much work as it saves, and creates a double-maintenance burden. Is there a fair test for these tools? I think so, and the next section describes it.

The Scanner Challenge

How many changes are required before the tool beats a pencil drawing scanned into Lotus Notes? The pencil (pen) is still the fastest drawing tool, and still can put the most information into a square inch. As changes are made to the design over time and the drawings are updated, a good drawing tool, or CASE tool, will start to pay for itself. I estimate that 30 to 40 major changes would have to be made to a single page of a pencil drawing before the CASE tool would pay back the initial cost of entering the drawing. If nonerasable marker were used, and the entire page had to be redrawn, then the CASE tool might pass the pen after about 15 changes to the page.

That in itself is not a fair comparison because the CASE tool drawing is made available to everyone on the project over the computer network, whereas the pen drawing is stuck in someone's filing cabinet. To make the pen drawing available, it has to be scanned into a distribution tool or document editor. It takes time to turn on the scanner, scan in the drawing, and paste it into a note. I would estimate that a CASE tool drawing might beat a scanned drawing at about 10 changes per page.

As CASE tools improve, that number should drop. And so it becomes a fair challenge to ask each year, "How many changes does it take before the CASE tool beats a pencil drawing scanned into Lotus Notes?"

Estimate how often you plan to update each page of drawings. That will help you see how much effort the CASE tool will cost you, or save you. On my last project, drawings were made four times: once before design review, once after design review, once before shipping to QA, and once on product release. The CASE tool did not pay its way in simplified changes.

Minimum CASE Tool Requirements

When will an upper-CASE tool offer value and not get in the way? When it meets the following three minimal criteria. They are not easy to meet, and to date, no upper-CASE tool I have seen meets them.

1. *Single point of maintenance.* The tool generates code from the drawing, but need not generate all of the code just from the drawing. It is permissible and probably necessary for the tool to support a mixture

of drawings, text, high-level notation, and programming language code. What *is* important is that each item (drawing item or text item) be the *only* source code for whatever it describes. It must never be necessary to edit two places for one change (this is called *single-point of maintenance*). If the drawing item changes, the program code should change also; if it is necessary to change some program text, the tool should preserve and protect that change. This requirement eliminates the double-maintenance burden of current tools. No tool I know of can do this.

2. *Tailorable mappings*. The code the tool generates has to be tailorable. Each project has its own programming conventions and standards, and within a single project, there may be different generation requirements for different kinds of classes (persistent versus nonpersistent, for example). At this time, some CASE tools support tailorable mapping.

3. *Logical versus physical views*. Drawing a line between two objects should not always result in code being generated. Sometimes a line means, "I don't yet know how this object talks to that object," or "We already know, and it is in the model, but I wish to hide how this object talks to that object to simplify the picture for the moment." The first is used in early stages of design, or analysis. The second is used to present a finished design in a "rolled-up" or "high-level" view. I know of no tool that does this.

Without at least these capabilities, busy developers will continue to ignore or resist the tool. There are other desiderata for such CASE tools. However, these three are already hard enough.

> *A useful tool records, tracks, or analyzes work to give people insights into what they did.*

The Cutting Edge

The newest, most marvelous idea in the industry will probably do you more damage than good.

In the early 1990s IBM's System Object Model (SOM) was hot, then it was Taligent's OO operating system, then SOM again, then the CORBA standard, Distributed Objects Everywhere, Visual Programming, and so on. Many organizations considering object technology felt that to be current, they were obliged to use or consider each of these. In 1996, Taligent suddenly quit. Companies dependent on Taligent had to scramble to work out a new strategy. Project Stanley (see Chapter 2) was one in which its

Project Stanley, 18

leaders' insistence on using cutting-edge technology was a major cause of its failure.

If you are an expert in an area, you know it. If you have done distributed programming, then you can evaluate Distributed Objects Everywhere, CORBA, Distributed SOM, Distributed Smalltalk, or distributed whatever. If you have not done distributed programming, then you cannot evaluate these technologies, and probably should stay away from them. If IBM and HP have not come to market with, for example, a CORBA platform, assume CORBA is not a good place to put your money just now. Select a cutting-edge technology only if you can handle the cut.

If it is not part of your specialty, buy it. This first part of the strategy is easy. Spend your development money where you have an opportunity to gain an edge on your competitors. Let a company that specializes in the new area work through the learning and development curve. You will be able to buy its solution for 1 to 5 percent of the development cost. If someone has not figured out how to bring it to market yet, assume you will not have time to do it on your busy project.

If you cannot buy it today, assume it cannot be done currently. The average project is less than two years long. If you rely on another company to deliver this new software in its *advertised* time frame, you add significant risk to your project. History is not on your side. Assume it will not become a reality during the timespan of this project. Investigate it again at the start of the next project.

Beware of programming houses and consulting companies eager to work on the latest industry fad using your dollars. Contracting companies habitually learn new technology by bidding it for your project. Visit a project for which the technology was previously deployed. If it has not been deployed yet, you are in the same situation as before. Try to work through this project without the new technology.

Be on the cutting edge only if you can handle the cut.

TRAINING AND GETTING ADVICE

Professional athletes use coaches to help them to play better. Doctors are required to take courses on medical advances each year. The best OO designers I know gather several times a year to trade ideas and pass on what they have learned. New bank tellers go through two weeks of full-time training before being put in front of a customer. Yet the average organization budgets perhaps one week of language training for their novice OO developers. Do you really want a $2,000,000 system built by people with one week of training? If a bank teller needs two weeks of training, how much should a developer get before tackling your OO project? A few organizations have worked out the economics of the situation, and send their new developers to about six weeks of training.

What to Teach

You expose your project to risk to the extent that your developers do not know the following topics. Arange for them to learn all eight.

1. How to think in objects.
2. How to make object design trade-offs.
3. How to program in the selected language.
4. How to use the tools.
5. Which conventions to follow on each deliverable.
6. What is in the class library.
7. What a framework is, how to use it, and how to document it.
8. Their role on the project and who is dependent on them.

The next sections discuss a strategy for each hazard.

Developers do not know how to think in objects.

YOU ARRANGE: Three days of instruction plus ongoing coaching

If your people do not know how to think in objects, the design will not have good encapsulation of design decisions, and so it will not be easy to extend over time. It will be, at best, a design that works once. You will miss the benefits of objects, without avoiding the costs (see Chapter 2). So:

possible benefits, 23
costs, 28

- Find an introductory course that teaches object thinking, plus programming or design. It should be a four- or five-day course because usually it takes three days to learn to think in objects.
- Hold periodic internal sessions for people to learn how good objects grow, or assign a mentor to do that task. New OO designers encounter a lot of pressure to use a nonobject (i.e., nonencapsulated) design. They have a great deal of time pressure, previous design habits to overcome, and few good examples to follow.

This process should go on for a year, until people are generating questions and answers by themselves.

Developers do not know how to make design trade-offs.

YOU ARRANGE: Another three days of instruction or mentoring on the project

If your analysts, designers, and programmers do not know how to make trade-offs in object design, then they will mistakenly think they are doing a good job when they are doing a mediocre job; the analyst will not understand when the designer/programmer rejects a "good" model because it is not appropriate for implementation. Send your database designers through this training also, so they understand the reasoning behind some of the rather different designs the OO designers come up with. Fix weak design by finding a course that explicitly teaches design trade-offs. Such courses are hard to find, I am sad to say; most teach everything *but* design trade-offs. However, there are some around. As an alternative, the mentor or one of the experts you hire will be able to provide this information on an ongoing basis throughout the project.

Developers program poorly or use tools badly.

YOU ARRANGE: Language/tool courses

Tools and programming instruction are the easiest to arrange. There are courses for every language and every tool. Smalltalk takes about one day to learn, C++ takes about one week. Each course typically is bundled with an introduction to object-think and class libraries. Find a C++ course that teaches C++ for object-oriented programming, not C++, the language (see section on C++ earlier in this chapter). The OO C++ classes *managing C++, 53* teach object-think *and* language. Graduates of regular C++ language classes still have to learn object-think and then must learn which of the nifty things from their C++ class they should *not* use.

Different programmers write differently, making the code hard to learn.

YOU ARRANGE: A half-day meeting or course on project conventions

Programmers write differently from each other because (1) they don't know what you expect from them, and (2) they tend to seek their own way and are somewhat skeptical of others' methods. You must deal with both of these issues.

Have the project's technical leaders negotiate and agree on a set of design and coding standards, a common, technically acceptable way of designing and programming. Meeting these standards is what you expect of your programmers. You might want to believe that all you need to do is send out a note with the standards, and then everyone will know what you expect of them. This will not work for reason (2) just mentioned.

Hold a half-day class or meeting to go over the standards. Let the programmers ask specific questions. It is important that the person answering the questions be someone they trust. You will save time by answering many of their questions at one time.

Some of the programmers will have legitimate exceptions to the standards; some will identify real flaws with them. Others will express fear that the standards will not be sophisticated enough to handle their situations. Good responses to their questions from the technical leads, along with well-designed standards, will allay most of those fears.

Another purpose of the meeting is to show the programmers that the project is really a team effort. This builds a culture, without which there may always be the nagging feeling on an individual programmer's part that "Maybe (the local superprogrammer) is not really going to use these, and I am the only sucker complying." I have seen decent standards ignored because such a meeting was not held, even though the standards were issued and signed by the local superprogrammer and team lead!

Developers create redundant classes because they do not know what is in the class library.

YOU ARRANGE: Courses on and reviews of purchased classes; design reviews

This problem is more difficult than the suggested fix makes it appear. Your language course should spend time on the standard class library. When a new class library is purchased, either the vendor or someone on the project should run a course on what it includes. Not surprisingly, people forget what is in those libraries, and have a tendency to create minor variations. This is part of the reuse problem (see Chapter 5).

polyBloodyHard
Reuse, 146

No one knows how to document a framework well.

YOU ARRANGE: For people to read various framework descriptions and experiment with writing them

Frameworks have been around since the mid-1980s, but still the documentation of them is unsatisfactory. Circulate the MacApp framework, the Taligent frameworks, and the Gamma et al. *Design Patterns* book. Have people discuss those and experiment with their own documentation. Software designers don't like to write or to read documentation, so try to bring up the level of writing using examples and simple encouragement. Make sure that your courses include understanding and *using* (not creating) frameworks.

Developers do not understand their role on the project and who depends on them.

YOU ARRANGE: Methodology review

If developers do not understand their role on the project, they will not make a decision they could make, or they will not pass on information to another person waiting for the decision or needing the information. Make sure all team members know which other people contribute to their work, and how their work affects other people. Hold a meeting at which you present the project's roles and the role interactions. This is part of your methodology and part of setting up communications.

When to Teach

Just in time, and continuously. Teach just before people need the knowledge, or else just after they have tried something on their own. It rarely pays to teach everything at one time. The exception is a six- to eight-week "boot camp" designed to turn out fully functioning OO developers. Such a camp will be organized (we hope!) so that material is introduced just about at the point when it can be integrated into the project.

Project Ingrid successfully used both teaching strategies: just-in-time and continuous training (see Chapter 2). The leaders introduced new concepts just before the developers needed them. OO concepts with simple language topics and class library contents came first; advanced language topics, framework design, and design patterns came later. On the job, the developers had a chance to digest and put the information into practice. A few months later, the more sophisticated design techniques and language were taught just about the time the designers were being given more significant design work.

Project Ingrid, 14

Continuous training was used to keep smaller quantities of information flowing to the designers over a long period of time. Project Ingrid conducted a weekly half-hour or one-hour study group to discuss particular topics. They chose examples of good and bad code, polymorphism, multiple inheritance, or alternatives to subclassing. The developers got used to asking questions and receiving information outside of class, and they were exposed to much more information over the long term. Those people are likely to continue to develop over time—which is what you want for your developers.

Teach just in time, and continuously.

Getting Advice

Make your own mistakes and learn, or pay for the advice up front. They cost the same, but learning the hard way takes longer. This is an unabashed recommendation to get advice. Many pitfalls have already been discovered, and it is a waste of time for you to rediscover them on your own.

You may need a consultant and a mentor. The consultant's role is to steer you away from pitfalls or to help you recover from those you have already fallen into. The mentor's role is to grow your developers by teaching them good habits. The mentor does not have to be the best developer, but rather someone with a good bedside manner, who is able to encourage and coach the trainees.

Market demand currently exceeds the supply of properly trained mentors and consultants, so take the time to investigate the experience and references of consultants and mentors you may want to hire.

LEGACY ISSUES

There are two particular issues to take up with regard to your legacy systems: mainframes and relational databases.

Mainframes

Most mainframe teams have different vocabularies and have been trained with techniques that are different from their object-oriented colleagues. Prepare for communication difficulties between the two teams and expect them to work in different ways. Many mainframe developers are used to working in a one-pass manner: "Give me the requirements; I'll do high-level design, low-level design, code, and test." Experienced OO developers are used to multipass, iterative development: "I'll tell you the requirements *after* we show it to our users twice" (see Chapter 5).

increments and iterations, 117

Partition the architecture so that the two groups can work in their own ways. Either get the mainframe developers comfortable with iterative development or develop a synchronization process that gives them their requirements only after the driving design is relatively stable.

The allocation of function to different platforms and languages may cause some trouble. The workstation and mainframe designers are likely to differ on which platform they believe a certain job belongs. This is not an object-oriented problem per se, but it is one that is likely to show up on your OO project. Defining the boundary of the OO system will require negotiation between the lead developers. Either they will have to agree or you will have to use a third party to work out the solution.

Consider using an "object-centered" design for the mainframe services to the workstation. Organize the services around the kind of requests coming from the workstation. The same objects are going to generate the same requests over time. Interestingly, object-centered design has twice been suggested to me by lead mainframe designers, not OO designers.

Relational Databases

Relational databases are fundamentally different from object databases and OO code. Here is a colorful allegory to illustrate the difference:

> You are parking your car in an object-oriented garage. You drive into the garage, get out, close the car door, and walk into your house. When you want to leave again, you walk into the garage, climb into the car, start it, and drive away.
>
> You are parking your car in a relational garage. You drive into your garage, get out, take off the car doors, put them onto the stack of doors; take off the wheels, put them onto the stack of wheels; take off the bumpers; and so on. You walk into your house. When you want to leave, you walk into the garage, take the doors off the doors stack, take the bumpers off the bumpers stack, take the wheels off the wheels stack, put them all onto the car's frame, climb into the car, start it, and drive away.

Putting relational data together is called *joining*. Joins are time-consuming, exactly as the allegory indicates. Fitting an object-oriented design to a relational database calls for additional table joins, usually to capture inheritance and many-to-many relationships. Reducing the number of joins needed is part of the strenuous work of fitting an OO design to a relational database. This one activity requires a great deal of communication, patience, and time. However, it is an important activity since it involves both the people and the models from the programming and the database communities.

The two communities and their models differ in a second key respect. Philosophically, a row in a relational table has no special "identity" beyond the data it contains. Any row that contains the same data is considered "identical." Not so for objects. Philosophically, each object has its own identity, so even when two objects contain the same data, they remain different. Naively putting objects into a relational database results in a clash, probably in the form of a long, drawn-out philosophical argument between the object and database designers over whether to add an identity field to the relational table.

If the relational database's purpose is to support the objects, it will have to have an identity column. Technically, this is simple: Just use the unique key that is automatically generated by the database management

---

◆ **Project Setup**   *C.D., Independent Consultant*

If I were to going to make recommendations for a large client/server project, here are a few things I would focus on given my experiences. I'm sure you will recognize a lot of these.

1. Find the right help. Don't be the guinea pig for a newly formed consulting group that has decided that "objects are hot," and that's where *they* want to be. If the consulting group you are considering can't provide references, it means that this is either their first project or that their other projects are "unreferenceable." Don't become their next unreferenceable project. If references are given, call them, or better yet visit them to see what kind of development environment and development process the consulting group left them with.

2. Be able to identify a technical architect for the project and make sure there is a commitment for that person to be involved in the project on a daily basis. Don't settle for a "two- to three-days per week" type of arrangement, and don't settle for an archi-tect who appears to be a "really bright person" but who has "poor communication skills." Hiring an architect who can't communicate *effectively* the hows and whys of the technical infrastructure to both managment and programmers is a recipe for disaster. Your project should not be the first project of its type for the architect. Again, demand references.

3. Realize that Smalltalk "out of the box" is not an appropriate tool for building complex client/server applications. Focus on transforming the completely generic development language/environment of Smalltalk into a business-specific development language/environment. Make sure that management understands the importance of this goal and is willing to allow for it in the project schedule and budget. If possible, develop your business-specific development environment over the course of several small projects. Whatever you do, don't hand your application developers Smalltalk and a database wrapper and let them "have at it."

---

system. The situation will be harder to resolve if the database has been there for a long time and it is not practical to add an identity column.

A third, greater hazard to your project when using a relational database is what is called the "persistence black hole." Rather than buying an OO database or buying a commercial framework for interfacing to a relational database, your team decides they can do the whole thing quickly and inexpensively by themselves. They say, "We'll just store the objects as rows. Easy enough."

A short while later, they find they have to optimize joins. Soon after, they find they have to handle transactions and transaction rollback. Then, they face checkpointing data and optimizing data transfer. Finally, they realize they have not adequately handled the object identity issue, and must retrofit that into the system.

In the end, they find they have built a small OO database system. It cost at least $300,000 for their two work-years of effort—perhaps triple that, if they were good enough to complete it at all. This little project-

4. Strive to develop and communicate standard approaches/solutions to common development scenarios. During the project, take checkpoints and surveys of the types of issues that application programmers are having to deal with on a daily basis. Make sure that the provided frameworks and standardized solutions address those problems effectively. If a framework doesn't appear to be solving the right problem or is getting in the way of the development process, cut your losses and purge it from the development environment as quickly as possible.

5. Document frameworks and solutions in a handbook you might title "Project ABC Developer's Guide/Cookbook." It should present an overview of business-object schema and behavior (when it becomes available) and technical architecture. Address the 15, 20, 30 most common application development scenarios/problems and their standardized solutions, with pointers to examples. The solution may involve a framework, or it might just be a standardized way of solving a given problem. Examples of common problems faced by client-side developers are: How to retrieve, change, and save persistent business objects; how to translate business rules into code; and how to surface the facets and services of business objects to the GUI.

6. Perform design and code reviews to ensure that new solutions aren't being invented for the problems that have already been solved/documented and to identify deficiencies in existing frameworks or the need for new frameworks or standardized solutions.

7. Make sure that opportunities for reuse between projects are exploited. Interproject communication is essential. Make sure that there is one solution developed and used for a problem that is shared by multiple projects; for example, technical infrastructure (persistence, validation, window management) and possibly even business domain objects.

Case material contributed by a third party, used with permission.

within-your-project swallowed your best programming talent for perhaps a quarter of your project's timeline. You would have been better off buying an object-oriented database to begin with.

If you do decide to use a relational database, search *extensively* for a company that has already built the persistence subsystem, then *buy it*. It will cost you much less, and will free up your best programmers to do your project work.

Beware of the "persistence black hole."

REVIEW

Rather than review all the things covered so far, I offer an Eyewitness Account above by C.D., a consultant, who asked to remain anonymous.

Chapter 4

Getting Started

Plan the project by milestones.

By now you have made your project selection. To effect it, you must create methodology, estimate, plan, set milestones, and start design.

METHODOLOGY

Methodology is, "how your organization repeatedly produces and delivers systems."[1] For you, it is the following:

♦ Who you hire, and what you hire them for.
♦ What information they expect from co-workers and pass on.
♦ What conventions they follow.
♦ What sorts of jobs you agree to do.

No one person should need to "read the methodology," because your methodology is the collected job descriptions of everyone on the project, what they do, and how (see Figure 4-1). As people learn their jobs, they stop referring to the methodology, except to check the project standards for the deliverables they produce. The rest is simply how they get their job done.

---

[1] The *Miriam-Webster* dictionary defines *methodology* as: (1) a series of related methods or techniques; (2) the study of methods. The *Oxford English Dictionary* contains only the second definition. Hence, American and English speakers disagree on whether to say "method" or "methodology." I use the American form.

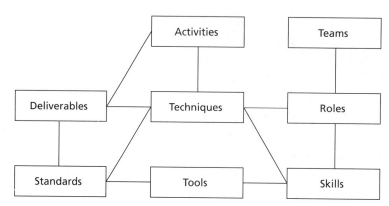

Figure 4-1 *Big-M methodology addresses all job descriptions*

I call this use of methodology *big-M methodology.* Major development houses use the term this way, and it is a powerful way to think. This chapter outlines a base big-M methodology for you, from which you can evolve your own, tailored version. Figure 4-1 and the following sections illustrate what I mean.

A second and weaker use of the term methodology is, "which drawing notation and which author (UML/OMT/Fusion/Booch/Shlaer-Mellor) do you follow?" I refer to this as *little-m methodology* because each author covers only a part of what you need for your big-M methodology. Do not spend too much time worrying over your choice of author or notation. Your little-m methodology will not be a critical factor in your project's success or failure.

Whatever you choose, you still have to decide who is going to do what activity to produce what deliverable, who will read the result, and what their interactions are. The little-m methodology, illustrated in Figure 4-2, is a fragment of the big-M methodology.

In this book, the term methodology always refers to big-M methodology, unless explicitly noted otherwise.

Big-M Methodology

Glenn House's EWA, 172

Developing a big-M methodology is crucial to the success of your organization. The Eyewitness Account by Glenn House in Chapter 7 conveys, as an undercurrent, how his company evolved a methodology slowly, expensively, painfully. Exactly as I promise here, they did finally develop one, which is serving them well.

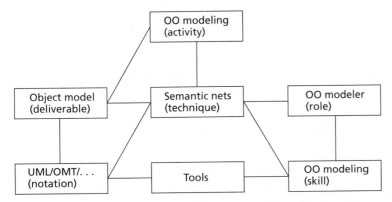

Figure 4-2 *Little-m methodology addresses one primary job description*

Your big-M methodology should consist of at least the following eight elements. Compare them to Figure 4-1.

1. *Roles*. The job descriptions you put into the ads when you need to hire more staff: JAD facilitator, project manager, requirements gatherer, business class designer, tester, program designer, programmer, writer.
2. *Skills*. The skills you expect those people to have when they answer the ads: as facilitator, planner, programmer, OO designer; familiarity with tools.
3. *Techniques*. The techniques you expect your staff to use in their work: JAD (Joint Application Design), session facilitation, CRC (Class-Responsibility-Collaborator) card exercising, Smalltalk or C++ programming, domain modeling, use-case modeling.
4. *Tools*. Which tools the people use in their jobs, either within a technique or to produce a deliverable according to the standard.
5. *Teams and Job Assignments*. How you group people and assign them to multiple roles. In the methodology outlined next, one job assignment is called *business analyst–designer*, and consists of the roles requirements gatherer, requirements analyst, business class designer, business class documenter. Another, *designer–programmer*, consists of business class designer, programmer, software documenter, unit tester. Each *business design team* has one business analyst–designer, two to three business designer–programmers, one database designer, one mainframe developer, and one system documenter. An *infrastructure design team* has one lead designer plus two to four designer–programmers.

6. *Deliverables.* What you want each person or team to hand off to another person or team: use cases; class, screen, test specifications; framework documentation; class diagrams; and interface diagrams.

7. *Standards.* What is permitted or not permitted in the design and in the deliverables. These include notation, project conventions, and quality concerns. Notation legislates things like selection of:
   - Use cases for functional requirements
   - UML or Fusion, or Shlaer-Mellor, or whichever notation for the object model
   - The programming language, its allowed variants and compilers

   Project conventions legislate things such as the following:
   - A use case having its name as the first line
   - Prohibition of many-to-many relationships in entity-relation models
   - Prohibition of "friend" classes in C++
   - Every program method or function having a public header description

   Quality concerns may legislate or simply raise awareness about things such as:
   - Completeness with respect to the requirements, modeling, documentation, and programming templates
   - Use of published design patterns in the design
   - Patterns of interobject communications in the design

8. *Activities.* The activities and milestones of the different teams and how they fit together over time to produce the final deliverables. Aspects of activities are covered over several chapters in this book.

Most OO book authors focus on one role, such as the designer, and then discuss notation for part of that person's deliverables, giving a few preferred technique fragments. Authors focus on slightly different roles and techniques, leading developers to combine little-m methodologies on a project.

Most popular books are not intended as project management texts, and so include only a simplistic process model, along the lines of "1. Gather requirements. 2. Find the objects. 3. Draw a model. 4. Describe the behavior. 5. Code. 6. Evaluate and repeat." This is as useful as the one-page instruction sheet I was given for building a dune buggy:

1. Take off old body.
2. Put on wiring harness.
3. Put on new body.

4. Attach controls.
5. Attach bumper cages.
6. Attach roof.
7. Drive away and enjoy your new dune buggy!

Your software development process deserves considerably more attention.

A methodology is organization-personal; each organization and company develops its own successful way of working. Therefore, a mass-market book can only scratch the surface of what has to become your organization's way of working. Various factors drive the development along different lines. Does the group:

- Do big projects or small projects?
- Aggressively incorporate new technology or play it safe?
- Have rapid or slow staff turnover?

These kinds of factors determine the detail to which you define your methodology, with many job descriptions or few. The following two sample methodology summaries, one for a small and one for a large organization, illustrate the difference.

> *Small-shop methodology.* We never take on a project that needs more than 10 people. We put 2 or 3 people on it first, until the architecture has been tried and is stable. We add people only after each partition in the system is defined and a lead technical person is either comfortable with its overall design or finds he or she needs help. Each team is made up of 2 to 4 people. There are no deliverables besides interface definitions and the final system, properly commented. Each team iterates at its own comfort level within a timebox. Risk/payoff lists are used to select each next activity.

> *Big-house methodology.* We use a project manager and assistant, JAD facilitators, requirements analysts, business experts, an architect, technology designers (network, database, server, OO, etc.), technical writers, testers, trainers. There are templates for each deliverable: use cases, business rules, domain class diagrams, interface charts, class and method/function specifications, test specs, test case results, and so on. Development teams follow an incremental process with four-month increments, with at least two full iterations per increment.

Which methodology is correct? Neither, or both. Each works under different circumstances.

A Base Methodology to Tailor: Crystal/Clear

A full methodology fills 300 to 1,000 pages, detailing roles, activities, techniques, and standards. There are small organizations with small *project purpose, 36*

projects and large organizations with very large projects. There are SWAT, Investigative, Production, and Full-Commit projects (refer to Chapter 3). There are as many methodology variants as there are organizations.

I present the following methodology outline for a medium-sized Production project in an industrial setting. The characteristics of such a project are the following:

◆ It is staffed by 20 to 40 people, total.
◆ It is of 1 to 2 years in duration.
◆ Time-to-market is important.
◆ There is a need to communicate with present and future staff, and a need to keep time and costs down.
◆ It is not a life-critical system.

It is a common sort of project, requiring trade-offs between complete, extensive deliverables and rapid change in requirements and design. I kept the number of deliverables low, to reduce the cost of maintaining them, yet included enough to keep the teams communicating. I tailored job assignments and teams to allow the fluidity usually needed on this kind of project. Many other sorts of projects also need provisions for fluidity and can take advantage of this methodology.

Discussion of the Methodology

This methodology is designed to let the technical development team deliver quickly. It is targeted to speed the communication from requirements through programming and back, without removing deliverables needed for future system evolution.

Some projects need more deliverables. A life-critical system needs more visibility into how the decisions were reached. A long-running project needs to preserve intermediate information because developers might never get to ask each other questions. Each document is expensive to create and maintain, which is the reason this methodology minimizes them.

Small organizations will want fewer job assignments, each containing more roles. Small organizations have extreme cost concerns, and rely on more face-to-face explanations between developers. Having fewer job assignments can sometimes mean fewer deliverables, which lowers costs further.

What you use on the first project will not be your final methodology. Rather, your first project will show you what you *really* need in the methodology, and how you must alter your first one to suit your organization.

If you choose to separate the requirements and design teams or the design and programming teams, you reduce the amount of parallelism and flux your organization supports. I dwell on this because team structure, creation of deliverables, and parallelism are items of contention between project management and software developers. Developers typically prefer minimal structure, few deliverables, maximum parallelism and flux. This reduces their workload and lets them get their work done faster. Managers typically prefer the reverse, to make the project easier to monitor, plan, and understand. It is not that one is correct and the other wrong. The team, monitoring, and deliverables structures determine the amount of parallelism and flux the project can support, or else are determined by the amount of parallelism and flux the project must support. When you choose one set, the other is no longer open to free choice.

The following quote, from Malan and Letsinger's description of Fusion methodology, illustrates a common misconception and pitfall regarding team structure, parallelism, and flux (see Chapter 6):

sentences you hope never to hear, 154

The [Fusion] method distinguishes three stages:

- *Analysis*—which produces a declarative specification of *what* the system does.
- *Design*—which produces an abstract object-oriented model of *how* the system realizes the required behavior.
- *Implementation*—which encodes the design in a programming language.

Fusion starts with an informal requirements document. Analysis transforms the information in the requirements document into a set of models that more precisely characterize the way the software system interacts with its environment. These analysis models are then input to the design process, which produces another set of models describing how the system is structured and how the system's behavior is realized in terms of that structure. . . . Finally, the classes and methods identified during design are implemented in an object-oriented programming language.[2]

The quote makes the development process sound much tidier than it actually is. Thinking that requirements, analysis, design, and implementation are easily separated adds a hazard to your project.

Many projects' teams find that there is a great deal of interaction between requirements, analysis, design, and programming, with fluidity

---

[2]Malan, R., Letsinger, R., and Coleman, D., *Object-Oriented Development at Work: Fusion in the Real World*, pp. 1-2 (Englewood Cliffs, NJ: Prentice-Hall), 1996.

in both the requirements and the design. Requirements shift while the designers design, often because of the designers' insights and questions. Further, most OO design modules consist of very few lines of code (often only 3–10), so that detailed class design almost *is* programming. This means that people change their understanding of the problem on the scale of days and weeks. Iterative development by itself will not keep pace with these changes, as iterative development operates on a time scale of weeks and months.

The methodology outlined in this chapter supports maximum flux by arranging only two people between requirements and code. These people share information on a daily basis, with no written deliverables required between them. One spends time in meetings, collecting and examining information for easy transmission to the other. The other keeps the detailed software design in his or her head. They negotiate over the business class definitions, one set of eyes focused on the business, the other focused on the software.

Finally, the methodology contains incremental delivery as a cornerstone, since that lets you make midcourse adjustments to everything else. At the end of each increment and at the end of the project, you evaluate what you learned: your priorities, what you would like to keep, and what you would like to change. That becomes your organization's personal methodology.

Here is the methodology.

Roles, Skills, Techniques

BUSINESS EXPERT. An experienced businessperson. Knows how the business operates and can answer questions about how things are done; what is stable; what is changing; what is essentially attached to each concept, habit, and term; and what is only conveniently associated with each.

> *Skills*: Knowledgeable in the operation of the business and the business plans
>
> *Techniques*: None related to designing the new system

USAGE EXPERT. An experienced user. Knows how the business operates from the point of view of the person who will be using the new software. Can say which system services are more important than others, which features can be dropped, which operational shortcuts can be taken, which alternatives can be created for procedures. Must know the user's job intimately. Is *not* an IS person who happens to have talked to a number of users, a manager who gives the software to the users, or the purchasing agent. There may be several usage experts for the several user groups targeted.

> *Skills*: Same as the users' job skills, plus the ability to articulate actions and priorities
>
> *Techniques*: None related to designing the new system

TECHNICAL FACILITATOR. Knows how to conduct a group discussion session, whether requirements gathering, joint design, or design review.

> *Skills*: Working with groups
>
> *Techniques*: JAD (Joint Application Design) or Group CRC card design, design review facilitation (CRC card design is described more in Ward Cunningham's Eyewitness Account later in this chapter.)

Ward Cunningham's EWA, 94

REQUIREMENTS ANALYST. Knows enough of the business to examine the users' requirements statements and enough of the technology to ask for alternative requirements when the solution looks too hard. Examines and catalogs interfaces to the new system, both current and planned.

> *Skills*: Communication skills, thoroughness
>
> *Techniques*: Common sense, domain object modeling (find the nouns, reduce them, check business rules, apply cardinality rules)

ARCHITECT. Knows how to design the system as a whole. Responsible for major subdivisions and interfaces within the system, performance targets, ensuring cleanliness and functioning of the overall system. Acts as reuse advocate across teams. Works with the project manager to prioritize and organize the project plan. Does high-level design.

> *Skills*: Ability to evaluate the entire system in her or his charge; ability to make global and detailed technical decisions
>
> *Techniques*: Systems analysis, performance modeling

PROJECT MANAGER. Knows how to gather and integrate information from all stakeholders in the project (executive sponsors, architects, developers, testers, etc.) and put it together into a workable plan. Knows how to fend off "feature creep" and other hazards of running the project. Responsible for the process, with input from the other roles.

> *Skills*: Motivation, observation, communication, planning
>
> *Techniques*: Project estimation, management-by-walking-around, team building

LEAD DESIGNER–PROGRAMMER. Knows how to create frameworks, knows the difference between strong and weak designs, can monitor and coach other programmers without demoralizing them. Reasonably good communication skills. Designs subsystems, applying design techniques to the requirements. Typically but not always the best programmer on the team.

> *Skills*: Framework design, class design, communicating with newer designers, programming
>
> *Techniques*: Domain modeling, framework design, design by responsibility allocation (CRC cards), design by client interface, design by theory building, or design by intuition

DESIGNER–PROGRAMMER. Knows how to design a complete and programmed set of classes from requirements and a sketched design. May know how to design frameworks. Could be an expert designer with little interest in communicating and teaching.

> *Skills and Techniques*: Same as lead designer–programmer

DESIGN MENTOR. Similar skill set as lead designer, but with stronger communication skills. Responsible for improving the level of design and programming in the group, and for coaching novices.

> *Skills and Techniques*: Same as for lead designer, plus the ability to articulate design considerations, coach novice and middle-rank designers

REUSE POINT. Either the architect or a designated designer-programmer with good programming skills. A part-time role. Identifies commercial classes to buy and classes being designed, which overlap and should be reconciled.

> *Skills and Techniques*: Same as lead designer–programmer

WRITER. Creates the external documentation, such as the class, screen, and test specifications, and first-draft user manual.

> *Skills and Techniques*: Good at writing, familiar with OO topics

TESTER. Knows how to create and run test cases, given either the requirements document or the class and screen specifications. Creates system test suites that can be run repeatedly (regression tests).

Skills: Creating test suites

Techniques: White box/black box test creation, disturbance tests, and test recovery

USER-INTERFACE DESIGNER. Knows how to create easy-to-use user interfaces. Knows or can learn the UI standards. Enforces simplicity and consistency in the UI design. May have special training in gathering feedback from users on the interface.

Skills: Able to learn the users' work needs and habits, and able to evaluate and test the user-interface design

Techniques: User-centered design, low-fidelity UI modeling, videotape- and questionnaire-based testing

Other roles might be present, such as test manager, training and rollout specialist, help desk operator, database designer, network designer, but the roles listed here are standard.

There is one other, less-than-obvious, job assignment I have found to work well. Combine part of the designer–programmer role with the requirements analyst to make the business analyst–designer, or analyst–designer for short. Having a business analyst–designer simplifies discussion and speeds feedback from design to requirements, as you will see.

BUSINESS ANALYST–DESIGNER. Responsible for talking with the users, eliciting requirements, cataloging interfaces, like the requirements analyst just defined. Creates the initial design of business classes, and negotiates and reviews final design of business classes.

Skills and Techniques: Class design, CRC cards; may help create frameworks for the business classes; responsible for seeing that the class diagrams match the final code upon system acceptance

Tools

Each role needs tools, including at least the following:

- Versioning
- Communication
- Programming
- Testing
- Project tracking
- Drawing
- Performance measuring
- Screen drivers for repeatable GUI tests

Work out the details of these tools and their templates as appropriate for your specific product and working environment.

Teams

The assignment of roles to people depends on the skills your staff members already have, the communication strengths and weaknesses particular to your organization, and your ability to alter the existing organization. Teams are created both along and across system decomposition lines. Here are those based along system decomposition lines.

FUNCTION TEAMS. A function team identifies and delivers user-based system functionality. Each consists of one or more usage experts, access to a technical facilitator, one business analyst–designer, one to three designer–programmers, a UI designer, a tester, and half or one writer. A database designer is included if there is a significant database to develop. Multiple function teams share the frameworks for the business classes.

The business analyst–designer and designer–programmers on a function team work as though they are one person in several bodies. To keep communications fast and allow fluidity in the requirements, design, and program, no documents are required to pass between them. The analyst–designer is responsible for researching requirements and interfaces, and passing on new information to the designer–programmers, perhaps several times a day. The analyst–designer will create the initial draft of the business classes, reflecting her or his domain knowledge. The designer–programmer starts work as soon as the functional requirements are "good enough to start." The designer–programmers alter the base design in negotiation with the designer–analyst to suit the evolving needs of the software. The analyst–designer reviews the final design, to reestablish validity with the user needs and business domain.

INFRASTRUCTURE TEAMS. The infrastructure teams create the subsystems that support the business classes: network, database, and user-interface support systems, for example. Each team contains a lead designer–programmer, several designer–programmers, a tester, and half of one writer. The infrastructure team is usually made up of those people having a strong computer science background, since severe and, often, subtle technical issues will have to be addressed. An infrastructure team may be responsible for simulating and evaluating the overall architecture.

EXTERNAL TEST TEAM. The testers create usage-based regression tests for the system. They may have close interaction with the function and technical teams, or they may work entirely from the technical specifications and documentation. Each way of working has its proponents.

The following are the teams that cross system decomposition lines:

SYSTEM PLANNING TEAM. Executive sponsor, project manager, architect, and one or more users. They identify and prioritize the work.

PROJECT MONITORING. Project manager and each team lead. They check where the next risks are coming from and how to reduce them.

ARCHITECTURE TEAM. Architect and lead designers. They ensure the overall system design stays coherent.

TECHNOLOGY TEAMS. One per specialty involved, consisting of the experts in each technology. Includes at least the UI design and the programming team. Most projects will also have a database design team, a writing team, and an internal test team. The purpose of each technology team is to set conventions and standards for their members, who are scattered across the function and infrastructure teams. For example, the UI design team makes sure that screens are consistent across Function teams in terms of the metaphors used, layout, and behavior. The programming team makes sure that design, coding, and documentation conventions are set and followed.

These teams require a lot of communication, which is normal. The OO teams will have additional communication, because of the frameworks being developed. A framework typically affects people in several teams.

Ownership

Ensure that each deliverable has an "owner." This means that each function to be delivered to the end user has a dedicated owner, and each class also has a dedicated owner (see Chapter 5 and Appendix A). The two may overlap, but there must be someone to answer for the ability of the system to deliver any given function, and one person to answer for the integrity of each class.

Ownership may be matrixed, with the same person owning both a function and a class. This is illustrated in Figure 4-3.

Deliverables

Although each team has deliverables, here I describe only the ones for the function teams.

- *The requirements document.* This includes the system purpose; the use cases; the business rules and relationships that must be preserved in the design; useability and performance requirements; and definitions

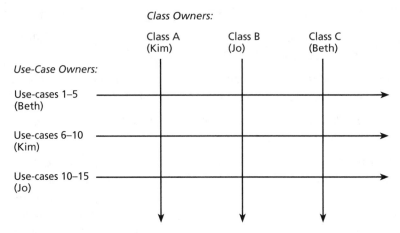

Figure 4-3 *Ownership matrix, function x component*

of needed interfaces to other systems or subsystems. This document is produced by the business analyst–designer and the writer. The purpose of this document is to communicate with the executive sponsors, the user community, the external test team, and the function team over time.

- *The user-interface design document.* This initially includes a description of the user metaphor, each screen's purpose, and the navigation between the screens. Over time, the details of each screen are added, along with details of error conditions. This is produced by the UI designer, analyst–designer, and writer.

- *The object model document.* This initially includes the major partitioning of the system into subsystems, each with its purpose, responsibilities, and interfaces. Over time, the purposes, definitions, and examples of use of each framework and class are added, along with a checklist of which major components are used for each use case. This is produced by the analyst–designer, designer–programmers, and the writer.

- *Specifications for other teams.* These include specifications for mainframe or other special programs that need to be written or specifications from the function teams to the infrastructure teams. These are produced by the designer–programmers and the writer.

- *Usage manual.* This describes how the users will use this part of the system. It is produced by the entire team, reviewed by the users, and used for external test and to prepare training material.

- *Code*. This comprises the source code and the compiled, bound code for delivery.
- *Test cases*. These are the regression tests applied to every class, subsystem, and total system.

It is possible for all deliverables to be started and undergoing change at the same time. The requirements document may still be fluctuating while business design is underway (see Monitoring in the Activities section later in this chapter). How much parallelism and simultaneous flux you can tolerate in your deliverables will depend on your team structure and the interteam communication (see Activities later).

monitoring, 92

activities, 92

Standards

NOTATION STANDARDS

- Use Smalltalk, with the proposed ANSI subsets where possible, for all of the business logic on the workstation. Use C on the UNIX server. Use COBOL on the mainframe. (This is just an example. Another company would use the ANSI-proposed C++, or Java, or Objective-C, or whichever language it preferred.)
- Use OMT until the forthcoming Unified Modeling Language is stabilized, then switch to that.

DESIGN CONVENTIONS

- The development team agrees upon and adopts design conventions for their deliverables (see the C++ program design conventions in Jeremy Raw's Eyewitness Account in Chapter 3, and the modeling conventions of the Brooklyn Union Gas project described in Chapter 2).

Jeremy Raw's EWA, 58

B.U.G., 13

- Other design conventions may require or preclude selected modeling techniques, programming language facilities, user interfaces styles, and writing styles.
- The book *Design Patterns*[3] might be required as a reference for common design problems. Whenever possible, the design solutions given in that book are preferred.

FORMATTING STANDARDS

- A standard template is created for the elements of each deliverable: use cases, business rules, screen navigations, interfaces, class definitions, function definitions, and so on.

---

[3]Gamma, E., Helm, R., Johnson, R., and Vlissides, J., *Design Patterns* (Reading, MA: Addison-Wesley), 1994.

- Programming standards describe what comments are needed with every function and class.
- New templates may be created on the first increment of the project, by joint agreement of the project teams. Old templates may be taken from existing standards.

QUALITY STANDARDS

Glenn House's EWA, 172

No quality standards are included here, but I suggest that you declare a small set based on your experience. Your team will discover more. Keep the set small (see Glenn House's Eyewitness Account in Chapter 7). Avoid gratuitous requirements along the lines of "every method must have 10 lines of code or fewer; every class must have 20 methods or fewer." These only push code elsewhere; they do not improve the quality of your system.

Activities

STAGING. Plan for a user-useable release every three or four months. Each release is one "increment" of the entire system. Each increment contains whatever each team feels they can deliver in the period, as orchestrated with the system planning team. It may include time for several revisions. Incremental development is described in more detail in Chapter 5.

increments and iterations, 117

REVISION AND REVIEW. Each increment contains several iterations, and each iteration consists of construction, demonstration, and review. A *shallow* iteration is construction, demonstration, and review of selected aspects of the team's assignment—perhaps just the screen design, the business behavior, or the database access. A *deep* iteration is construction, demonstration, and review of a slice of the team's assignment, working from end to end. A deep iteration for a function team has user function running from the user interface through to the database and back.

Use three deep iterations within each increment. Any number of shallow iterations are permitted. The purpose of the review at the end of the first deep iteration is to let users recheck their assumptions, and react to the basic design. At the end of the second iteration they get to double-check and fine-tune the design. They may remember additional assumptions, but should be discouraged from making major changes. The third iteration results in the subsystem going to test and delivery. The scheduling of each iteration is left to each individual team.

MONITORING. Monitor each team's deliverables with respect to both progress and stability. Progress is measured in milestones, which are sequential; the stability states are not necessarily sequential.

PROGRESS MILESTONES

1. Start
2. Review 1
3. Review 2
4. To test
5. Deliver

STABILITY STATES

1. Wildly fluctuating
2. Fluctuating
3. Stable enough to review

A common sequence of stability states might be: 1–2–3–2–3–2–3. A deliverable rated "to test" may get relabeled as "fluctuating" if some unexpected problem were encountered that questioned the design or the requirements.

PARALLELISM AND FLUX. Any dependent task can start as soon as all the predecessor deliverables are "stable enough to review." The team structure just given is tuned to permit this sort of parallel flux. The designers can start working out their basic needs, but should not start serious design, while their requirements are "wildly fluctuating."

As soon as the requirements are "stable enough to review," designers can begin parallel design. As soon as the design reaches "stable enough to review," serious programming can begin. (Tentative programming may have been done earlier, to assist in creating the design.) As soon as the business object model is "stable enough to review," database design can start. And so on. This maximizes the parallelism in the production of a release, while permitting flux in the deliverables.

The function and infrastructure teams work in parallel. The project monitoring and architecture teams review their work plans, stability, and synchronization points.

You can read more about big-M methodology topics and the foundations of these ideas in *Software Development as a Cooperative Game*. *Crystal/Clear* (in preparation) presents a lightweight methodology for small teams, of 3-8 people. Steve McConnell's *Rapid Application Development* and Jim McCarthy's *Dynamics of Software Development* contain many practical tips to adjust your team's way of working.

Find out how your organization has learned to produce systems.

◆ **Building Consumer Understanding of the Design**   *Ward Cunningham, Cunningham & Cunningham*

Things had gone well. The customer was satisfied, excited, and constructive. The review team, consisting of bookkeepers and accountants, cared about the objects inside the prototype and understood why they mattered. They, unlike previous review teams, could see past the little flaws in the hastily built interface. This was what an IT program manager told me when she called after demonstrating her phase-two prototype to her internal customers. Here is what we had done to make that happen.

I met the team of 16 people—customers and developers—on the first day of a four-day design workshop early in the project. They had already gone through introductory training in Smalltalk, which included an introduction to CRC cards. Had anything sunk in? They weren't sure.

On Monday, we wrote cards for lots of business data. This was easy. Most of the group knew the current system and the several volumes of requirements that had been written for the next one. If a noun appeared anywhere, we probably had it on a card. By the end of the day, everyone was tired and a little worried. There wasn't any sense of progress. I wasn't expecting any.

Tuesday began the same way. We kept going over the same material without decision or conclusion. People stopped looking at me, the facilitator, and started looking at each other. I looked where they looked, at the real decision makers. Then came the protest. Why weren't we writing "responsibilities" and "collaborators" on the cards as they had done in training? I had to be honest. We had the wrong cards.

Our 50 cards just barely scratched the surface of the problem (their assessment). We were going to need hundreds more just like them to get to the first prototype. If we were going to write that many cards, we might as well write another book and put it on the shelf with the rest of the requirements.

On Tuesday afternoon, I announced that we were going to have to start over. I took a stack of blank cards and moved to the far side of the conference room table. Our carefully arranged work-to-date lay out of reach and almost out of sight. I wrote out three rather generic cards. I challenged the group to work the now familiar scenarios using these alone. We stumbled. Some wondered, were we making progress or going backward? Our decision makers cautiously nod-

communication between developers, users, and executives, 24

I leave this topic with Ward Cunningham's Eyewitness Account of the use of CRC cards. CRC cards can be used not only to create a design, but also to communicate it with businesspeople. Ward's experience is that businesspeople of all kinds can understand, appreciate, and criticize the design using CRC cards. This strengthens communication between developers and businesspeople, and hence strengthens the project (see Benefit 4 in Chapter 2). CRC cards are described in more detail in the original 1987 article by Beck and Cunningham and in other recently published books.[6]

---

[6]Beck, K., and Cunningham, W., A laboratory for teaching object-oriented thinking, from the 1987 OOPSLA *Proceedings* (pp. 1–3), published by the SIGPLAN group of the Association for Computing Machinery. Also see Wirfs-Brock, R., Wilkerson, B., and Wiener, L., *Designing Object-Oriented Software* (Reading, MA: Addison-Wesley), 1990.

ded just often enough to keep everyone on board.

By Wednesday, our small design had grown to six cards and had been dubbed the "framework" approach. I liked the name. We worked through scenarios from half a dozen flipchart pages that we had pasted around the room during a lull in "progress" the previous morning. I watched for nods and excitement. I was getting some.

On Thursday, our last day with the customers, we set out to tackle the tough problems quoted on the two remaining flipchart pages. They turned out to be easy: more of the same as yesterday. By mid-morning, the decision maker among decision makers (the most important customer) said to the program manager, "If you could make the first prototype do these six objects, that would be worth seeing." We were done. We broke at lunch so our guests could do some American style Christmas shopping before heading back across the Atlantic.

The last task I had to do was make sure those six cards were not forgotten. I didn't want the first-time Smalltalk developers to lose sight of what we had accomplished. Six objects: How long could that take? One of the developers and I wrote them up that night in heavily stubbed Smalltalk code. We walked through it Friday morning.

We were beat but we had done it. We all knew what we had to build. No one wanted to admit that we had reduced volumes of requirements to six index cards. Because . . ., well, we hadn't. What we had done was to bring 16 professionals together and get them communicating on the same level about the same things. Then, looking into ourselves, using all of our professional experience, we searched for and found the essence of the desired system, the part that had been overlooked in the previous generation.

The schedule called for prototype releases every couple of months. There would be plenty of time to review requirements, documented and otherwise, throughout development. The whole team had connected once and would do so again often. I caught my flight Friday afternoon knowing that the team had a skeleton, one they knew to be the right skeleton, and were well prepared to flesh it out with the continued help of their customers.

Case material contributed by Ward Cunningham, used with permission.

ESTIMATES

The best way to estimate your project is to ask someone who has done it before. I assume you would do that if you knew such a person. Usually, however, you find yourself in a new situation, at least regarding team and tools. This section contains some estimating and planning tips that have helped other projects.

First, use your common sense. Consultants comparing notes are continually astonished at how often otherwise rational people schedule a new project, with new technology and new staff, to ship in one-quarter of the time or less, just because the project contains the word "objects." Object technology improves productivity somewhat, but not by a factor of four on a new project.

Next, use an incremental development strategy. Your first estimate is sheer guesswork. After the first increment, you can make a much better estimate, based on the track record of the first increment. There will be improvement as the team learns. Your third estimate is based on the track record of two increments, and so on. You will have the best possible basis for your estimates as the same team creates the same kind of system with the same tools.

To make the initial guesstimate, develop a few rules of thumb. The following are not foolproof, but they will serve to start your planning discussion. Collect your local OO experts in a room and let them debate your project with respect to these initial estimates.

Two Weeks per Noncommercial Class

One rule of thumb says that a class intended for use on only one project takes about two workweeks to develop. For commercially resaleable classes, double that to four weeks per class. Could 10 developers working for a year (40 weeks) deliver a system with 200 classes? Yes, that is a plausible figure, averaging across classes.

The hard part is not in developing a class every other week, it is guessing how many classes there are going to be!

Domain Classes

Perhaps you can start by guessing how many domain classes there will be, then multiplying it by a factor. Brainstorm the "nouns," the concepts, or the components of the system you are building. Start with `Customer`, `Address`, `Product`, the different stages of a product, or whatever your system's topic is. An `OrderForm` has a `Header`, a `Footer`, a `LineItem`, a `ServiceLine`, a `SummaryLine`. You will find your list of business components adds up quickly. Spend some time going over the list to combine and split as you think you might. Database analysts are fairly good at this, as are your experienced OO designers. If you have done only a cursory job of naming business components, multiply your estimate by another number, say 1.3, to get a more reasonable guess. Start by allocating two weeks per class.

Screen Classes

The number of screens you have is not directly related to the number of domain classes. An order form will probably have a screen to itself. An order line might or might not. A subtotal will not. Screens arise according to the needs of your users, not the classes. Therefore, estimate how many screens you will need directly from your functional requirements. Each screen will have a class to drive it, and perhaps several to support its needs. Allocate three weeks per class.

Utility Classes

You will write generally useful classes beyond the ones you buy in the class libraries. You may write money, time, transactions, recursive trees, and other things. Guess how many you will need; allocate two weeks per class.

Frameworks

You will develop some frameworks. These are much slower to develop than business classes, and more important. You might create a framework for persistence, for queries, for errors, for managing screens, for transactions, for common domain object behavior, for business abstractions, or for algorithms. Estimate how many you will need, and perhaps add one or two.

How long it takes to develop a framework is dependent on the person doing the work, so this is harder to allocate time for. Allocate six workweeks for a small framework, initially. If you are developing your own persistence framework, allocate 60 workweeks just for that framework (see discussion of this in Chapter 3).

legacy issues—persistence black hole, 74

The actual time it takes to develop each class depends on the staff you have available. Great programmers develop faster than the times just suggested; novices develop much slower. Fred Brooks cites a difference factor of 10 between best and worst programmers on a single team.[7] List your framework designers by name, because they will determine the pace of the hardest part of the design.

The screen classes are the next most difficult to design; the domain classes are typically the easiest. I know of no way to carry out the estimating exercise without knowing or planning on what kind of people are going to be on the team. The final work/time estimate and the final staffing plan are closely interrelated.

Periodically, after your project starts, count how many classes of each kind you have per requirements item. See how long it takes your team to create the classes for the requirements items. Discuss the quantities and the estimate with the teams after each release. Learn the following:

---

[7]Brooks, F., *The Mythical Man-Month*, p. 30 (Reading, MA: Addison-Wesley), 1995.

- What kinds of classes there are.
- What kinds of people are needed to develop each kind of class.
- How many of those kinds of classes can be developed in the next release.

From this, using incremental development, you can improve work estimates as the project progresses.

The work estimate and the staffing plan are connected.

PLANS

Not having a project plan is embarassingly common. The following are several reasons why it happens:

- Your staff does not have the discipline to sit down and think through the project.
- You have normal planning procedures, but you do not know what will be different with object technology.
- You are taking on several technology changes at once (client/server, graphical user interfaces, object technology, iterative development). You do not know what changes to make in your normal planning procedures.

If your staff does not have the discipline to sit together and think through the project, then your project hazard is exactly that. The project will take unexpected twists and turns and encounter unexpected delays. To help ward off project disaster, develop enough discipline to predict, just slightly in advance, what sorts of twists, turns, and delays are about to hit you. Work through a project plan using milestones. Although the plan will contain some errors, having your people talk through likely scenarios lets them understand the team's interdependencies. Measure and adjust the plan to anticipate the surprises. Chapter 5 in this book, on the project timeline, the ideal study project, and tuning the project, will give you ideas about what to expect.

If you know how to produce a project plan for your software and are just adding object technology, then the starting point is *plan as though the code were not being written with object technology*. Although surprising at first, this strategy will become "obvious" after close scrutiny.

Exactly what is different in an object project? Only the actual design of the object-oriented components. For the people doing the design, that is different, indeed. From a project planning perspective, it is a small difference. By the time you factor in the education for your team and all the nondesign parts of the projects, the difference between using OO and any other design technique will seem small. Your team will analyze the needs; create the requirements; examine them for technical and business dependencies; separate the work into releases; create a base architecture; get educated; and then build, examine, refine, test, document, and deploy each release. The fact that your designers are using object design techniques may show up in different numbers being suggested for the design part of the work effort, but that will not affect the way you put together your plan.

Here are three specific reasons that you can go ahead and plan the project as though "just any" design technique were being used:

1. An enormous amount of learning goes on during the project, which slows down software development to offset your productivity gains in using objects.
2. There are a dozen different time elements in the plan, of which design technique is only one. If you already have a planning formula that takes into account human nature, then you are better off using that than trying to guess a new formula.
3. The project will use an incremental development strategy, and so plans will improve after each increment. The first plan serves primarily for sizing, to see whether the project fits within its constraints.

Therefore, use your standard design-time estimates to put together the initial plan.

Every kind of project, whether SWAT, Investigative, Production, or Full-Commit, shares this: It should produce results at approximately three-month intervals. The SWAT project can produce the fastest—that is its purpose—and might be asked to show results monthly. The Investigative project, which involves a lot of training, can show the training results as a small bit of function at the three–month point, and a more substantial piece of function with better design at the six-month point. A Production or Full-Commit project is in danger of hemorrhaging in learning, paperwork, and communication; it should be forced to show delivery every three to four months to keep it moving.

project purpose, 36

The Eyewitness Account that follows is about a planning session I participated in.

Have the project show working results every three to four months.

◆ **An Estimation and Planning Session**   *Alistair Cockburn, Humans and Technology*

Before beginning the project proper, but after spending two weeks gathering over 100 rough use cases, we made our first project estimate. Our four best OO designers, the project manager, and a few other experienced, non-OO people made up the planning team. We split the session into:

◆ Estimating the size of the system
◆ Estimating work time according to the type of person we would need
◆ Suggesting releases, by technical and business dependency
◆ Balancing the releases into approximately similar sizes

We used an "open-auction" system to get to a size estimate. Each experienced OO designer wrote on the board the factors he thought would determine the project effort. One wrote, "technical frameworks, use cases, UI screens"; another added, "business classes"; another added, "database generation tool." Each added a column with his guess at how many of each type would be present. Then the first person added a new column with his revised estimates based on what he had learned during the first round. We did three rounds this way. Some used multiplication factors from the estimate of

business classes, some used use cases as a base, some used UI screens as a base. There were about 20 to 25 factors in all.

We discussed whether we had achieved convergence, and what the differing factors were. In the end, we agreed on some numbers and understood where we disagreed. The key drivers for the estimates were the number of (1) business classes, (2) screens, (3) frameworks, and (4) technical classes (infrastructure, utility, etc.).

Second, we decided what type of person we would need for each type of class. Frameworks are hard, and there are only a select number of people who can write them reasonably. We decided that the business classes would be relatively easy to write, but would require business knowledge. Technical classes would be harder, but would not require business knowledge. In the end we settled on:

◆ Expert developers for the frameworks
◆ Intermediate-level technical and UI developers
◆ Relatively novice business developers who could learn the domain

We split the table of classes to be developed into those three categories, summed the

MILESTONES

As you work, there is an awkward sense that everything depends on everything else. It seems that requirements cannot be completed until the second deep iteration, that UI design and component design are not complete until programming is complete and the whole thing goes to test. This hardly makes for a satisfactory project plan. The response is milestones:

◆ If you are paying attention to your risks, you may discover the need for a prototype of some portion of your system. The evaluation of that prototype is a milestone, for it will tell you something new about your system.

classes per category, and decided how many classes per month that level of developer could develop. We gave the framework developers 10 weeks per framework, the technical and UI developers 3 weeks per class, and the business class developers 2 weeks per class.

The sum of all those weeks gave us our first project time estimate. We hemmed and hawed over that for a long time, comparing it against other reasonability measures, such as the rate we could hire and train people. In the end, we kept the estimate.

Deciding on the releases was straightforward. Nothing could be delivered until most of the infrastructure was done, so that went into release 1. We created a dependency graph of the business functions, by technical and business dependence. From the size estimates, we circled areas of similar size. That gave us our release plan. We already knew we wanted a release every four months. At this point the session was essentially complete.

I created a separate lines-of-code estimate [see Chapter 7, Productivity], using different curves for the various productivity levels people have. Productivity per month changes over time with learning, peak productivity, and saturation as the project grows in complexity. This second estimate gave the startling prediction that 6 expert developers could develop the system in the hoped-for timeframe, but 4 experienced people and 15 novices could not. As it turned out, using 6 experts was not an option, and we were going to have to use 3 to 4 experts and 12 to 18 novices. I pulled this chart out at several times over the course of the project, and found it was tracking accurately.

As the project progressed, we learned that we could not come up with a detailed estimate from the requirements alone. Within each increment, we had to develop an initial size and shape of the object model to estimate business-related classes. We also had to develop an initial size and shape of the user interface to estimate the UI-related classes. Then we could make a meaningful estimate from use cases, UI classes, business classes, and technical classes

The good news is that this matched our original estimation formula. The numbers shifted as we learned more about each release and tuned the plan.

- The moment at which your developers have enough requirements to start work is a milestone that helps you plan staff parallelism.
- The moment your users get to see the first working version is a milestone, which will tell you how much more work needs to be done on those functions.
- The second user review, the design review(s), and the review for compliance to standards are milestones.
- The day the work is bundled and sent to test is a milestone.

Here are nine basic milestones you may find useful, more or less in the order in which they are encountered:

1. Start of requirements gathering
2. Start of design (when only part of the requirements are gathered)
3. First user-interface review
4. First design review
5. Object model and database models reconciled
6. First user review of working function
7. Final user review of working function
8. Design, code, and documentation meet standards
9. Pass into test

These milestones, or ones like them, can be applied to each cluster of functions you are delivering on this release. Keep it in mind that prototypes, reviews, and documentation are valid milestones.

> *Plan by milestones, each showing sufficient results
> to let the next work start.*

MEASUREMENTS

According to Pfleeger et al. ". . . researchers have not yet been able to find measures that are practical, scientifically sound (according to measurement theory principle), and cost-effective to capture and analyze" (p. 32).[8] So decide *why* you want to measure before trying to decide *what* to measure on the project. In Glenn House's Eyewitness Account in Chapter 7, read about the hazard of measuring too much.

*Glenn House's EWA,
172*

Be aware that most people take measurements for the next project, not the current one. We feel so bad about not knowing how to estimate this project that we want to reduce that feeling on the next one by measuring what happened on this one. I wish that worked. However, the next project will almost certainly have different clients, different developers, and different technology from this one, so the numbers on this project are unlikely to help much. That does not mean not to take those time measurements; it only means you need not make them as accurate as you might otherwise think—which simplifies your work.

Avoid the most obvious unit of measurement: number of hours spent on each domain class to reach each milestone. This one will drive both your developers and you mad, even though it is the obvious measurement to request if you do not know the actual question you want answered. It is an extremely detailed question, and most developers do not have any idea

---

[8]Pfleeger, S., Jeffery, R., Curtis, B., and Kitchenham, B., Status report on software measurement, *IEEE Software*, 42(2): 32–43, 1997.

how much time they have spent on each class at the end of a day or a week. I have seen dedicated developers take their time cards home with them over the weekend to see if they could puzzle out what they did all week. Dilbert fans use a random number generator to fill in their timesheets.

Measure only what you need, after you decide which question you really need answered, why you need it answered, and what information you need to answer it. Here is an example:

> **What I need answered:** What percentage of the total development time went into
>
> 1. Gathering requirements?
> 2. Performing analysis?
> 3. Designing domain classes?
> 4. Designing user interface classes?
> 5. Designing infrastructure classes?
> 6. Testing?
> 7. Fixing discovered errors?
>
> **Why I need this answered:** Those percentages reflect the different skill pools I have to hire and the relative efforts of each. I need to create such an estimate for every increment of this project. Also, given these percentages, if I can reasonably guess any one of the numbers from looking at the original project description, I can then guess the rest.
>
> **The measurement I need to make is:** Weekly hours spent on those seven categories.
>
> **The work intrusion of this measurement is:** Small; most people will be working only in one or two of those categories each week.

What should you measure besides elapsed time? As Glenn House notes, measurements can misdirect energy and cause anxiety. The leader of Project Ingrid (see Chapter 2) tried various ways to measure the project's technical contents, to correlate them with the project's results. He concluded that nothing really works except to measure client satisfaction at the end. Here is what happens if you measure:

Project Ingrid, 14

◆ *Development hours per class, errors per class*. If your developers tell you it took six weeks to develop two classes, should you think they did a good job or a bad job? If they tell you they developed 20 classes in two weeks, did they do a good job or a bad job? By not thinking hard, they can quickly create large numbers of redundant classes. By using copy-paste techniques, your developers can produce huge amounts of code per day. Development hours and errors per class tell you something either about your problem domain or your designers, but it is not clear which or what.

◆ *Lines per method/methods per class.* This is known as "pushing the bubble around under the plastic." The solution your team just designed has a certain complexity, which you can push around just as you can push a bubble around under a piece of plastic, without ever removing it. If you require that all methods or functions be under 10 lines long, they soon will be—and you will have huge numbers of methods in the class. If you publish, shortly thereafter, that all classes should have fewer than 30 methods, they soon will, and your system will then have a huge number of smaller classes. You will have the measurements you demanded, but without improving the system.

I sat with a designer who was wondering out loud how much to charge for his new product. The other people in the room thought about it and asked some questions, and eventually one of them had to ask, "How many lines of code is it?" The designer answered, "Three thousand. Does that make a difference?" The rest of the people in the room looked around in confusion. How could they tell whether 3,000 lines of code was an easy solution to an easy problem or a brilliant solution to a hard problem, whether it deserved a little money or a lot of money?

If you are interested in reducing the complexity of the system, *hire a better requirements analyst to find simpler requirements,* or *hire a better designer to design a simpler solution.*

TAKE THE TIME TO DESIGN

Team leaders complain about absence of design in all languages. Take the time to design, whatever your implementation language. Programmers suffer from a cultural resistance to careful design, which extends back to their earliest programming days. They tend to program immediately and then fiddle with the program, without constructing a design. Do not do this. The design is harder to see and discuss in the program than it is on whiteboard or paper. Changing definitions on-line is slower than changing it on whiteboard or paper. In my experience, even the best— especially the best—developers think through their designs before they step to the keyboard. They recognize that typing *captures* and tests the design. They then evolve the design using the maleable development environment.

I have visited projects composed of 20 to 200 people in which the developers cited "iterative" development, but never designed their system. They spent months changing their code, while the rest of the project waited for a stable design so they could get on with their work. Therefore, take the time to design.

This chapter ends with an Eyewitness Account about two Smalltalk projects; it was prepared by an experienced Smalltalk teacher, programmer, consultant, and a former COBOL/CICS programmer. He asked to remain anonymous in order not to cause either company mentioned any discomfort (the initials K.L. are fictional).

K.L.'s Eyewitness Account attests to the benefit of designing as opposed to just typing. He worked on two projects at approximately the same time. In one, there was a weak design, with lots of typing. In the other project, the experienced Smalltalk developers took several weeks to work through their design. The weeks of design paid off when the project expanded to include new developers, who extended the original design. Note the presence of other key success factors on the first project: user involvement, architecture, incremental development, expert teams.

K.L. is cautious in his optimism for a first OO project, although clearly committed to the technology. I have found this to be a common characteristic of people whose job is not to sell the technology, but to ensure its success.

◆ Design, and Two Smalltalk Projects *K.L., Independent Consultant*

I worked on two Smalltalk client/server projects similar in purpose, domain, requirements, and tools. They could not have ended up more differently.

On the first project, the users had never used personal computers or graphical user interfaces. The scope of the project expanded significantly. The databases had been patched over the years, so that many attributes had overloaded meanings and undocumented inconsistencies.

The project was managed primarily by the user organization. The IS organization wished to have the project killed. The project manager had to respond to frequent political "firefights."

The project manager knew the organization and its politics, the client's legacy technology and object technology. He was a pretty good Smalltalk programmer to boot. He and another consultant worked for about a year doing technology assessments, prototypes, and cost-benefit analyses, and generally "sold" the system from the grass roots through to the executives. He then brought in to design and implement the first release of the system four Smalltalk programmers with an average of more than four years Smalltalk experience, plus experience with the legacy technology. We used and improved frameworks from our previous projects. Our domain expert was one of the better users, and was assigned full-time to the project. He was not an IS person. Several COBOL programmers wrote the host server transactions.

Phase 1 was a success. IS recognized this and, with the cooperation of the user organization, reorganized so as to manage subsequent phases. The project manager rolled out more and more function to the users, often at a faster pace than the users' organization could accommodate with planning and training.

I personally learned (or confirmed) several lessons from the project:

◆ The management team needs to understand both the business and the technology.

◆ Several highly skilled Smalltalk developers, working closely with domain experts, can develop more than a hoard of "architects," "methodologists," "designers," and "coders."

◆ System architecture and performance must be focused on from the very beginning. They cannot be saved for later.

◆ The testing architecture can save your project. Ours let us capture test-case suites and facilitated communications between Smalltalk and COBOL programmers. It let us quickly resolve problems or adapt to changes.

♦ Design and code reviews are mandatory. The project is still struggling to clean up and rewrite code written by a person who wrote Smalltalk that could not be understood by anyone else.

The second project was the prototypical large team of about 50 people: senior architects, designers, analysts from the customer's organization, mainframe programmers, and half a dozen, mostly novice, Smalltalk programmers. Some senior staff flew in for a few days every few weeks and confused everyone. There was a hidden subproject to design and build a new OO case tool.

Project management changed twice. Technical experts came and went. The few experienced OO people did not work on basic architecture. There were no initial Smalltalk frameworks from which to build. New Smalltalk programmers received little coaching, and their code was not reviewed.

The project delivered late, was scaled down, and slow. The case tool was used only for diagramming. Key frameworks were still evolving at the last minute, which caused havoc to the application developers. A seasoned (non-OO) project manager said she thought development in C would have taken less time. I agreed. From this project I concluded:

♦ We do not yet understand how to leverage Smalltalk development to a large development organization with lots of junior programmers. Doing what we did with COBOL didn't work.

♦ Try to organize a team that has been successful with projects about 80% the same.

♦ Do not expect the first version of a framework to be good. Evolution is the only proven course. At the same time, Smalltalk programmers will always prefer to write frameworks and tools instead of application code. Good project managers concede to this, but only in limited quantities.

♦ Analysis, design, and programming are interdependent with the rest of the development process. Analysis and design do not stand alone, and quality code will never be produced accidentally by new Smalltalk programmers. Mentoring and reviews are critical, and need to start on day one.

Case material contributed by a third party, used with permission.

Chapter 5

Making Corrections

Learn what you don't know you don't know.

The ideal project does nothing wrong; it simply delivers the system. However, that kind of project does not show you how to get past your own unique difficulties. For that reason, as a study project I have chosen one that went wrong in worse ways than your project will, yet turned itself around to deliver a useful system with skilled staff.

A STUDY PROJECT

Project Ingrid is ideal as a study project because you can learn the most from it and model your own recovery after it. I have applied the lessons from this project to good effect, and think you can, too. Use it as a starting point, to let yourself make mistakes, and to motivate you to adjust your project according to those mistakes. It is by correcting mistakes that you survive. The project went through the five stages described in the following sections.

Stage 0: The Usual Ignorance

The Ingrid Project began under common circumstances. A new, client/server system had to be built. There was plenty of mainframe programming talent, but no OO experience on the team; there were COBOL and C programmers. C++ was chosen as the target language, because "everyone knew that C++ was the OO language of the future," and C++ was considered just another programming language, one that the programmers would be able to learn easily. The project was staffed with about two dozen programmers, under two managers.

The leaders of Project Ingrid provided themselves with one escape avenue, which led to their eventual success: They insisted on a fully incremental process, to the point that they would not even say what their requirements would be for the next increment! Each increment would be four months long, and include, at the beginning, a requirements determination phase. This process went against the standards for the organization, and the leaders had to fight long and hard to get exemption from the usual process. The reason they asked for the exemption and got it was that they had never done a project like this and simply could not commit to a schedule, or even to the requirements. The project was sufficiently critical that it had to be done, and the decision had been made to do it in object technology.

Stage 1: Disaster

The result of the first increment was (no surprise) total disaster. The project was way over schedule; the programmers had not mastered C++, the two teams were at odds with each other, morale was down, and the system was not functioning, even for the limited requirements they had set themselves. This is when the incremental process came in.

Stage 2: Rebuild

The leaders replaced 24 of the 25 programmers. I thought this was rather severe, and asked, "Wasn't it rather hard on them, being let go like that?" The reply was, "Oh, no; they were happy to go back to something they were good at!" Clearly, not everyone wants to become a novice after having been a master. The new group they hired included many young people, who had less unlearning to do and less ego to subdue.

Next, they addressed interteam friction. They "tied" the two managers together: Any note from either manager was signed by both managers, so that there was the semblance of just one manager.

*methodology:
ownership, 89*

Third, they ensured that every end-useable function and every class had an owner, whose job it was to maintain the integrity of that end-useable function or class. Some people owned end-useable functions as well as classes. This did not seem to cause any difficulty.

Fourth, they arranged for several months of training, delivered in pieces over time. Finally, they rescheduled their work. They had to rebuild the first increment as part of getting the requirements for and delivering the second increment. They made a schedule, and were 50 percent over plan, but delivered a working release.

Stage 3: Improve

After delivering the second increment, they decided they were on a safe course. Certain people had evolved as leaders in each of the teams. They created an architecture team, consisting of the leaders for each of the subsystems.

They established a weekly self-teaching meeting. In it they worked on the use of polymorphism, inheritance, state variables, coding style, and so on. These meetings allowed all members to hear, discuss, learn, and build a common style of work. It let everyone on the team improve continuously over the year.

They fine-tuned the process, the teams, the work allocation, the estimating techniques, and set the requirements and schedule for the third increment. It delivered on time.

Stage 4: Functioning

At the time I talked with them, the team members were able to get their work done in a little under their scheduled times, and were getting good internal reuse. It had become a successful project.

Internal reuse meant they did not have to write as much code as they had expected, because they could take advantage of previous work. Internal reuse should be a goal of every project.

The project was also successful with respect to methodology. They had learned how to put out systems. Their comment on published (little-m) methodologies was that they had investigated them but found them not useful. They had the same comment for the OO CASE tools at the time.

Stage 5: Overconfidence in Scaling Up

This is a forward pointer to Chapter 7. The key phrases are, *"Don't forget what made you successful,"* and *"A successful smaller project does not ensure a successful big project."* Project Ingrid was expanded to include 150 people across a number of sites. The last I heard, the project members were experiencing difficulties in dealing with these large numbers of diverse people over long distances. I suspect that the characteristics of observation, focus, and flexibility that served them so well in the beginning will help them adjust to the newer demands of the large project. The point is hazards do not stop just because you have mastered one project.

expand, 165

Lessons From This Study Project

Let us go over the project again to see what lessons can be learned.

Lesson 1: *Work in increments.* Without increments, Project Ingrid would not have been able to change its team, its management, its process. Incremental development is a critical success factor; lack of incremental development is a prime failure indicator.

Lesson 2: *Keep your eye fixed on delivering the system.* The goal of Project Ingrid was not to train the original two dozen programmers, but to deliver a system. It would have been easy for them to have kept the original staff and then failed, just as it would have been easy to follow the organization's original process guidelines and then fail. Each change they made was done with the goal of delivering sooner.

Lesson 3: *Be willing to change anything.* Project Ingrid changed nearly everything. They were fortunate to have leaders who were able to recognize errors and fix them.

Lesson 4: *Get training; keep learning.* Not only did Project Ingrid get initial training, they established internal study meetings. Continuous learning is a key factor in building a successful development organization. Even the masters of object technology continually meet to trade ideas and learn. One week, even four weeks, of training does not constitute "enough learning."

Work in increments; focus after each; rebuild with agility.

MANAGING PRECISION, ACCURACY, AND SCALE

Having seen a project go wrong and then rebuild itself, let us start considering ways to avoid mistakes, and then recover from them.

Your team can get into trouble from being too precise, just as from being too vague. Define levels of precision, accuracy, and scale—even imprecisely—to improve the ability of your group to keep discussions on target and produce the information needed at a particular moment in time. Keep relevance and tolerance in mind.

Let me clarify what I mean by relevance, precision, accuracy, and scale. *Relevance* is the items you decide to include in the discussion. *Precision* is how much you care to say about a particular item. *Accuracy* is how correct you are when you talk about the item. *Tolerance* is how much variation you can handle. *Scale* is how many items you collect into one term. I use the acronym PARTS to remember these: precision, accuracy, relevance, tolerance, and scale.

We are familiar with these terms from everyday life. When we lay out the plan of an office, we may talk about the *size* of the furniture, rather than weight or color; we have selected for relevance. In software design, we might talk about the domain classes and omit the others from discussion. For the purpose of a conversation, describing a bookshelf to the nearest foot is *precise* enough. So we refer to "the 6-foot bookshelf," when the bookshelf is actually six feet, one and a half inches long. If we say, "the 4-foot bookshelf," we are *inaccurate* describing to the nearest foot. Working on the initial design of a house, it is useful to work to the precision of the nearest foot. When cutting the lumber, we need to be accurate at greater precision, perhaps the nearest inch, half-inch, or eighth of an inch. Accuracy is meaningful with respect to the precision needed at the time. There is no point in worrying whether the second decimal place of the bookshelf size is .04 or .05 if we have not yet decided if it is to be 4 feet or 6 feet long.

Scale means changing how much to include in one thing to be able to cover more material in the same amount of space. We don't, for example, have space on paper to draw a house at a 1:1 scale. To fit the drawing of the house onto the paper, we use a small box to represent a large space. Scale interacts with relevance and precision. Once we decide to draw the whole house on a single piece of paper, we become limited in the precision we can use. We omit from the drawing everything whose overall size is below our level of precision. Thus, light switches would not show up in the drawing. Typically, at this scale, light switches are not relevant.

On a software development project, these terms have analogous meanings and analogous uses. Every deliverable, from requirements to project plan to hardware and software design, can be described at various scales, to varying precision, with varying accuracy. Working at the inappropriate scale means working with inappropriate information. Let us look at these more closely.

Precision is the most significant of the three terms. It defines the amount you care to say about a particular item, so it controls how you connect work on the project. Most deliverables have three or four levels of precision.

◆ For the project plan, the first level of precision is to state the releases, the basic functionality in each, and the development dependencies between them. The second level of precision is to state clearly which functions are delivered in each release and which team is developing each, and to name the specific dependencies between the teams.

Delivery dates for the next several releases fit into this level. The third level of precision states the milestones and the dates of each deliverable involved in the release.

- For the functional requirements, the first level of precision may include just the name of the function or use case being delivered; the user group expecting it; and the anticipated value, urgency, and development cost. The second level of precision may include details about the basic usage scenario, the business events and business rules involved, frequency, and performance. The third level may include all other details about the function's requirement.
- For the object design, the first level of precision is the name and main responsibility of each class. The second level is detailed responsibilities and collaborations used. The third level is attributes, relations, and function signatures. The fourth level is the code.

It is especially important to note that when someone draws (or shows) a class diagram describing relations, functions, and attributes, he or she is operating at the third level of precision. There are times when trying to create that diagram or to show that diagram is inappropriate, and less precision should be used. These times occur both at the beginning of the project and when presenting it in summary form.

For a given amount of precision, there is a desired amount of accuracy, at which point the question "when is it good enough?" is raised.

- During initial development, each deliverable needs to be accurate enough only at a given level of precision to permit work to start on the next level. Striving for too much accuracy early can waste time, since your work at higher precision will turn up new information, which may alter the previous description: Working through the various failure scenarios and error conditions of a use case may turn up new use cases; working through interteam deliverables may change the development priorities; working through a design may change the original planned collaboration structure. The earlier low-precision work needs to be done, and it needs to be done just accurately enough to permit the next work to be estimated and coordinated.
- Accuracy feeds the iterative process. The purpose of an iteration is to create the best deliverable possible at that time; that is, making it as accurate as possible. Luke Hohmann, in his Eyewitness Account later in this chapter, uses the metaphor of cooking pancakes. When he says he "just wants to see a burnt pancake," he is saying that accuracy is not needed at this time; movement through the process is. When his team asks him, "How edible do you want it to be?" they are asking for

Luke Hohmann's EWA, 128

clarification about accuracy. Edibility is a good measure for accuracy, because people have an intuitive understanding of its meaning and consequences.

Scale is a matter of getting more of the system into view at one time. It has the following three aspects:

1. *Using lower precision.* Just as a 1:30 or 1:100 scale drawing of your office will not show the keys on your computer keyboard or the support boards on your bookshelf, so the 1:30 or 1:100 scale drawing of your software design will not show all the attributes of each class. This way, each item can be shown smaller.
2. *Selecting items for relevance.* To get more of the domain model into view, you can choose to omit the nondomain classes entirely. This is similar to a cartographer omitting bus lines and houses on a city map.
3. *Bundling multiple items together.* Numerous component-bundling schemes have been proposed in the literature, such as *class categories*, *domains*, *ensembles*, *subsystems*, and *fat objects*. There is no consensus yet as to the best way to bundle classes. In project management, a *release* is a useful unit, bundling many functions and deliverables; and use cases may be clustered to gain an overview of the function sets.

Once the project has more use cases, dependencies, or classes than can comfortably fit on a few pages, developing a larger-scale view becomes necessary. Unlike precision and accuracy, it is not necessary to the development process per se, but it is necessary for understanding the overall shape of the project. As the project becomes larger, it becomes more necessary.

Managing Work According to Precision and Accuracy

There is no point in trying to get the milestones right until the release dependencies are documented. Similarly, it is counterproductive to argue over the creation behavior of a link between objects before subsystems have been carved out or basic responsibilities have been assigned. How you sequence your work affects the progress of the team.

The value of monitoring precision was not clear to me until I worked with groups of people who insisted on working at high precision too early.

The domain modelers were interviewing business experts, who had been gathered at great expense and under time constraints. The domain modelers had decided to capture the information at very high precision. If they drew a line one way, it would have one meaning; drawing it another way would give it a slightly different meaning. While the expert was talking, the modelers could not draw a line at all, because they did not have enough information to decide between the two styles of line! As they pursued the information they needed to the precision at which they needed it, the conversation got sidetracked and the attendees lost the thread of the overall conversation. At the end of the allotted time, the business experts vanished, without the modelers having the critical information they needed.

These modelers' priority should have been to capture the information that they needed to proceed, and that they could only get from these experts gathered in this room. They could have and should have worked at a lower level of precision. It would have allowed them to cover all the territory they needed to cover, and mark those places they needed to come back to.

It is common for developers to program or draw class diagrams immediately, before working out a basic design. In their haste, they forget that the less precise design can be reviewed sooner, much more easily, and changed more easily, if worked out only to the level of name, responsibility, and collaborators.

It would be soothing to say that one should finalize the lower level of precision before working more precisely. That is not the case, however. History has not been kind to those who developed all the deliverables at large scale and low precision before touching the next scale and precision. Too many surprises lie in wait, and it is to diffuse those surprises that we use prototypes, iterations, and increments. Therefore, managing the level of precision employed at any moment takes some effort.

Here is a sample ordering of work that illustrates managing the level of precision. It fits within the first increment and shows how low-precision deliverables can free teams to work in parallel, thus optimizing the use of their time.

1. Collect the functional requirements to the first level of precison: user goal and user group. Estimate urgency, value, and cost of each (note that this is medium-accurate and low-precision information), plus technical dependencies. This gives you the system spec at the first precision level.

2. Estimate how you will release the system, ordering the releases by technical dependency, priority, and ease of construction. This gives

you the project plan at the first precision level, medium accuracy ("edible"), and scale of perhaps 1:100.

3. At this point, you can create teams by function and release, and let them work in parallel.

4. Let the teams gather requirements to the third level of precision, capturing main and failure scenarios for the functions selected for the first or first two releases. Also capture external systems for the interface drivers that will have to be developed.

5. Split the teams into management, user interface, domain, and infrastructure, and let them work in parallel. The management team will create dependencies and milestones. The user-interface group, domain-modeling group, and technical-infrastructure teams all have enough information to start their work. All teams move their deliverable sets to the next level of precision.

6. If some aspect of the project needs a quick investigation, this should show up about now. Some people *always* like to do a quick prototype here to discover what surprises are ahead.

Decide how much precision is appropriate for each discussion. Generally, move from lower to higher precision over days and months to master the intellectual complexity of your task. Dive briefly into high precision, as in a prototype or detailed examination to evaluate risks and uncover unknowns. Use the acronym PARTS to remember the issues.

Decide when to work at low precision and high precision.

INCREMENTS AND ITERATIONS

Increments are so important that we should be clear as to what they are and are not. Here are three questions to consider:

1. What is the difference between increments and iterations?
2. What is the purpose of doing increments?
3. What is the purpose of doing iterations?

The short answer is:

- Increments let you fix or improve the development process.
- Iterations let you fix or improve the quality of the system.

Although both are necessary to produce a good system, increments are usually necessary just to survive.

Increments and V-W Staging

Incremental development is a *staging strategy* in which portions of the system are developed at different times or rates, and integrated as they are completed. It does not imply, require, or preclude iterative development or waterfall development, which are rework strategies. The alternative to incremental development is to develop the entire system as one lump deliverable.

The phrase "incremental development" does not, by itself, indicate which deliverables are developed incrementally and which are developed en masse. Often, requirements are done en masse, with design and deployment done incrementally, although Project Ingrid created requirements incrementally.

The rewards of doing incremental development are great, including the following:

- *Education.* People do not know what they are heading into when they start a project. Incremental development lets them go through the entire development cycle once, and use that newfound knowledge immediately.
- *Discovering what you don't know you don't know (WYDKYDK).* You think you know what you are up against, but your project has surprises in store for you. The increments let you find out early.
- *Fixing the way you work.* Finding out early what the surprises are gives you a chance to change your way of working. Each increment boundary is a chance to improve everything you do.

Staff, techniques, and tools change on every project. People who have not been through the entire process really do not know why they are gathering requirements in your particular way or how well they are doing. They do not understand the analysis, design, documentation, testing, or delivery tasks. Going through the entire process gives them an "aha!" feeling of comfort about how the project works. This is what Grady Booch calls the "gestalt round-trip."[1] It lets them start the next round of development with an understanding of what is going to come and how the early activities affect the later activities.

If you can manage it, put your new staff on a very small, two- or three-week development assignment, just so they can experience the entire process. Several project groups have told me they have adopted this as a standard way to get newcomers comfortable with the development cycle and process.

---

[1]Booch, G., *Object-Oriented Design with Applications* (Reading, MA: Addison-Wesley), 1991.

Most project leaders are confident at the start that they know how to do the project. However, the development processes in most projects do not work very well initially. The discrepancy between the two is that the people do not know what it is that they do not know about the project. They are in for a surprise. Where will the surprise occur? No one knows. That is why delivering the first increment is so important. This first increment is covered in more detail later in this chapter.

project increments, 129

Even after the first increment, there are surprises in store and things to fix. Incremental development allows you to find, fix, and improve those things every few months, before they cost you too much.

The drawings that follow are a schematic rendition of incremental development. Figure 5-1 shows a box in the center representing the portion of the system being built in one increment. The other four boxes are sections that will have to be integrated with the center one later on. Figure 5-2 shows the sequence in which parts of the system are built; here, time flows from left to right. The figure also shows the infrastructure being built in the first increment. The second increment might be started in parallel: the user interface (UI), the system functions, and the database. After they are all deployed using the infrastructure, a second set of functions may be deployed. The infrastructure can then be extended.

Figure 5-2 illustrates that all four parts of the system will be under development at the same time and that all will continue to grow over time. The pieces are integrated into the total system as they are completed.

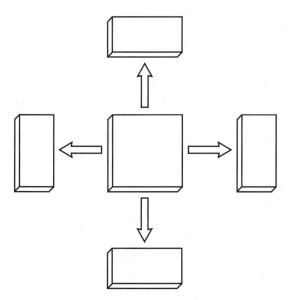

Figure 5-1 *The center box is the portion of the system built in one increment.*

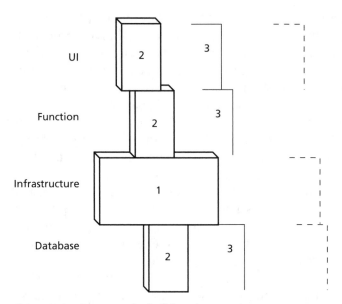

Figure 5-2 *Sequence for building the system*

Figure 5-3 shows how incremental development fits onto the project timeline. Once again, time flows from left to right across the diagram. One increment follows the other, usually at two to four months per increment. Within each increment, the well-known activities of setting requirements, designing, testing, and shipping follow each other (I show how to modify this shortly). At the end of each increment, set aside some time to learn what to improve on the next increment. This time may be as short as two to four hours in a group discussion, or it may go several days as you try to invent new approaches to solving your existing problems. Hold the meeting, however short, because that is when you get leverage on development.

But wait a minute! Isn't that waterfall development shown in Figure 5-3? Among object-oriented developers, this is considered a terrible accusation, and so we must deal with it fairly. The diagram in Figure 5-3 illustrates a simple fact of life: You cannot ship any part of the system until you have tested it; you cannot test it until it is designed and built; and you cannot design it without requirements. That particular sequencing of activities is simply a fact for any part of the system; I call it *validation-V.* The validation-V sequence holds whether you use increments, iterations, rapid prototyping, or waterfall development. *Waterfall* development is when there is only one copy of the V, no matter how long the project is. Incremental development requires having a series of Vs, so

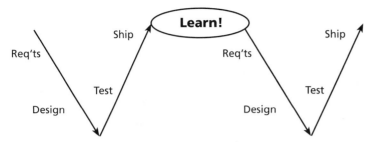

Figure 5-3 *Incremental development on the project timeline*

that lessons from one V feed the next. Because the connecting Vs form a W, I refer to this form of project segmentation as *V-W staging*.

V-W staging is a general strategy that subsumes incremental development and iterative, spiral, and prototyping strategies. It provides a way for the project manager to:

- Uncurl the spiral of spiral development so that the activities lie flat against the project timeline.
- Arrange prototypes and iterations without sacrificing the notion of continuous progress.
- Derive effective progress indicators based on delivered function rather than on "phase deliverables."
- Manage subcontractors on delivered increments instead of phase deliverables.
- Get the value of "gestalt round-trip" without having to study Zen.

In V-W staging, different parts of the system are put through the validation-V sequence at different, specific times. The Vs can be arranged to overlap or to sit within one another.

Suppose your highest-level management has given you 10 months to create each segment of the system—a long period to hold everyone's interest. You decide, therefore, to split the 10 months into three increments of four, three, and three months, respectively. This is illustrated in Figure 5-4. Each increment produces a chunk of the system you could deliver if you chose to. You get continuous staging of your system, which raises morale, lets you fix process problems (including dealing with antagonistic developers), and gives you dependable progress measures. The increments also assure you that you will be able to show your executives the system segment at the end of 10 months—the period they consider as one increment.

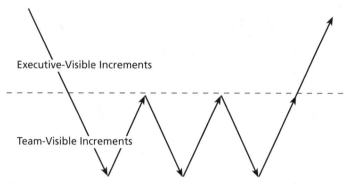

Figure 5-4 *Splitting one increment into many*

V-W staging also gives you a handle on managing multiple teams in parallel. One person from a 150-person, multiyear project told me that all the teams defined their increments on a two-week grid. Each increment was 2, 4, 6, 8, or 10 weeks long, as needed. Based on the dependencies between the teams' deliveries, they worked out a schedule and an owner for each newly integrated version of the system. A team participated in the creation of the new version only if their increment ended on that 2-week boundary. Thus, the Vs needed by the various teams differed in length, as their problem required, and the project manager had the interesting task of managing the dependencies and integration activities. A multiteam V-W is shown in Figure 5-5.

One project I know successfully used increments of one week long! Participants worked in an environment in which priorities were constantly changing. To keep up with the changing priorities, they broke all work into one-week chunks. Each Monday morning, they met to arrange their work assignments for that week. While this situation is extreme, and a bit confrontational for most developers, the technique did allow them to track the company's needs and get the necessary software out. Most

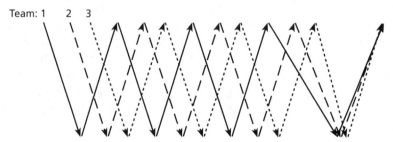

Figure 5-5 *A multiteam V-W*

project teams say they feel comfortable with increments one to four months long. The overhead of picking up and putting down work causes them to prefer the longer increments.

Increments let you improve your development process.

Iterations

Iterative development is a *rework scheduling strategy* in which time is set aside to revise and improve parts of the system. It does not presuppose incremental development, but works very well with it. The phrase "iterative development" does not, by itself, indicate how many deliverables get revised or when the revision happens. You have great freedom in choosing whether to revise requirements or only design, whether to treat the revisions as separate increments or embed them within the increments. Iterative development does not mean a free-for-all with no delivery targets, and you should not accept an argument that says it does.

Iterations are difficult to schedule because you recognize that your knowledge is inaccurate, without knowing exactly in what way. The following are some of the rewards of doing iterative development:

- *Reduce risk.* You thought you heard what your users want and need, but did you, really? Your team assures you that the new technology will handle your workload, but will it really? Iterative development gives you a chance to schedule a first look at key parts of the system without having to ship it. In many cases, that saves you from an embarrassing first shipment, or even a nonshipment.
- *Improve quality.* Even if you are close to correct on the algorithm or user interface, it is fairly inexpensive to add two weeks during initial development to get the algorithm, design, or user interface tuned properly before shipment.
- *Improve communication.* Scheduling a prerelease look at the system lets the users, executives, and other teams see what your team is doing.
- *Ensure that you are delivering what your clientele can use.* People sometimes ask for a feature not knowing what it will mean to get it. Often, they can only tell if it is what they really need after they see it. Iterative development ensures that what they request is what they can really use.

You want to reduce risk when you are using a new, key algorithm; when you are trying a new technology such as objects, client/server, or networking; when you are using a new vendor; when you have new staff;

and when you are trying a new process. You may not know the performance of your database. You may not really trust the users who are giving you your requirements. You therefore deploy the system in an early release to let people examine it.

You may think you are confident in your staff, and that you don't need to plan rework time into the schedule, but how confident are you? What is your fallback strategy should you discover, just before delivery, that the response time through the network and database is unacceptable, that the users really do not like the system?

The *system integration* period is the time frame when faulty assumptions come to light. It is, however, an expensive time to discover mistakes and to make things come together. It is less traumatic to plan a period in which to discover where the system pieces do not fit, and to schedule a rework period after that to get them to fit.

Quality will certainly improve if you set aside time to evaluate what you have done, and to redo parts of it. Almost certainly you will need this improvement at the user interface. Not only are you unlikely to get the screen optimal the first time, but experience shows that you are unlikely to get the functions of the system right the first time. People giving requirements just forget to say some things, or say them with an unknown bias; or the people listening miss something, or hear with an unknown bias.

Quality improvements also come in the infrastructure. Both algorithms and technical design get better over time. The improved architecture will be easier to learn and more efficient. Object-oriented frameworks are designed to support variation, but it is almost impossible to guess correctly just what variation will be encountered. For framework development, therefore, plan for revision.

Early examination is a two-edged sword. You reduce risk by finding out early whether your design is adequate. This saves you failing to ship or shipping a defective system. On the other side, you add risk by permitting the discovery that you need to rework something. The added risk is a worse schedule delay than you anticipated.

The drawings that follow are a schematicized rendition of iterative development. On the left of Figure 5-6 are two portions of the system being developed incrementally. They are dotted to show that they are relatively complete, but they also contain question marks to show that there is some open question about them. They have been developed according to schedule. The next stage (the darker dotted boxes) in the schedule calls for them to be evaluated, so the question marks can be removed. The right part of the figure shows them reworked, ready to be fit in with the next portion of the system.

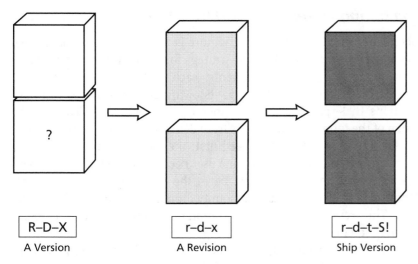

R–D–X	r–d–x	r–d–t–S!
A Version	A Revision	Ship Version

Figure 5-6 *Iteration is converting partial knowledge into a system.*

Figure 5-7 shows the iterations unrolled, using V-W staging. As usual, requirements precede design, which precedes testing. Testing, in this case, means examination. After examination, the sequence is repeated until the risk is low and the system is ready to ship.

Both incremental and iterative strategies provide a chance to reduce ignorance and to improve. An incremental strategy lets you improve your process, while iterative development primarily lets you improve your product. They work well together. Iterative development certainly does take more time than delivering a low-quality system, but planning the iterations allows you to predict and control those costs.

Iterations let you improve the quality of your product.

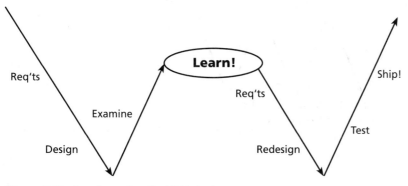

Figure 5-7 *Iteration using the V-W staging*

Combining Increments and Iterations

Increments and iterations do not require each other, but, as just stated, they work well together. A useful strategy for the end-user functionality is to create four-month increments, each with three iterations (see Figure 5-8). The infrastructure has its own increments, but it will have iterations that span the function increments, because feedback to the design of the infrastructure comes from delivering functionality.

Ask what the users really need first; then ask what they must have second, third, and so forth. Combine user needs with the technical dependencies to determine what must be in the first release, or increment. Choose the smallest acceptable amount of functionality for the first increment. The architecture and first iteration of the infrastructure belong in the first increment.

Within each increment, allow a period of quiet time for design to happen. As soon as there is a design of the screen and screen flows, show them to the users to learn how closely the design meets need. This is the first *shallow* iteration of the user function. Build that function as well as you know how, then show the working system to the users. This is the first *deep* iteration. At this point, plan on surprising users and developers. They may have thought they communicated well, but now they will find how they misspoke and were misinterpreted.

Do a second deep iteration, and show the newly working system to the users. This shows that the necessary corrections were made, and catches remaining small errors. The third and final deep iteration results in putting that portion of the system to test.

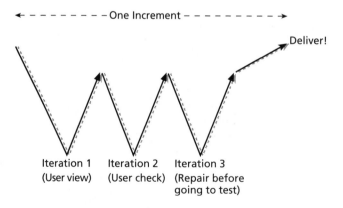

Figure 5-8 *V-W staging—iterations within an increment*

There are two particular dangers to iterations:

1. Prototypitis
2. The death spiral

Prototypitis is a well-known and distressingly common ailment in which the development people never stabilize their design or interfaces, but simply rework a prototype in the hope that it will eventually become a product. Project Manfred (see Chapter 2) fell into this trap. Prototypitis can befall a project of any size. I have seen it on a 200-person project.

Project Manfred, 15

The response to prototypitis is incremental development *with delivery*. Have the development team commit to a delivery. Nothing sharpens the mind like having to deliver in two to four weeks. If the design is mildly insufficient, it can be improved on a subsequent release. If it is badly insufficient, that will show up. Even if delivery has to be canceled, the key issues will become apparent and you can address them.

The *death spiral* is less well known. It attaches to iterations through the worries of the management. The death spiral runs like this:

1. Management asks for a schedule. Team creates one.
2. Team develops iteration 1.
3. Management gets worried, asks for a schedule. Team creates another.
4. After the pause to create a new schedule, team starts working on iteration 2.
5. Management gets more worried because the pause stalled development. They ask for a new schedule.

. . . and so on. The project dies because there is never enough time to make progress on the design. There are two steps to getting out of the death spiral, both of which fall under the general strategy Distractions: Someone Always Makes Progress, as discussed in Appendix A.

distractions: someone always makes progress, 224

The first is a *timebox*. During a timebox, you permit no interruptions to the development, whether to change requirements or ask for future schedule estimates. The timebox gives your team a period of protection for some progress to be made. The other part of the strategy is Sacrifice One Person, also covered in Appendix A. When a schedule needs to be made, the team draws straws or otherwise selects one person to create the new schedule, while the rest of the team keeps progressing. Getting out of the death spiral is as difficult as ending prototypitis. Take both seriously.

distractions: sacrifice one person, 230

The following Eyewitness Account by Luke Hohmann relates how he shifted people from a single-Vmodel (waterfall), to a multiple-V iterative

◆ **Burn Some Pancakes** *Luke Hohmann, SmartPatents*

In one assignment I had to find a way to change the development process of a team of developers. As you can guess, prior management enforced an extremely strict waterfall model. In a waterfall process, you are expected to create complete outcomes from each process before moving to the next. The only problem was that my predecessor had elevated the practice of waterfall development to an anal-retentive art: Developers were expected to produce nearly perfect outcomes! As I tried to change their overall development process from waterfall to an iterative one, I encountered extreme resistance. In the past, the staff learned if they did not practice waterfall, they would be punished. How could I change their attitude? The only thing I could think of was to introduce them to the burnt pancake process model. Burnt pancakes?

I am not the best cook in the world, but every now and then I like to make pancakes. The trouble is, I always seem to make the skillet too hot for the first pancake. By now, I have accepted the fact that I will, with a high degree of probability, burn the first pancake, throw it out, fix the temperature, and start again. To encourage my staff to get an initial system completed, I would ask them to "burn some pancakes" (i.e., create an initial system), with the assurance I wouldn't "eat" (i.e., judge) the first pancake. At first, they responded tentatively. But the idea was quickly adopted when they learned I meant what I said: I would not judge them on incomplete outcomes.

Within a few weeks, they had fully adopted the approach, making it a part of the culture of the group. When asked for an outcome, staff members would respond: "How edible does it have to be?" If I responded with "fairly edible," they knew I was looking for a rather complete outcome. On the other hand, if I responded with "completely burnt," they knew I wanted to briefly assess their activity to ensure they were headed in the right direction; in no way would they be judged on the outcome. Soon, the entire team was talking about pancakes, and productivity started to improve.

Case material excerpted from Hohmann, L., *Journey of a Software Engineer.* Used with permission.

model.[2] He did it by giving them permission to be wrong at certain times in the project.

Following Luke Hohmann's lead, I introduced the burnt-pancake model into a project where the participants were extremely sensitive to being wrong or producing an incomplete system, and found it to work well. The *burnt-pancake* model is a way of managing expected "accuracy" on a project, which is useful while getting started with iterations, as discussed earlier in this chapter.

*managing precision,
accuracy, and scale,
112*

Use iterations within increments to reduce risk.

---

[2]From Hohmann, L., *Journey of a Software Engineer: The Sociology of Software Development* (Englewood Cliffs, NJ: Prentice-Hall), 1997. Copyright © Luke Hohmann. Used with permission of author and the publisher, Prentice Hall, Inc.

PROJECT INCREMENTS

This section shows a Production project as a first increment, a second increment, and a succession of next increments. The first two are different; the rest should look much the same. Each increment is approximately four months long.

project purpose, 36

The SWAT-type project and Investigative-type project have different timelines, and were discussed in detail earlier in the book. A Full-Commit-type project can be modeled on the Production project plan.

In the sections that follow, I reintroduce the fearsome being that some of your parents scared you with as children—the "boogeyman." According to the old story, the boogeyman is a terrible person who hides in dark places. When you are not behaving yourself, he will jump out and carry you off. In normal life the boogeyman is apocryphal, but on a software development project he is real—he is what you don't know you don't know (WYDKYDK).

Although the boogeyman is indeed waiting for you on your project, if you follow this project setup, you will find out where he is hiding, and be able to deal with him. The early parts of your project have two goals, and one of them is to find the boogeyman (learn WYDKYDK). If you do not take care of this, he will indeed jump out at you when you least expect it.

Increment 1

The purpose of the first increment is to:

- Establish an architecture for the software.
- Deliver feedback to the project sponsors and users.
- Develop good patterns of programming and designing.
- Find the boogeyman and learn WYDKYDK.

There are many possible ways of running a successful first increment. I give here one, which builds on the earlier descriptions of teams, incremental development, methodology, and staffing. I also state the intentions of the plan, so that when you choose to do things differently, you can protect the intentions.

First, split people into two teams: (1) the architecture team and (2) the training team.

The Architecture Team

The architecture team consists of your best designers. They will do the following three things, which will hold the project together over time.

1. They will create the "large design" of the system, and decide how critical details get handled. All of this I refer to as the *architecture of system*. It includes partitioning across platforms and functions, the philosophy of handling errors, the philosophy of handling persistence, the philosophy of handling user-interface commands. These things must be known in order for a group of developers to reinforce each other with their different work styles, as opposed to competing with each other.

2. They will both design and build a base infrastructure, the "plumbing" of the system, which contains the object-oriented frameworks that carry user-interface commands, transaction completion, error notification, searching, and so on. It is built and tested.

3. They will design, build, and deliver a few of the end-user functions. This has two uses. First, it ensures that their architecture works. They will find and repair any flaws in their design faster than anyone else. Second, it establishes a pattern of programming for other programmers to follow. Your other developers will see how your best designers design and write code. They will use these designs to establish their own design habits. Probably, they will copy the sample code and modify it to their need. Make sure there is good code for them to copy!

The Training Team

The training team consists of a mentor for every 5 to 10 novices. Their purpose is to spend the first increment becoming fluent in object design and programming and to deliver a very small piece of function. The mentor should spend at least an hour each day working individually with each trainee.

The training team will attend several weeks of classes, where they will learn the language, OO design thinking, and the tools. They may spend another two weeks working on a small problem from start to finish, to get the feel of an entire cycle.

Finally, the training team will be given a relatively simple section of work to do. The mentor will work with the architecture team to set up design and coding templates that can be copied. The training team can get started, but they will almost certainly have to make changes along the way to accommodate the changes in the templates as the architecture team makes fixes.

The Intentions

If you set up the first increment differently, try to preserve these intentions:

1. Develop a strong statement of how the system is put together. This "architecture" provides coherence as the project staff changes.
2. Develop acceptable templates for designing and programming. Most developers find it easier to work from existing code than to develop afresh. Setting good templates in place early allows novices to learn faster and everyone to work faster.
3. Deliver something to the users. It may not be much, but it shows the project sponsors that the team delivers, and it shows the users what they are getting, which enables them to make better suggestions on the next cycle.
4. Work through a full cycle of development. This provides the learning effect of increments described earlier in this chapter. The second increment will go more smoothly once everyone knows what the full cycle looks like.

increments and iterations, 117

5. Find the boogeyman (WYDKYDK). As you start, you simply cannot know where your big problems will be. Will it be that the users are constantly changing their minds? That the developers cannot follow standards, or will not document? Or that the error rate is very high? Or that the test-fix cycle goes on forever? Or . . .? Going through the entire cycle through delivery lets you examine every component of your process and discover the ones that need attention. Finding the boogeyman is a critical success factor. Find him early, and develop a response. If you do not find him within the first six to eight months and take steps, he will jump out at you later, at some unexpected and critically bad moment.
6. Develop the habit of delivering. This is a second critical success factor. It anchors in everyone's mind the very important notion that "this team delivers." The presence of that thought, or its opposite, determines what the project team thinks it can do.

Two Stories

Earlier in this chapter, we studied Project Ingrid, which failed its first increment: It exceeded its schedule, had poor morale, and no apparent chance at recovery. However, the team had failed at only one increment, and were able to detect this failure after only four months. They found their boogeymen: their staff, their teaming structure, and their process. In fact, their boogeymen included everything except the project management and the incremental work plan. They recovered the project by revising staff, teaming, and process. Project Ingrid did deliver on the second increment. The team learned they could deliver, and learned how to deliver. At the end of the second increment, they were on sound ground.

a study project, 109

Project Winifred started off badly too. The first increment was delivered, but reduced in function. There was no architecture to speak of, and quality, communications, and morale were all low. But delivering established that they could deliver, and set the foundation for the eventual success of the project. They also discovered their boogeymen: the absence of architecture, absence of a technical leader, and a long quality assurance/ test cycle.

On the second increment, they created an architecture concurrently with adding function. They delivered on time again, and with slightly higher quality and morale. By now, the team was sure that they could deliver their system. They found other boogeymen, which included an overly rigid process unable to handle shifting requirements. However, there was not much question they could adapt to solve these problems.

Over the increments, the architecture, the design, and code quality improved. The Project Winifred team found various problems on the different increments and were able to change much of the way they worked. In their case, persistence became a habit. If they had not put out the first, "bubblegum" release, it is likely that the project would have been canceled.

I include these two stories to impress upon you the importance of completing and delivering the first increment.

Establish the architecture, deliver one function,
find the boogeyman.

Increment 2

The purpose of the second increment is to:

- Repair the major mistakes discovered in the first increment.
- Establish or tune the software architecture.
- Create a process and team that works for you.
- Settle on good development habits.
- Deliver more function to the users.

Pause and Learn

Review the first increment. This may take half a day. Remember that the boogeyman was what you didn't know that you didn't know. What unforeseen things kept you from performing the way you thought you would? What mistakes did you make? To get your project to succeed, you may have to change some of your closest-held wishes and beliefs. When I was a programmer, I thought that project managers, project plans, and object diagrams were all useless. Obviously, I have changed those beliefs. Some managers believe they must have all the requirements and time estimates before they can step into the project. Those managers will fail until they change their beliefs. Before starting your second increment is your best chance to locate possibly faulty habits and start new habits.

If you are forced to change something you hold dear, consider all the new strategies as "hypotheses." By doing this, you reserve the right to change back or change to another approach. That attitude alone may save your project. Review these aspects of the project:

- *Process*. Most large projects have too much paperwork, which slows communication, flexibility, and learning. What can you do in the process to let learning propagate faster through the teams? What paperwork can you drop? Conversely, some projects have too little paperwork, with the result that one team's decisions do not get communicated to the people who need it.

- *Team structure*. Why are decisions not getting communicated between teams? Do you need to put people who are apart together? Perhaps you have teams that fight each other. Consider creating teams around function if they weren't before, or around design components if they weren't before, or making them cross-functional.

- *Standards*. It is common at this point to discover that there is too much diversity in design and programming styles. Get the technical leaders together to settle on writing, designing, and programming standards. Think about how you will get the standards followed.

- *Linkage to the users*. Did you really deliver what the users need? How often did real users come and see the system? Most projects need to strengthen this aspect.

- *Architecture*. Often, the first increment's architecture is built on wishful thinking. What do you know now that you did not know then? Decide what your new architecture should be.

- *Training*. What do you now know that your staff needs to know? Usually, this is the time to set up more training.

Move On

Everything that was true about the first increment is true for the second, except that now you are starting with an architecture and people who know what they didn't know the first time. Deliver again, to develop the pattern of delivering regularly. It will become a habit. This second increment is the start of your way of working successfully.

Pause and learn; revise and persist.

Increment N

By the time you reach the *N*th increment, you have the habits and patterns of success. There are only two dangers to watch out for: falling asleep and overexpanding. If you have paid attention to this book, you will not fall asleep; rather, your project will get more efficient over time.

Project Ingrid overexpanded. It became so successful that it was cloned, split, copied, and distributed. The original 24-person team grew to over 100 people spread over several locations. However, the techniques that worked so well on the single-site project did not work when scaled up that way. Which points us to Chapter 7, on larger projects, and more people.

Always recall how you became successful.

USER INVOLVEMENT

Without direct user involvement your project may survive, but chances are that it will not be considered a success. The best way to discuss this is to review the paper on customer-developer links by Mark Keil and Erran Carmel.[3] In 1994, Keil and Carmel visited 17 companies, and collected data on 31 projects. They focused on 14 project managers who had each managed successful and unsuccessful projects. The managers were asked about the differences between the two, in particular, how much use they had made of 15 types of links to the user.

> Results of the analysis revealed that in 11 of the 14 paired cases, the more successful project involved a greater number of links than the less successful project. The mean number of customer-developer links used in the 14 successful projects was 5.4 compared to a mean of 3.2 in the 14 less successful projects. This difference was found to be statistically significant in a paired t-test ($p<0.01$).

The authors recommend using more links up to a point, perhaps six or seven. The study results also gave them an interesting second recommendation:

> *Reduce reliance on indirect links: Intermediaries and customer surrogates.* . . . Many of the development managers that were interviewed perceived that the problems associated with less successful projects resulted, at least in part, from overreliance on intermediaries or customer surro-

---

[3]Keil, M., and Carmel, E., Customer-developer links. *Communications of the ACM* (May 1995): 33–44.

gates. It is on this basis that we suggest managers reduce their reliance on indirect links, substituting direct links between customers and developers where possible.

There are at least two reasons why intermediaries and surrogates are poor substitutes for direct links between customer and developer. First, intermediaries can intentionally or unintentionally filter and distort messages. Second, intermediaries may not have a complete understanding of customer needs.

The comments from the study participants are powerful and revealing. Here are four from different projects, as quoted in the paper:

> If we had gone to the end user and not relied on these intermediaries, I think it would have made a difference [in the outcome of the project].

> Unfortunately, we never involved the people who would be using the system. They were not aware of the project and there was no ability for them to come back and say, "Hey, you haven't thought about this or that." It was shoved down their throats.

> The [surrogates] were people who used to be [in the field] and have now moved into a staff position . . . some of these people were three to five years removed from that function.

> These are marketing people who have been in the ranks for a number of years, believing they know the product and understand customer requirements. They basically said: "Here are your requirements; build a product." It was a dismal failure.

The article names 15 forms of links you may use: facilitated teams, support lines, user-interface prototyping, surveys, requirements prototyping, interviews, tests, bulletin boards, usability lab, observational study, MIS intermediary, marketing and sales, user groups, trade shows, and focus groups.

So, get real users linked into the project. The upcoming Eyewitness Account by Jon Marshall explains the difference between just showing an interface to the users and having the users really involved in its design. But first read what K.L., the author of the following EWA, has to say about directly viewing the users.

Jon Marshall's EWA, 58

There are several ways to link users into the project. Beyond the ones mentioned in the Kiel and Carmel article, here are three I have seen work effectively.

1. *Put one or more experienced users on your development team.* This is the best. Give considerable authority in defining the services and interfaces to those whose lives the system will affect. Jon Marshall's account gives an indication of the power of this.

◆ **Watching Users**   *K.L., Independent Consultant*

. . . [O]ne of the things that proved valuable was that my partner spent about two weeks sitting in on real calls with the sales reps. None of our requirements came from the IS people (I have found that such organizations often don't understand their users very well). We then built UI prototypes with the help of our domain expert and showed them to the users.

One of the things that almost immediately showed up after working with the users was that the biggest problem with their old 3270 application was the classical issue that they could do only one thing at a time. Navigating menus and switching modes was a major cause of frustration. I remember having a conversation with my partner, during which we said something like: "We could probably give them any user interface as long as they could do multiple things at once. In fact, they would probably be thrilled if they could just have multiple 3270 sessions at once!"

One of our design goals, therefore, was that the system would be as amodal as possible, allowing multiple windows of multiple types at once, while allowing the user to decide the flow of control (a "messy desk" metaphor). This feature was thoroughly denounced by the IS staff, who said that the users, who had never used GUIs, would just be confused. We felt vindicated when, after the system was installed, we saw the users easily flipping between many windows so quickly that even we couldn't follow them.

Case material contributed by a third party, used with permission.

2. *Hold weekly or biweekly user meetings or interviews.* You need one user from each category of the future users' system for two hours per week for each interview. The first meetings will provide you with system requirements. Later, you will discover the shortcuts it needs to provide them. The users will be able to react early to the assumptions you have about the user interface. When you find you cannot easily create some functionality in the requirements, they can help you find ways to simplify the system and get around the problem.

3. *Have the developers become trainee users for a few days.* The developers will return with a deep appreciation of the lives of the users, the ways they get interrupted, the shortcuts they need. They will be able to interview the users better, and their first design will be closer to the mark.

Get the real users involved.

PROJECT TEAMS

You are likely to find that the teams you initially established need altering at some point during the project. Such midcourse correction is natural and reasonable. Teams were discussed in Chapter 4, where a particular team structure was nominated. Appendix A, Collected Risk-Reduction Strategies, explains two project management patterns, *holistic diversity* and *owner per deliverable*, which I shall draw from now. Jim Coplien's Eyewitness Account of various team structures is in Chapter 8.

methodology, 77

Jim. Coplien's EWA, 198

Ownership

Team structure may be one place where object-oriented development causes a difference in managing the project. An object provides not one function or service, but a set of services to the rest of the system, which means that the developers of the class are involved not in just one element of the system's functionality, but several. They will have to understand several aspects of the system's functioning, and they will have several other teams coming to them asking for enhancements to that class. This means that different traps await you if you organize your teams entirely by function or by class.

Who would be accountable for ensuring that the overall function works if you organize your teams entirely by class structure? Nobody. You would have an *ignored area* (see Appendix A). This is a fairly common mistake, but it is easy to detect, because you will have the familiar situation of people pointing to each other saying the missing function belongs in the other's classes.

ownership, 89

ownership: owner per deliverable, 220

Suppose you then organize by function. You end up with a *common area*, a place rather like the refrigerator in a shared apartment. Just as no one person in the apartment knows what in the refrigerator can be thrown out, so no developer knows what in the class can be deleted. Developers put into the class whatever they need at the time, and the class grows in complexity, out of control. No one person can clean it up.

A particularly sharp team of three people recognized they had done something wrong when, after only a few months of work, they had to sit together for a morning to work through all the classes. They all had to be in front of the screen to make any decisions about the classes. They had created a common area. After that, they decided they had to have both function and class ownership.

There are still many ways to organize teams, even given that every functional requirement and every class should have a designated owner. Here are two, both of which satisfy Owner per Deliverable, and relate to the team structure suggested in Chapter 4.

methodology, 77

◆ Involve the Users   *Jon Marshall, ParcPlace-Digitalk*

An application was being designed for a company's market planners, who visually scanned large amounts of data looking for trends, conditions, and correlations. They changed service delivery schedules to optimize revenues, based on their discoveries. Although the design was progressing, the users were not too happy, and the development manager felt some outside help was needed. They asked me to guide part of their user-interface development.

The design team was eager to show me their user interface and get my approval, along with some helpful tips. I told them my approval didn't matter; what mattered was their users' approval. I asked them if they had been involving their users in the design. Their answer was, "Oh yes; we show the users our design every two weeks and we get their feedback!"

To their surprise, I told them that this was not involving their users. I asked how much of the design their *users had actually created*. They reacted predictably: "The users don't really know what they want. They would just tell us minor improvements on their old way of doing things. We listen to what they want, then we work it into the design if possible."

The designers were surprised when I said this was a false presupposition. They didn't yet know *how* to involve the users in the design process.

I assume you know the old saying: "If your only tool is a hammer, everything looks like a nail." When I asked the group to show me their design for the user interface for this marketing system, *it looked exactly like a Smalltalk Class Hierarchy Browser, complete with unlabeled list panes papered across the screen!*

"Do you think that marketing analysts think in terms of unlabeled list panes paneled across the screen?"

"We are putting in training programs for the use of this product."

It was then that I knew I had my work cut out. I worked with the design team for two days every other week for three months. The first thing we did was to select a user representative to attend the user-interface design meetings.

1. We taught the user what was possible to do with the computer.
2. We asked the user to sketch an ideal scenario of the use of the computer.

These were not done in a strict sequence. Rather, they were woven together through a series of discussions. My primary job was to continually assist the user in expressing his blue-sky, no-holds-barred ideal of what the

Total-Ownership Teams

Total Ownership teams are appropriate for smaller projects. Each team consists of two to four people, and each team is responsible for everything from requirements gathering to testing and documentation. They own a set of use cases (functions), and those use cases correspond tidily to a set of classes that they will own. The restriction is that there must be clear ownership of componentry by team.

Matrixed Teams

This is the matrix of the teams, Functions × Components described and diagrammed in Chapter 4.

methodology, 77

system would be like to use in their own business process. The hardest part of the job was to get the engineers to keep still and stop interrupting the user with their ideas as to how they could do things.

A breakthrough occurred when I gave the engineers the technical challenge of implementing the user's ideal, rather than constantly subverting it into a design they had already conceived. I asked "Are you guys smart enough to figure out how to do what he's asking for?"

Suddenly, the nature of the meetings changed. Instead of seeking to show the users how their design would satisfy their needs, they began to challenge themselves with implementing the user's seemingly outrageous design.

The design *was* outrageous, viewed by a programmer; but to a marketing analyst accustomed to physical things like paper and in boxes, the design was very natural. The users had simply moved their office and all its objects on to the screen. And they had moved their conceptual work processes there as well.

We went through a series of usability tests. The useability testing helped tune the design and locate inconsistencies not seen before actual use.

The system was implemented using the new GUI design, largely invented and sketched out by representatives of the users. The engineers took on the technically quite difficult challenge of implementing the users' ideas. The resulting product was judged highly successful by the users, the manager of the user group, and the manager of engineering. Significant productivity and useability gains were achieved.

The lessons
1. Involve the users, letting them define their ideal work scenario.
2. Involve the users by teaching them what the computer can do, so that they can be contributing members of the design team.
3. Let the users design a majority of the user interface.
4. Assist the user in discovering the objects in their work environment. These include the objects they work on and with, and the objects they use to work on their work objects (i.e., physical and conceptual tools).
5. Challenge the engineers to solve the users' "outrageous" design.
6. Eliminate the engineers' wish to come up with a great design by themselves.
7. Do usability testing to discover design flaws in actual use.

Case material contributed by Jon Marshall, used with permission.

◆ A group of people are made owners for each subset of the functions. Each ensures that the business object model, the user interface, and the program code all support their subset.

◆ A group of people are made owners for each subset of the classes, or components. Each person ensures that his or her classes stay "clean" and correct and understandable.

It is common, and probably a good idea, to use the same people for those two groups. That way, they will have some understanding of what it means to have functions satisfied and still keep the classes clean. In the successful projects whose members I have interviewed, it was the case that these two groups were made up of the same people, although the project leaders did not draw any significance from this. I suspect that if the function owners are different than the class owners, quite a bit of friction will build between them, as they will each develop their own vocabulary, values, and interests.

Ensure each deliverable has an owner.

DOMAIN MODELING AND REUSE

Domain modeling and reuse are two contentious issues that will show up repeatedly over the course of the project. Each requires attention from both the managers and the developers.

The Domain Model

Prepare for heated discussions about "modeling." Currently, experts differ as to whether *enterprise modeling*, *entity-relationship (E-R) modeling*, *domain modeling*, or even *business process reengineering* are essentially the same, different only because of old development habits, or fundamentally different. If you are not careful, you can sink a great deal of time and money into one or more models without getting full benefit.

Hazardous Situations

The following sections describe four hazardous situations you may find yourself in.

MODELERS BECOME ENEMIES. It is possible that the object and database modelers will become enemies. The object modelers claim that their model is fundamentally different from a data model, while the data modelers claim that the two are fundamentally the same but that the object modelers created a poor model. The result is that they cease to communicate.

My experience is that the structural part of the object model is fundamentally the same as the conceptual data model, and must be so. This is a position I retest each year, because of the strong reactions it provokes. The biggest difference seems to be between data modelers who model the business in conceptual entities and data modelers who model data on the disk. The domain object model most strongly resembles the conceptual data model.

PROGRAMMERS IGNORE MODEL. The programmers ignore the domain model. While your business experts are carefully modeling the objects in the business, your programmers create whatever they want in the software. In the end, the programmers win, since their code runs your business. If the program code does not match your business, your system is basically flawed. Create an "audit" task in your development process to resolve differences between the two.

TOO MUCH TO MODEL. You are trying to define the entire business model at one time. This is like trying to boil the ocean. History has not been kind to organizations that have tried to model the enterprise in one go, for two reasons:

- There is no feedback to the enterprise modelers from the programmers as to how well they are doing. Of the many possible valid models of the enterprise, some transfer well to software and some do not. Since the program code and the domain model must match, it is important to give feedback continually to the modelers.
- The enterprise keeps changing. By the time the full enterprise model is complete and ready to hand to the program designers, the rules have changed. Since change is inevitable, create a model/design/build process that gracefully accepts shifts in the business.

CONVERTING THE DOMAIN MODEL. You try to convert the domain model directly to a software design. There are many valid models of the domain. The first domain model you create may not make a good software design; however, whatever final design you create must be a legitimate domain model. It is straightforward to convert a good design model to a readable business model, but not to convert just any readable business model to a good design model. Beware of any advisors who advocate the latter path.

How can you create a reasonable domain model? *Incrementally*, with *audits*, and using a *common domain model*.

The Common Domain Model

The program code must represent a valid business model that is also a good software design. That fundamental requirement drives the rest of the discussion.

First, create a high-level model of your business. This should take no longer than two to four weeks. Use a skilled object modeler and three to six business experts. The business experts do not need to know anything about objects to begin with, although they will become skilled by the end of the work period. Applying use cases, CRC cards, semantic modeling, or some other techniques, create a model of the business with not more than a dozen key classes and several dozen supporting classes. Identify the most important four, six, or eight classes. This small model serves as a guide as you evolve and detail the model. The main four to eight classes are the key abstractions that will show up over and over. Refer to this initial model as time goes on.

Second, decide what your first release will contain. Model just enough of the domain to develop that release. This first model may be built by your business experts with an OO-skilled technical facilitator or by your OO analysts, depending on your teaming structures and skill mix. The result of this work is conventionally called the *analysis model*. I refer to it, or any similarly created analysis model, as *version 1 of the common domain model*.

Third, let your OO software designers and database designers create *version 2 of the common domain model*. The requirements for version 2 and every subsequent version of the common domain model are that:

◆ It must be a good software design.
◆ It must be a valid and understandable domain model.

The relationship between the later versions of the common domain model and your programmers' design model is that the design model may contain extra lines, extra data or methods, and extra classes to clarify details of the software design. However, the common domain model should be obtainable by erasing the nonbusiness terms, collapsing communication routes that run through nonbusiness objects.

Version 2 of the common domain model does not have to look like version 1; it does, however, have to be accepted by the business experts. From this point on, the business experts serve as advisors on the common domain model.

Fourth, as the design and programming progress, late-breaking design issues will cause the OO designers to change the common domain model. At every point, it must be a good software design and a valid, understandable domain model. The business experts must concur that the model does not violate the rules of the business.

Fifth, audit the program code periodically. Programming almost certainly will change the model. Most of the time, you will update the common domain model to reflect the program code. Sometimes, you will find that the program code is simply incorrect as a model of the domain. Change the program, to get it back to a valid domain model.

Repeat the preceding process for every release. The second time through, the business modelers can take advantage of knowing which changes were made in the first release. When you put your system into production, the program code will match the common domain model.

Why Are There Multiple Valid Domain Models?

There are many ways to describe the world. It is not that some are wrong while the others are right; it is just that there are many ways to characterize information. I am often asked to give an example of a domain with multiple valid domain models, whose designs differ significantly. In the interest of stimulating argument and comparison, here are three I have encountered: *checkbook entries, organization structure,* and *flavors of soda.* They are described in the following subsections.

CHECKBOOK ENTRIES. Perhaps you are not a bank, but your system needs the concept of a checkbook to keep track of entries. You need a dozen different kinds of deposits and about as many kinds of withdrawals. Your users must be able to void out a checkbook entry after creating it.

- Does your domain model include "deposit" and "withdrawal" as kinds of objects? Probably so.
- How about "checkbook entry"? Also probably so.
- Is there a different model that avoids checkbook entries altogether? Yes, you could model the system with transactions and logs of transactions, instead of using a checkbook.
- Do you model a void of a deposit as a deposit or as a withdrawal? I have found that the answer to this varies considerably with the person being asked, and that there are many more than just two answers. I was not even able to understand some of the answers, so I cannot list them here. Try this out on your friends and colleagues, and see what you come up with.
- Is a voided entry a subclass of entry, or is it so different that it is simply a separate kind of object?
- Do you display a voided deposit in the deposits or withdrawals column?
- What will you do when the users change their mind about whether a voided deposit should be considered a deposit or a withdrawal?
- How would you place a void of a void of a deposit?

When we first encountered this problem on a project, we created the class, CheckbookEntry. We gave it two subclasses, Deposit and Withdrawal. There were about a dozen classes listed under Deposit, and a similar number under Withdrawal (see Figure 5-9). There was no debate about this initial design. Everyone considered the model obvious and true. Then we encountered the voids. Each week, as we interviewed more people, we got new and different answers to the fourth question, to the point that we felt we could not trust the stability of any answer. It was,

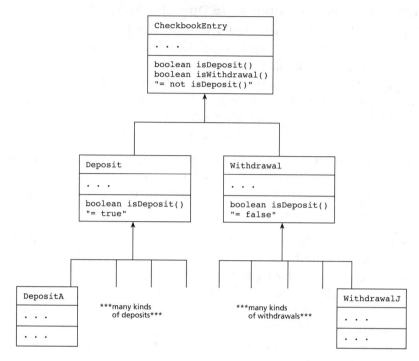

Figure 5-9   *Initial class structure for checkbook entries*

however, clear that the users wanted to see a voided deposit in the deposits column.

We decided in the end that while we could trust that the two dozen kinds of checkbook entries would continue to exist, there was nothing intrinsic or stable about the classes Deposit and Withdrawal. Each entry had to be able to answer whether it was a deposit or withdrawal, and we were clearly going to change our minds often as to how a voided deposit would answer that question.

Eventually, we created about two dozen subclasses under the CheckbookEntry class, one for each entry type, including voided entry (see Figure 5-10). Rather than locking into the class hierarchy the answer to "Are you a deposit?" we gave each entry type a method to answer whether it was a deposit or withdrawal. The reason for moving the question from the class structure to a method is that changing the class structure is a serious alteration to the system, while changing a method's answer from true to false is minor.

Once we created this design, we stopped worrying about the answer to the question, "Is a voided deposit a deposit or a withdrawal?" That could change every week without holding up the project. To this day, I do

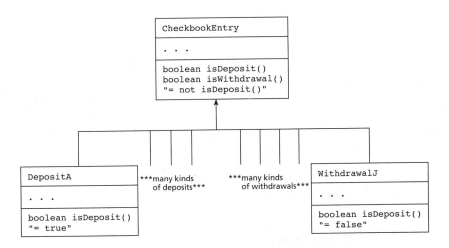

Figure 5-10 *Eventual class structure for checkbook entries.*

not know what the final answer was, nor do I worry about it. The software design was adequate, timely, stable, efficient, and a reasonable model of the business.

ORGANIZATION STRUCTURES. An organization consists of suborganizations, down to a department, which contains people. There are many similar kinds of organizations: legal, sales, corporate, and so on. Is it better to model the organization as a recursive structure or to model the levels of the organization explicitly?

Both are valid models of the domain. Some analysts prefer the recursive structure, because it gives a simple and general model. The experienced designer–programmers I know prefer the explicit structure, because it gives an efficient software design. They say that by the time you encode the allowed behaviors of the different organizational levels, you have done all the work of writing it explicitly, but have hidden your solution so that it is harder to see and change.

On one project, I really wanted to use the recursive solution—because it is universal, beautiful, and so cool. Hearing from the developers that it would also be harder to understand and maintain, we did a careful impact analysis. In nearly all cases, the explicit solution showed itself to be simpler and easier to modify than the recursive structure. The only case in which the recursive solution worked better was the least-likely and least-frequent-change situation. Reluctantly, I decided not to use the recursive solution. Since then, I have come to prefer the explicit solution over the recursive one, for reasons of design and maintenance.

But both are valid domain models, so I shall have no trouble revisiting the decision on a future design.

FLAVORS OF SODA. A restaurant serves many kinds of food and drink. These can be modeled as classes and subclasses. There is, for example, the Pizza class, with possible subclasses for special toppings. There is also a class, Soda. Does Soda have subclasses for various brands or flavors and for the sugar content of each? Or does the class Soda just use a name to differentiate the particuar sodas? After you decide, consider whether the nature of your business makes any difference in your answer.

Integrate domain models while delivering increments.

PolyBloodyHardReuse

Why did I pick this term, *PolyBloodyHardReuse?* Why not just say "reuse"? Because there is an ingrained tendency to relate the difficulty of a topic to how long the word used to describe it is. The topic of reuse is so diabolically difficult that the short word "reuse" actually gets in the way of dealing with it. If we cringe at "multiple inheritance," "genericity," and "polymorphism," we should cringe more at "PolyBloodyHardReuse."

When you get reuse right, it becomes just "use." We say, "I use the hammer to put in the nail." "I use this spreadsheet to do my project management lists." We use the delivered development environment; we use the Smalltalk collection classes; we use the C++ Standard Template Library; we use the C standard I/O subroutine library; and so on. When reuse is operating properly, we think of it as use. That is your goal.

In 1995, Frakes and Fox reported on the results of a questionnaire sent out to discover what affects reuse positively.[4] They reported on 16 questions and test phrases, only a few of which I include here:

- *Programming language.* The question was, "What percent of the life-cycle objects your organization creates are typically composed of reuseable parts?" The answers were compared against the organization's programming language. The researchers concluded: "Usage of languages usually thought to promote reuse, like Ada and C++, shows no significant correlation with code reuse levels. . . . Our conclusion is that choice of programming language does not affect code reuse levels."

---

[4]Frakes, W., and Fox, C., Sixteen questions about software reuse. *Communications of the ACM* 38(6): 75–87, 1995.

- *CASE tools.* The test phrase was, "CASE tools have promoted reuse across projects in our organization." The researchers wrote, "We conclude that CASE tools are not currently effective in promoting reuse. . . . [They] may not be used; they may not be used correctly; or they may not be effective in promoting reuse even when they are used correctly."

- *Fun.* The test phrase was, "It's more fun to write my own software than to try to reuse." Frakes and Fox reported, "Most respondents (72%) do not have the NIH [Not Invented Here] syndrome. We conclude that most developers prefer to reuse than use from scratch. This result contradicts conventional wisdom in the software engineering community, but is in agreement with the findings from another recent study."

- *Recognition rewards.* Frakes and Fox compared reuse among respondents reporting no rewards against those with recognition rewards. They reported: "We found no significant differences between them. . . . Our results contradict the common belief that recognition is a sufficient reward for reuse." Regarding the possibility that cash, not recognition, might be a sufficient motivator, they reported a "lack of respondents in organizations with cash rewards."

- *Perceived economic feasibility.* The test phrase was, "Reuse is economically feasible in my organization." The responses were compared with the organization's reuse level. They reported, "The boxplots show a clear trend toward higher reuse as belief in the economic feasibility of reuse increases. . . . This result implies that it is important to convince software engineers that reuse is economically justified. Management must bear the responsibility for educating software development staff that reuse is a desirable and economically viable practice."

- *Reuse education.* Frakes and Fox tested two other statements: "I was educated about software reuse in school," and "My organization has an education program about software reuse." Both statements correlated with higher levels of code and design reuse. Frakes and Fox concluded "that education about reuse, both in school and at work, improves reuse and is a necessary part of a reuse program."

Overall, Frakes and Fox investigated whether any of the following correlated with reuse levels: programming language, CASE tools, perceived economic feasibility, reuse education, fun, software engineering experience, recognition rewards, common software process, legal issues, reuse respository, industry type, company size, project size, quality concerns, use of reuse measurements.

Of all those factors, perceived economic feasibility and reuse education were the two that correlated best with increased reuse. There was a weak to moderate correlation that "there is more reuse in organizations with a common software process that promotes reuse." Such a process provides education, perceived value, and standards of behavior. There was a secondary correlation between reuse and certain industries, telecommunications coming out best.

In light of the study, let us review some issues that you will encounter. You might have read, as I have, that OO technology gives you reuse. Neither my experience nor the study article supports that claim. Object technology gives your developers three new reuse mechanisms; that is, three new mechanisms for them to ignore. Even OO developers feel compelled to write afresh. It became immediately clear when I visited several organizations just starting out in object technology that the developers were going to write everything themselves, object-oriented or not. Reuse fails due to people, not technology. So a successful reuse program takes the human factor as well as the technology into account, which is why education and increasing perceived economic value correlate with greater reuse.

One reuse mechanism already exists with standard languages: the reference to existing functions or subroutines. Use of classes to collect data and functions, polymorphism to add to existing functions, and inheritance to add to an existing class are part of object technology. The combination of all four results in a framework, which is hardest to understand, but provides the most leverage. The following sections discuss three issues that complicate reuse.

Conflicting Reward Systems

The sponsoring executive and end user get little reward from a new design mechanism. So you might think that the industrial pressures would drive the professional software programmer to use existing software. But professional programmers get little reward from using someone else's design. It does not advance their career or give the same intellectual satisfaction as developing their own design. They have, after all, been trained to "program" and hired as "programmers." If they do a good job, they will become "senior programmers" or "senior designers." In other words, you hired designers–programmers and now are telling them not to design–program!

I have met few people who can imagine saying, "This is our senior programmer. She is so good, she never programs anything. She just buys it." This is the conflict between the profession and the need. Therefore, do not expect developers to search out opportunities for using someone else's solution. It goes against their reward system.

Given human nature, we should not expect that putting an artificial reward system into place is going to make much difference. Whom do you reward: the person who puts a package into the library or the one who uses it? Oddly, most companies reward the person who puts it into the library. That encourages an individual to submit his or her own solution. But how do you reward people for using someone else's classes? Will the developers subvert your reward system?

Lack of Trust

My experience is that lack of trust of other developers is one of the greatest inhibitors to reuse. If a programmer does not believe that (a) the other person did a decent job *and* (b) the other person's problem was actually very close to the current problem, then looking through a library of other people's solutions is clearly a waste of time. It is the rare programmer who trusts the work of another programmer. Trust shrinks in the time it takes to walk the distance of a single hallway, and more rapidly after that.

I Can Write It Faster Myself

It is frequently a true statement that the time it takes to design and program a solution is about the same as the time it takes to locate, learn, and use an existing design. That statement, however, does not take into account testing and documentation. The person who makes that statement may have an unspoken second half to the sentence: " . . . because I am not planning on testing or documenting it." The average programmer's time horizon is the length of time it takes to type in the first three-quarters of the solution. Study time, and testing time and completing the solution and documenting it are somehow not in the scope of the comparison.

Let us work the arithmetic, briefly. Assume the programmer costs the organization $120 an hour, or $1,000 a day. Currently, this is a reasonable, fully burdened cost figure. Word has it that a class costs 10 days to develop for just one project. Double that if the class is going to be sold commercially or marketed for reuse; that is, a single class costs $10,000! A simple solution to any interesting problem is going to include at least 5 or 10 classes, making a simple solution cost $50,000 or more! Someone selling the solution commercially is planning on selling to hundreds or thousands of customers, so the selling price is much lower, probably $500 to $2,000 for a similar solution. Comparatively, the purchased solution is a negligible cost compared to the home-brewed solution.

That is not a fair comparison, however. It will take your developer perhaps a day to find the solution, another two to three days to learn it, and another three to four to use it (and that will have to be tested). So the developer is comparing five days of fun developing his or her own solution (not including the other five days of unpleasant testing and documentation) with five days of less fun reading someone else's solution to the same problem. Hence, "I can write it faster myself."

Where is the hope? The ideas in the following sections may help.

IMPROVE THE ATTITUDE. Of the factors Frakes and Fox investigated, *education, perceived economic value,* and *a common software process that promotes reuse* correlated with the amount of reuse. In other words, attitude. Most people wish to be good citizens when they can. Let it be the case that good citizenship means looking for ways to use existing work instead of reinventing it.

Project Winifred revisited, 188

ALLOCATE TIME FOR SEARCHING. On Project Winifred and a few others, there was one person charged with discovering class libraries. This person had it in his or her job description to spend time reading magazines, talking on the phone, and trying out advertised classes. When that person found something useful, he or she bought and installed it, and worked to get it accepted in the architecture. Not all the purchased classes were used; typically, they were used when they solved a hard rather than a trivial problem. The time saved on not having to invent a solution for the hard problems more than made up for the money spent on the extra classes not used. Note that the suggested big-M methodology in Chapter 4 contains a role called *reuse point.* Allocate time for at least one person to search for classes.

Big-M methodology, 78

MAKE REUSEABLE CLASSES SKINNIER. Even a class intended for reuse almost always does some special favors for its first client. Just what those extra services are is not usually discovered until the second client tries to use the class and finds it does these various extra and unwanted things. Making the class more reuseable means taking those extra services out; that is, making it skinnier, not fatter! The problem is that it is very difficult to detect which services are going to be the ones considered extra by the next client; and it is very hard to work in such a disciplined manner.

The final form of a reuseable class is apparent only after it has been reused in different contexts several times, and been thinned. Hence the saying, "If it hasn't been reused, it is not reuseable."

CONSULT THE *DESIGN PATTERNS* CATALOG. The book *Design Patterns* contains several dozen thoroughly tested ideas for design reuse.[5] Your training program should include time on key design patterns, when to use them, and how to document use of them. "Re"use of these designs not only will save time and money in development, but will probably result in a better design. As with commercial class libraries, you cannot expect the developers to learn these simply by having the book. Put some time into the plan for study groups to learn how to use them.

OTHER IDEAS. I wish I had seen other ideas work. I certainly have heard enough talk. However, I do not expect the fundamental psychological or reward structure to change in the near future, and so I do not expect reuse to become easier.

> *Improve the attitude; if it hasn't been reused,*
> *it cannot claim to be reuseable.*

FURTHER READING

For more on adjusting your project in midstream, consult Steve McConnell's book, *Rapid Development* (Redmond, WA: Microsoft Press, 1994). It contains numerous ideas and best practices for basic project management such as micromilestones, incremental development, prototyping, and continuous delivery. For more on the slippery topic of software reuse, read the book by I. Jacobson, M. Griss, and P. Johnson, *Software Reuse: Architecture, Process and Organization for Business Success* (Reading, MA: Addison-Wesley, 1997). Buy your designers the book *Design Patterns* by Gamma et al. and get them to the point where they can both recite the patterns and describe their designs in terms of the patterns.

---

[5]Gamma, E., Helm, R., Johnson, R., and Vlissides, J., *Design Patterns* (Reading, MA: Addison-Wesley), 1994.

Chapter 6

Advice From Hindsight

Learn what you wish you had known.

Pretend for a moment that you have now completed your OO project, and are about to look back at what you just experienced. What do you wish you had known before? What would you say are the actual costs and benefits? If you could travel back in time to the start of the project, what advice would you give yourself?

COSTS AND BENEFITS REVISITED

The one-sentence summary revisited: *The cost is training, the benefit is agility.* Yes, you really did spend something like $6,000 per person to get three weeks of training. Or you spent double that letting your people wander around on their own without a teacher. Possibly, some of your newly trained developers left the company when they discovered they were worth more on the open market. I hope you kept them by giving them a raise or an interesting assignment, in recognition of their new value.

You also spent something like $100,000 on consultants, trainers, and mentors, or equivalent lost time; you bought new software development tools; and you experienced iterative development. If you were alert, you learned to build time for revision into the plan.

What did you get for this? Hopefully, you got the following:

- Better encapsulation of design decisions. It is now easier for your software to follow your company's changing directives.

- Quicker response to changes. Your developers can roll out a new variation of the software faster than before.
- Improved communication between the developers and the end users and executives. They now all speak in business terms.
- Easier implementation of some technical parts of the system such as memory management or drag-and-drop user interfaces.
- Improved programmer morale and vitality—for most of your programmers. Some still prefer to work the old way.
- Improved time-to-market, which is the sum of the preceding.

You also came to terms with incremental development and, perhaps, iterative development. You saw the size of the reuse problem.

Probably, your reuse program is not working yet because people still prefer to write their own classes and frameworks instead of looking for an existing one. You still don't have a global enterprise model; you have a model of a particular section of your domain, as was needed for the project. You still don't perform analysis of the domain and then simply program it up.

You were expecting magic? Of course not. Object technology is ultimately just a different way of packaging software—although it is a way that allows developers to think differently. The technology allows the programmer to create a program structure that matches the structure of the problem and then program by differences. That shift in working permits the rest.

SENTENCES YOU HOPE NEVER TO HEAR

The following sections describe six common, seriously spoken, but dangerously flawed statements. You are likely to encounter one or more of them during projects. See if you can diagnose what is wrong with each.

Writing 500 Lines of Code per Day

"C++ is so productive I can write 500 lines of code a day with it!"

Name four things wrong with that sentence! First, anyone, aside from the rare genius, claiming to write 500 lines of code a day either is not spending time thinking, or is probably copying large chunks of code from place to place, giving you "code bloat."

Second, almost certainly, there is no internal reuse going on, but rather use of lots of copy–pasted code or boilerplate code. A good sign of internal reuse is when the line count stabilizes and then starts to go down. One expert programmer says that he reaches the total line count about one-third of the time through development. Why? At that point, his understanding per unit function is at its lowest: he knows the least about the structure of what he is creating, compared to the amount of function. From there on, he learns more about the structure of what he is creating, and replaces existing bloated program pieces with leaner and neater structures that do more. The line count fluctuates, but at the end, the code is about as large as it was one-third of the way along.

The person who says he or she writes 500 lines of code per day is not learning as he or she might. The code is getting "fatter" with time, and losing, not improving, its structure. The final system will be harder to maintain.

Third, people who take design seriously prefer to be happy about small, tidy designs, rather than large ones. This creates two rather interesting dilemmas for the serious OO designer: How can your people boast about their work? Should they say "We wrote all 2,500 lines of code in only one week!" or "We did it in only 200 lines?" It makes for rather subdued and sometimes awkward discussions. It is not clear how to talk about the superiority of the design and mention code volume at all.

How do you measure the productivity of the designers? If your designers are producing 500 lines of code per day, do you reward or punish them? If they are producing 10 lines of code per day, do you reward or punish them? Are they creating great designs, getting superb use of existing classes, or reading comic books? Trying to quantitatively measure designers and programmers is very difficult, the operative word being "quantitatively." It often becomes clear quickly who produced a neat design that solved a problem or that other people can work easily with.

The fourth thing wrong with the sentence is that it indicates code bloat. Simplistically put, bulk is bad. The more bulk in the code, the more testing will have to be done, along with more documentation and more learning. At the rate of 500 lines of code per day, the bulk is adding up very fast.

I sat next to a great C++ programmer at a conference. While listening to the speaker talk about the 250,000 lines of code in the latest release of some software tool, the C++ programmer leaned over and whispered to me, "I can't even see how they can write 250,000 lines of C++! All the systems I and my friends have written together have much more function and still don't add up to that many lines! Something must be wrong in their design!"

Getting back to the person extolling the wonders of C++, that it let him produce 500 lines of code per day: I was not at all surprised to hear that the project was having major difficulties a few months later.

Model the World, Then Code

"To do OO, just model the world, then code it up."

the domain model, 140

Project Tracy, 19

The final object design almost certainly models the world, but modeling the world does not produce the final object design (see Chapter 5). There are still some people who claim that object-oriented design simply means to model the world and then code it up. See Project Tracy in Chapter 2 for notes on a project that tried this. Project Tracy's failure was not due only to this, but they felt afterward that trying to "model the world and then code it up" was a serious error.

It is worth some effort to understand why this sentence is both wrong and dangerous. The key is twofold:

1. The path you took to get the final model was not straight; the model changed numerous times on the way.
2. When you have the final design, you will notice that it models the world.

There are many valid models of your world. Some lead to robust and efficient software designs and some do not. When you create your first valid model, you cannot know whether it will lead to good software. Odds are that it will not. The process of doing design is first to add the various constraints of maintainability, efficiency, and respect for resources, and then to find *another* valid model that is also a good software design. The model may shift dramatically in these stages, and you will be wise to let it. If you did not have to make the model run efficiently and support future modifications easily, then there might not be sufficient economic motive to revise the original model; however, that economic motive is strongly present.

Designers who have experienced this process make several observations. The first is that, after a great deal of arduous work over weeks, the result looks as though it should have been obvious from the beginning. The final model is simpler and clearer than the intermediate ones, often so simple and clear that it is embarassing not to have seen it from the beginning. The second observation is that they often encounter resistance to reworking the model at all. Business experts or analysts feel that the first model is adequate, because they understand it. They are pleasantly surprised when a clearer description emerges from the subsequent work. The surprise is doubled when they find that the design better supports future needs.

Design the Screen, Then Code

"To do OO, just design the screen, then code it up."

This is the other side to "just model the world and code." The objects on your screen should match objects in the domain and in the software design, but it is not clear that your first attempt to name the things on the user interface will prove to be the best ones for the software. "Design the screen and code it up" is likely to produce a superficial design.

The strategy is proposed for three reasons:

1. It sounds easy.
2. It leads to a prototype quickly, without requiring deep thought.
3. It actually works for a while.

The downfall is just a continuation of the discussion about modeling the world. Your software needs to be designed to withstand pressures of computing resources and evolution—and that *does* require deep thought.

Iterate Prototypes

"To do OO, just iterate prototypes until you are done."

This sentence leads one to believe that the team feels that there is not enough time to think through architecture and design, and to review the designs. The two dangers of prototyping are:

1. *Lack of quality.* A prototype should give you information that you could not get by just thinking for a similar period of time. After getting that information, a design should be possible, and your team should publish and review that design. The peer review will rapidly provide some assurance about the quality of the design. The reviews take less time than building another prototype.
2. *The process may not converge.* We want the architecture and design to stabilize so that the other teams can move on with their work. With continued prototyping, there is no commitment to a stable interface or to a converging of the design.

Project Manfred (see Chapter 2), ran into exactly those problems. I visited another project running this way with over 100 people on staff. Several dozen designers on other teams waited in increasing frustration as the base design team iterated for months without commiting to a design or an interface.

Project Manfred, 15

I wish to distinguish between managed iterations as a necessity in software design (as discussed in Chapter 5) and the hazard signaled by the

increments and iterations, 117

more on iterations, 159

quoted sentence, which gives the sense of an absence of control and an absence of design (see next section in this chapter).

Classes?

"Do we need classes?"

At one time, the few people using C++ were doing so to try out OO programming. By 1996, most C programmers' compilers were C++ compilers. Today, even if they write C code, it is called C++ code. C++ now refers to: ordinary C programming, template-based C++ programming, and object-oriented C++ programming. A similar statement can be constructed for Ada 95 and OO COBOL.

If you hear this sentence, you know that one of the other types of programming is being used, which is okay, if your project is not intended to be an OO project. But if the purpose of your project is development using objects, then you need to address the source of the problem:

◆ Are your developers getting enough time to learn and apply OO design techniques? Some developers have told me that they felt they had to resort to programming in their old way because of schedule pressures.

◆ Are your developers getting enough training to do OO design? OO design is not something that they can pick up from reading the language manual. Make sure they get either two weeks of dedicated OO design training or one week of classroom training, plus one hour a week of project-internal discussion time.

Reuse Is Easy

"Reuse is easy; I always design reuseable classes."

The person who made this statement was a senior designer who went from project to project writing reuseable classes. It soon became clear that he did not stay around long enough to know whether anyone ever used the "reuseable" classes he wrote for them (see the section in Chapter 5), nor did he use other people's classes, not even his own from previous projects. His reuseable classes almost certainly were not. Unfortunately, there are quite a few senior designers like this around.

polyBloodyHard Reuse, 146

PolyBloodyHardReuseable classes are polybloodyhard to create, and take their final form only after their original forms have been tried, altered, and reduced to their essence. It is very hard to predict which parts of the original class are superfluous. Only your next project can tell you that. Making a reuseable class has this in common with making 20-year-old whisky: You have to wait. You cannot say, "Today I shall write a reuseable class" any more than you can say, "Today I shall make a 20-year-old whisky." You have to wait as long as it takes for the class to be used, unaltered, just like you have to wait 20 years for the whisky.

MORE ON ITERATIONS

You ran your project in what you thought were iterations. But some things went wrong. First, some people on your team decided that iterations meant rampant prototyping. They refused to accept requirements, saying that the requirements would show up after several iterations. Some claimed that deep design was not necessary, that the prototypes would "evolve" as the design became clearer. They cited publications that reported that it is difficult or impossible to get designs right the first time. They claimed documentation was not necessary until the very end, since it would always change anyway—and they never produced it at the end. In short, your project was never schedulable or controlled.

Even if that did not happen to you, you still did not know how many iterations to do. Did Alistair say that three is the magic number and you have to do three? Is doing only one the same as "waterfall" and therefore evil? How many is the right number; how do you decide? Again, you felt you were not running the project; it was just "happening" around you.

Schedule a second iteration when you are suspicious about the quality of information you have at the start of the first, or when you detect that something is critically unsatisfactory about the first version. Remember that a second iteration is expensive, therefore it is preferable to get high-quality information before or during design, and then simply create the proper design. A second iteration adds two costs: one for the time spent evaluating the first version, and one for the time spent redoing it.

Realize that people almost certainly will not get the first version right, and therefore something will be critically unsatisfactory. The difficulty is in getting high-quality information before building the version. Here are two places where we know by now to expect rework.

1. It is notoriously the case that we get the user interface wrong in some significant way, however hard we try. It is, therefore, a good place to plan a second iteration.
2. We know the design and programming will have errors, so we schedule a "repair" or "integration" or "QA" time, which is nothing more than a planned iteration.

There are other times when the information we have is suspect. As soon as the information is reliable, the next version should be the last. You manage the project by paying attention to the quality of information the developers have on different topics.

Iterative does not mean "sloppy." Good requirements gathering, design, coding, and communication reduce the need for and cost of further iterations.

SELF-TEST

Here is a test to give yourself once you are partway through the project. Using cheers and groans, how do you currently stand on your project? You should know by now what to look for in the answers. The next sections contain eight possible answers to the question, "What is happening on your OO project?"

Two Increments Delivered

"We have just delivered the first two increments."

Yay! That means you are using an incremental strategy, that you have delivered something, and that you have established a pattern and habit of delivering. Your team knows they can get the system out the door. Now you are in a position to make changes to improve whatever it is you feel needs improvement.

Thirty People

"We have just started a project with between 30 and 100 people."

Groan. I hope you have done this before and succeeded so that you know what you are doing. If not, ask yourself this:

- Is it clear what all those people are going to be doing right from the start?
- Do you have a solid architecture in place?
- How are those people going to communicate and coordinate with each other?
- Could you perhaps do the work using only half the people—the best people?
- Could you perhaps send all but six of them off to do other work while those top six people set up patterns of design and programming?
- Is it too late to reconsider your plan and make adjustments?

On Project Udall (see Chapter 2), the team spotted this situation, and told all but six people to do something else for the next several months. Some took this opportunity to get training, so it was not wasted time. As the six people established the architecture, they carefully selected a few others to join them. As the months went by, the number and sizes of teams slowly grew, always after the previous section's design had been laid out and they had a technical leader for it. Project Udall moved from a catastrophe waiting to happen to a successful project.

Project Udall, 20

Analysts, Programmers, and Tools

"We have a group of analysts, a group of programmers, and we just bought the latest OO CASE tools."

Groan. Please reread Methodology in Chapter 4 and Project Teams in Chapter 5. You are likely to run into the following hazards:

methodology, 77
project teams, 136

- Poor communication channels and poor mutual respect between the two groups
- A "throw-it-over-the-wall" mentality
- An analysis model not well suited to software design
- An analysis model out of synch and ignored by the programmers
- Money wasted on the CASE tools

If you are in this situation, consider pairing up analysts with programmers to get full, two-way communication, as discussed in Chapter 5. Recheck with both groups just to confirm what you expect the CASE tools to do for you—and listen to both teams. If you know what you really need, you can probably get your CASE tools to deliver that.

project teams, 136

Learning OO From the Compiler

"We just bought the latest C++ compiler; our programmers are good, and they'll just learn and do it."

Groan. That is a first indication that you have bought trouble. Watch out for these pitfalls:

- Insufficient training, leading to weak designs
- Letting programmers model the business
- An inappropriate method of choosing technology
- A lack of development discipline
- Weak communications

Please reread the stories about Mentor Graphics and Project Ingrid in Chapter 2, and the sections on Technology, Training, and C++ in Chapter 3. Many good organizations have succeeded with C++ projects, just as many other good organizations have failed with C++ projects. Reread those chapters and recheck your assumptions.

Programmers Between Projects

"We don't want to risk much on this OO thing. We have some programmers between projects, some users between tasks . . ."

Groan. Your goals are imprecise and your commitment is not commensurate with the cost you will expend. You are on track to be a failure story for the next edition of this book. The cost of any project is large, at least because you block the use of those people and that time on a better project. Reread the Project Reginald and Project Alfred stories (in Chapter 2), and Chapter 3.

On the Cutting Edge

"We are going to develop distribution and CORBA within the system infrastructure."

Groan. The cutting edge always looks very attractive because it promises to solve some problem you have. But reconsider. Unless it is part of your core business or core competency, odds are that you are underestimating the difficulty and cost, and overestimating the benefit. If you think that implementing distributed, multilanguage, multiplatform technology is part of your project, please reread the section in Chapter 3.

As it says there, "Select the cutting edge only if you can handle the cut. If it is not part of your specialty, buy it. If you can't buy it today, assume it can't be done at this time." In other words, let someone else figure out how hard it is, and then sell you the solution for 1 percent of the development cost.

Designers and Programmers Separated

"We put the designers over here, and the programmers over there."

Groan. It is a myth that designers design and programmers program. Everyone designs, and the programmers have the last word on the design. The programmers are a critical mental resource and should be included as part of the design team. The designers are better off programming because they will see their mistakes a lot sooner. Please reread Project Teams in Chapter 5.

project teams, 136

Six-Month Pilot Started

"We have a six-month pilot going, with a non-IS business expert, three programmers with two weeks of training, and a mentor."

Yay! You have set up what there is to set up at this point. Assuming you do not change the ground rules and you pay attention to what they encounter, the project has a good chance of success. Plus, you have a good chance of finding out how to fit object technology into your organization.

Chapter 7

Expand to Larger Projects

There are new traps with bigger projects.

There is much to say about surviving a big OO project, but for the most part, it has little to do with objects, or it is a repeat of what has been said earlier in this book. To survive larger projects, remember the following:

- A successful small project does not make a successful big project.
- A big OO project is more a big project than an object project.
- Try not to do a big one, because it is risky and expensive.
- Hire someone who has done a big OO project before.
- Do everything suggested in the earlier sections of this book; particularly, study these project stories in Chapter 2: Brooklyn Union Gas, Mentor Graphics, Project Stanley, and Project Udall.

YOUR FIRST BIG PROJECT

What is a *big project*? The most salient definition I can give is, "one that is twice as big as the biggest one you have successfully managed in the past." If your largest previously successful project had three people, then eight people will introduce you to big-project problems. If you have done 20-person projects, you should be able to figure out a 30-person project, but there will be surprises with a 50-person project. If you have successfully delivered 150-person projects, then please write and tell me your story! Some organizations understand large projects quite well and deliver them regularly. I have little to teach such an organization in this book.

In this chapter, I use the stories from Brooklyn Union Gas, Mentor Graphics, Project Stanley, and Project Udall as a base. Glenn House of Mentor Graphics was kind enough to add an Eyewitness Account (later in this chapter) about that company's experience of moving to C++. The main conclusion I drew from the larger projects I visited is that they do not show a different pattern of success and failure from what I wrote about in the first part of this book. Two items show up, though:

Glenn House's EWA, 172

1. Project planning and team coordination are considerably more important on a large project.
2. The key success and risk factors are much more critical. Perhaps you can get away with breaking the rules on a small project, but you will not be able to on a large project.

Let us take a walk through a large project and reexamine topics from other chapters in the book, plus one new one, class duplication.

Project Charter

You may end up with a big project because the problem you are solving is big, or because your charter is to train people. One training strategy is to overstaff your project by a factor of three, just to provide OO experience for two-thirds of them. If this is your project's charter, allow the extra time in your schedule, and keep it clearly in mind when setting up the teaming plans. Create separate training teams and progress teams, as described in the Day Care[1] strategy in Appendix A, but with more teachers to keep the project moving.

training: day care, 232

Clarify your project charter, and set up your project to work within that charter. Do not confuse delivering a large system with training a large number of people and delivering a medium-sized system.

Communication

Twenty people do not talk together in the same way that three people do; 50 do not talk in the same way as 20. Your task is to keep people working in small clusters whenever possible, and to keep communication going whenever it is needed, which calls for the management skills to establish project spirit and morale.

---

[1]Day Care: Your experts are spending all their time mentoring novices, so . . . put one expert in charge of all the novices and let the others develop the system.

You will need to track communication with groupware communication tools. Separating workers into smaller clusters calls for your architects to partition the system so that teams of three to five people can sit together and talk on a minute-by-minute basis, exactly as on a small project.

Your communication checklist should include communication (1) with users, (2) between analysis and design, (3) between developers, and (4) between program modules. All of this is as for any large project. I am only reminding you.

Staffing, Skill Dilution, and Project Teams

Without trivializing the issues, two points to make about large projects are these:

1. Sometimes a small, good team is not sufficient for the task and you will have to use a large team.
2. It is possible to make a large team less effective than a small team.

Later in this chapter, in the section on productivity, I discuss how 6 outstanding people can outperform 20 or 27 people of mixed proficiency. This is clearly the way to go when you can. But, there comes a point when even the ideal 10-person team cannot produce the system you need in time. You may have to use 200, 500, or 800 average people.

productivity, 177

The way people are teamed can result in a difference in how well they perform of several hundred percent. Thus, a large staff can perform worse than a small staff. Here, and later in this chapter, I reiterate selected factors to prevent this from happening.

training: day care, 232

- Work out teaming mixtures based on the technical architecture (see also, Chapter 4).
- Let your experts develop simple frameworks for others to use.

methodology, 77

- Grow training teams into highly competent expert teams (you will have time for them to become experts on a multiyear project), and keep them out of the way of the experts while they are learning (the Day Care strategy).
- Use some of the ideas in the productivity section in this chapter to set up alternative teams based on proficiency.

productivity, 177

- Read *The Mythical Man-Month*[2] and *Rapid Development*[3] for other ideas.

---

[2]Brooks, F., *The Mythical Man-Month* (Reading, MA: Addison-Wesley), 1995.
[3]McConnell, S., *Rapid Development* (Redmond, WA: Microsoft Press), 1994.

◆ Make sure a leader on the project has worked on a problem of similar size before. My sense is that a person can extrapolate his or her experience up 50 percent, so having worked on a project two-thirds the size of your project may be sufficient. Consider having someone who has worked on a project this size, but not in object-oriented software.

Methodology

For a large team, the deliverables and standards portions of your methodology are much more significant than on a small project. Consider using conservative standards to reduce risk. On the Brooklyn Union Gas project, Tom Morgan related that they made the following two fairly strong decisions about modeling conventions:

Tom Morgan's EWA, 28

1. They used only one-to-many relationships, optional on both ends, when modeling their domain classes. This precludes arguments over the questionable many-to-many relationships and even the less questionable one-to-one relationships.
2. They did not subclass any domain classes, even if it meant copying code.

Why would they make those choices? The project took place in 1986, when few people had experience on large OO projects. The first convention was designed to prevent hours of argument over small details; the second was designed to protect their database from changes in the class hierarchy. In retrospect, Morgan said the first convention was good because it did prevent arguments and remained sound. They could have been a little more adventuresome with the second, he said; it did, however, serve its purpose. Morgan concluded: "There are, no doubt, many other ways to organize the project conventions; we chose these, and they worked for us."

Your methodology should specify how teams are to synchronize their work, along with what deliverables are reviewed by whom. I interviewed the technical leader of one successful large project, call it Emily, that had well over 100 people. He said that each team could select its next increment duration as any multiple of two weeks. Not every team had something to contribute every two weeks, but there was a synchronization across all teams that were finishing an increment. For each build, one team was selected to be in charge of the process and coordinated the other teams. Thus, they were able to incorporate incremental development, vary the increment sizes, and devise a synchronization mechanism across teams. This is just one way to lay out a project synchronization plan.

The organization's methodology does not have to become bloated, or waterfall, just to accommodate the larger project size. It does have to take into account the increased communication needs, and should provide explicit protection for discovering surprises partway through the project.

Plan periodic methodology updates on a large project. You will learn that some deliverables are too time-consuming to produce, that teams need to be structured differently, that communication channels need to be strengthened, and that additional synchronization points are needed.

Increments and Iterations

Increments and iterations are designed to let you recover. They are more important on a large project, because there is more to recover from. Project Emily (described in the preceding section) demonstrated that you need not fall back on a waterfall, one-build process simply because your project is big. In fact, just the opposite is required.

Measurement and morale on a project is better if complete functions are delivered every few months than if a long time is allowed to go by. With each increment, your team learns how to put a working system together better.

The Cutting Edge

There are enough risks on a large project, so avoid any technology risks you can. Brooklyn Union Gas attributed part of its success to being conservative with the technology whenever possible. Project Stanley took the opposite approach, continually reaching for the newest ideas and technology, and failed largely because of that.

Domain Modeling

The value of domain modeling increases as the project grows. The reason is that there are more people inventing things, so it is more valuable to get an expert to identify the properties of the business abstractions to be used. You still need to ensure that the domain model matches the final code—the code is what ships, runs, and is maintained. If it does not describe in a valid domain model, there is probably something missing in the design.

the domain model, 140

Risk Reduction

collected risk-reduction strategies, 201

Everything in this book comprises risk-reduction techniques. The basic strategy always is: Look around; find and attack the items that are most likely to derail your project (see also Appendix A).

PolyBloodyHarderReuse

PolyBloodyHardReuse gets harder on a big project. Communications are worse, more people are inventing, there is less trust between developers who don't know each other well, and human character is the same. What can you do? I have the following suggestions:

♦ *Create a class administrator or reuse "czar."* The system architects and team leaders make good, local reuse czars, because they are in communication with other leaders and care more about getting the system out than they do about "cute" designs.
♦ *Work from local reuse outward.* People will use designs from someone they know sooner than from relative strangers.
♦ *Raise consciousness on the subject.* Look for ways to remind your people to check constantly for existing solutions.
♦ *Encourage good citizenship, particularly of the team leaders.* Include the question, "Does this abstraction or framework exist already?" in the design review. Be sure to have the project OO architect review code for unnecessary duplication of effort.

Class Duplication

Class duplication is a failure of your reuse mechanism. Duplication may also happen on a small project, but on a small project, the communications lines are a lot shorter, and team members can find out and respond more quickly and easily. On a large project, duplication is more likely to go undetected.

Certain sets of classes are useful to many teams, and hence may be discovered and invented by different groups. Examples include money, time intervals, transactions, and relationships. For some classes, it does not matter much if several teams invent their own variants; for others, such as time stamps and currency, failure to detect duplication can cause system failure. Allocate the critical classes to specific teams and have the project architect and team leads ensure that the official classes are used.

A big OO project is more a big project than an object project.

TRAINING THE TIDAL WAVE

We are about to revisit the bleak subject of training (see Chapter 3). If object technology follows its current course, how many people will be learning it in the next five years? I have not seen a reliable estimate, and the answer depends on what you call object-oriented work. It would be safe to say in the range 10^4 to 10^5; that is, somewhere between 50,000 and 200,000 trainees! That means on the general order of 10,000 people a year going through those early steps. How will the industry, and you, deal with this tidal wave of trainees?

training and getting advice, 67

Some of you will be using these trainees on a small project, some on a big project. Consider:

◆ At one mentor for every 4 trainees, 2,000 mentor-quality experts still can handle only 8,000 trainees. At this time, there are not 2,000 mentor-quality experts available.

◆ At $6,000 per person for courses (3 weeks at $2,000 per course) and 6 months of lost time until they are earning their salary again:

  – For 6 people, that is $36,000 and 5 work years.
  – For 200 people, that is $1,200,000 and 100 work years.
  – For 3,000 people, that is $18,000,000 and 1,500 work years.

IBM has stepped up to this challenge. The company now has an internal, six-week-long Object Technology University, and several sites have announced they are going completely OO. Other companies are doing something similar.

Must you also step up to this level? I believe object technology will become a primary way of creating software. We can look at the history of hardware development to learn what this means. There were vacuum tubes, then transistors, RTL, TTL logic, and custom-integrated circuits. Many, but not all, of the designers simply had to learn the technology. They were not very effective at first. They took on small projects, sometimes at home, sometimes in school, sometimes at work. Then they tackled larger projects. Schools produced junior designers who specialized in the technology, who became the new staff for new projects. Learning the new technology became a fact of life. Eventually, most designers learned the new technology.

◆ **Ten Lessons the Hard Way** *Glenn House, Formerly Vice President, Mentor Graphics*

In 1988, Mentor Graphics was the largest and most successful electronic design automation (EDA) company worldwide. It had profited from an extremely well-integrated set of tools built on a commercially available workstation, the Apollo computer. The original software was in Pascal, and it used platform-specific graphics optimization routines. This formula of tight integration of tools and leveraging the networking and graphics acceleration of the workstation produced a nearly unbeatable product offering in the market.

In the normal course of events, new competitors entered the workstation market, most notably Sun. Sun used a more open architecture than Apollo. This meant the company was faced with a horrendous porting job or a rewrite. Since the original offering was now becoming dated, Mentor Graphics management decided to make a real technological breakthrough for their customers, and they embarked on the most expansive development program in the company's history: project 8.0.

Naturally, we selected an innovator language—C++ (we were Pascal-based)—using the cutting-edge C++-to-C translation technology (no compiler was available). We had to build our own windowing technology because X-Windows was not commercially available. We also had to change platforms, operating systems, development environments, defect tracking systems, and documentation development systems for our new foray.

Lesson 1: *Do not assume language features provide an architecture: Less is more.*
Just because the language designer provides a feature is not a reason to use it. There were many features of C++ that enticed us: encapsulation, inheritance, polymorphism, to name just a few. Our initial implementation of the general string class supported every string operator imaginable. It even

supported international variants like Kanji. It was beautiful. It was huge!

Unfortunately, when compiled and linked into an application, the lights dimmed. Then, numerous individuals started linking in the string library and, because there was only minimal support for shared libraries at the time, the binaries just ballooned.

Lesson 2: *Training in a new methodology cannot be done by reading a book.*
Make sure your team gets professional training and that initial projects are "disposable" until competency is reached. We have found that the professional programmer needs about one to three months to absorb the OO paradigm.

Talented engineers and managers can convince themselves that reading a book or taking a one-week training class can make them effective and productive. In our situation, C++ and the methodology of object-oriented programming was in its infancy. There were few books, tutorials, and training sessions available that provided real methodological guidance. We were lured by the promise of OOP. We ultimately benefited from that methodology, but only after a lot of product code had been written. The initial code had many elementary mistakes and flaws in OOP style. This had a very negative effect on quality.

Lesson 3: *Heed encapsulation: Design and obey interfaces.*
Many of the issues we encountered could have been avoided if we had adhered to a proper form of encapsulation. Just because C++ allows you to define public, private, and protected variables and functions does not mean that your developers will use them appropriately. Programming standards would have helped us here. As an example, the string class just mentioned could easily have been corrected by changing the underlying implementation. Yes? No! Because

some users of the string class complained of speed problems, the string class owners made some internal variables public—and the rest was history.

Lesson 4: *Do not be an innovator adopter in more than one segment of technology.*

Although it may be fashionable to adopt new technology in your business, limit adoption of new technology to only those areas in which it is absolutely necessary. Innovator technology, by its very nature, is fragile and fraught with not well-thought-out issues. It is not what is in the documentation that you should worry about, but what is *not* in the documentation. In the early days of C++, the order of constructors and destructors was not defined under certain conditions. Our programmers came to rely on how CFRONT (our C++ translator) ordered them. When we switched to other commercial compilers, this created quite a mess. If we had worked to the initial ANSI standard, many of these traps could have been avoided.

Lesson 5: *Food chains are great in nature but not in large-scale project programming.*

A food chain is when the code of developer H has to be there for developer G to do integration testing. Add programmers A to F the same way. Translate each programmer into teams of programmers and you get the food chain. All 1,000 developers must line up in total eclipse to get an integration build. Not a pleasant task, and the time lost is immeasurable. Keep reuse broad and shallow.

Lesson 6: *Change one thing at a time.*

This seems like the most simple concept. But it is the hardest one to fulfill in practice. If you change language, compiler, linker, environment, OS, or whatever, do one at a time. The penalties of not following this rule are lengthy debug times and endless fruitless experiments on never-ending permutations of source. Time and financial pressures will always press you for widespread change, but change only one variable at a locality so that isolation of the problem is simple; it will pay dividends.

Lesson 7: *Stay with commercially available development tools and compilers.*

When your developers insist they can build a better translator, compiler, linker; when they say they must modify so and so to improve performance and capacity; if innovator technology is involved, run for cover. The pity here is that the engineers are probably correct. They can do it faster and better. But who is going to support nonstandard anything three years from now? As the technology matures, you can count on the fact that the technology providers will do it as well and different from you. You will be stuck having a difficult and costly transition to off-the-shelf products. If you really, really need innovator technology, then leave it alone as much as possible.

Lesson 8: *The development environment is as vital as the implementation language.*

The check-in/out, bug-tracking, testing harness, and related technology are as important to project success as the programming language selected. Because we had strayed from commercially available compilers and linking, we could not use simple debuggers, leakage tools, and profilers. The need for us to write internal tools became even greater. The development environment discouraged even the most patient engineer. At one low point, it would take 24 hours to turn around a single line of C++ from code to working executable. Make sure that the development environment is designed from the start and that it is maintained on a par with the language compilers and linkers.

Lesson 9: *Do not be a slave to process and metrics.*

When you are in the middle of a major implementation and the implementation

◆ **Ten Lessons the Hard Way**   *continued*

starts to have its challenges, it is not time to deploy every new process you can think of, and to require rigid adherence. The development and deployment of 200 metrics do not help the engineering staff to think; it makes them wonder why they became engineers. Introduce process in metrics in measured steps and then only to cure significant difficulties in the middle of a development project. When executive management started to realize how late project 8.0 was going to be, their answer was metrics: we had metrics to measure everything. From metrics you start to have targets. When you have 200 metrics and, say, 100 targets, then directors of engineering start spending their time trying to decide which targets to miss. Not a very good use of their time. Decide on a very few (fewer than five) metrics and give fewer targets (two or one), and make the target metric customer-focused.

Lesson 10: *Do not be proud, never give up, and demand success.*
This lesson is last. Never be too proud to throw something out even if you have slaved to get it. Some code we developed had to be thrown out and redone; some underpinnings had to be redesigned, some tools had to be refitted, some metrics had to be killed; and some targets had to be removed. Over time, managers and executives wised up.

Demand success of the project and the people will respond. Remember the adage: "There is never time to do it right, but there is always time to do it over."
Be a believer. Our product set was two years late, did not meet our performance and capacity expectations, and was very expensive to maintain and extend. It took two more years to cure all the 8.0 issues. These lessons have changed the way we think about development and adoption of methods and tools. We still believe in taking risks and adopting technologies before the mainstream. Version 8.0 was the price we paid for a very expensive education. But how else do you get educated when you are at the bleeding edge of technology adoption, when no one has done it before?

Several years later, Mentor Graphics sits with project 8.0 more and more of a memory. We have returned to being a highly productive engineering company. Our developments are better planned and executed, and more innovative today because of our experiences. We have become more than an EDA company; we have become a software company.

Of couse, neither you nor any of your developers would ever violate any of these lessons. You are all too smart for that! Good luck.

Case material contributed by Glenn House, used with permission.

I expect much the same scenario to play out in object technology. However, at the time of this writing, schools are not yet producing many OO programmers, so the burden is still on you. You can choose between two strategies:

1. Train fewer people.
2. Whomever you train, train them more effectively.

Train Fewer People

This is one of the mitigating factors in the bleak scenario I alluded to at the start of this section. These are the three reasons for not requiring that every programmer learn object design techniques:

1. Your C and COBOL programmers will be needed for network and mainframe programming for some time. The mainframe has not gone away, and COBOL has moved to the workstation. Many C programmers will still write C code, even if they are using a C++ compiler.
2. Application generators will become more powerful, so that you will have to write fewer lines of code to deliver the same functions to your users.
3. Finally, users will do more of the work themselves. Spreadsheets and laptop databases will be tied in to the corporate database so that users can enter and query directly. They will create and trade macros, and large chunks of computing will move out to individuals. Some of them will learn about object technology, but neither they nor you will be involved in the issues of this book.

That still leaves a very large number of people to train.

Train More Effectively

Chapters 3 and 4 contain most of what I have to say about training. You can add effectiveness by being creative. Here is an example:

training and getting advice, 67
methodology, 77

> The president of a small company told me that they had only about five programmers. He sent the senior programmer to C++ school for a week. That person became responsible for staying up to date on C++ and for teaching, mentoring, and setting design and programming standards for the other four people. This was an effective strategy for that small company.

This company has established the following necessary roles:

- There is a source of standards.
- The setter of the standards is someone the others respect and will follow.
- There is ongoing learning.
- There is a full-time mentor.

They are found in the same person, but, nonetheless, they are accounted for. For a larger group, you may have to hire a full-time mentor. This person should be able to create training and review teams and work across teams. Review the section on training in Chapter 3, and use your creativity to make lean but effective training structures.

Training 50 or More People

Here are some ideas to consider if you need to train 50 or more people at one time. I offer them as suggestions for your staff to argue over to help produce better ones. Notice this is set up as a way to grow OO skill at a steady rate that will exceed 50 people per year.

Set up a Full-Time Classroom Program

You probably have enough people for three or more classrooms. Each person needs a total of six weeks of training: two for language, one for OO design, one for tools use, part of one on the class libraries, part of one on methodology, and one for a group assignment.

training and getting advice, 67

Create a classroom facility with a full-time teacher. Spread the six weeks of training over a 6- to 12-month period. Set up an ongoing study group that meets one hour per week (see Chapter 3). For 50 people, that works out to about 20 full-time workweeks for the instructor. She or he will need the other 26 weeks to tune and prepare the classes, and to stay up to date with the industry.

Set up 6 to 10 Connected Projects

Treat the training as a large project consisting entirely of novices. Organize a set of projects with teams of four to eight people under one or more mentors—the Day Care strategy, without the progress team (see Appendix A). Connect the projects, but not tightly, to ensure that each team makes progress. Run the projects so that they use each others' systems. The interlocked projects will allow the students to learn and appreciate design, documentation, synchronization, and incremental development, and also will give the mentors a chance to keep mental control of what is happening across projects.

training: day care, 232

Use a Full-Time Mentor

The mentor/coach/architect/teacher approves design standards and conventions, and coaches them. This person obviously should be a senior OO designer, with mentor characteristics. A superprogrammer with poor communication skills will not do you much good here.

The mentor should allow the group to set some of their own standards and conventions so that the students will come to appreciate the creation of standards. The mentor's job also is to review designs and code, to see that the people are gaining skill, and to suggest avenues of development.

Maintain Tight Standards and Review Policies

Adopting design conventions and standards is part of building a culture that will hold your organization together as the people in it grow. Letting the students suggest, settle on, and use those conventions is very important.

Let your people develop the organization's "way of writing." Use peer review, code and design-document walkthroughs, design reviews, and group study periods to develop a style. As that way of writing settles in, the developers will be able to move more easily from one place to another in the organization, understand what is going on, and communicate with each other.

Rotate People

To build and reinforce your company's way of writing, and to share design experiences, let each person in the training groups work on at least two projects over an 18-month period.

To manage the next 200,000 trainees, be creative.

PRODUCTIVITY

This section contains some productivity models that can help you select between alternative project staffing strategies. I separate the discussion of productivity from that of estimation (see Chapter 4), because two projects with identical people will produce very different results depending on their team structure, their communication habits, their morale, when and how they come onto the project, the project staging strategy, and even the system design itself. In his Eyewitness Account in Chapter 8, Jim Coplien describes how those factors interact with each other to push the productivity curves around. Typically, just two or three factors will dominate the productivity you get. I have picked out some of the dominant ones to discuss here. You will find it useful to find out what factors drive your project.

estimates, 95

Jim Coplien's EWA, 198

Size

Functioning properly, a large team can do more than a small team. In *The Mythical Man-Month*,[4] Fred Brooks gives a simple calculation, which

---

[4]Brooks, op cit.

shows that sometimes a project requires a very large team. The following paragraphs summarize that calculation, and then generalize it.

Although you might be able to get the very best people to work on a small project, as soon as you need more people, the odds of your being able to staff with only the best people diminishes. I refer to this decrease in skills as *skill-dilution*. The difference between people is great, and you might notice a difference of 5, 10, or even 20 in contribution between people. Fred Brooks used an example of 1,000 people on a project, with a skill-dilution factor of 7 (that is, the average contribution per person on his postulated 1,000-person project was only one-seventh of that on a small, top-notch team).

The curve describing skill-dilution should drop steeply at first and then flatten out. This captures the notion that the very best people are rare, and that the group will slowly tend toward an average. I modeled with various functions, which gave similar results. Here I use for Average Skill the function $1/\log(n)$, where n is the number of people on the project. This is a nice, simple function that captures the notions just described. I omit the various constants and factors for any one project, because there can be so much variation across projects.

The other important factor is *communication overhead*. As the project grows in size, people will have to communicate with more and more other people. For this, Brooks again used a productivity drop to one-seventh in his 1,000-person project. I use the function $1/\log(n)$ again for Average Productivity, this time based on a hierarchical communication structure. Again, I omit constants and factors.

The two factors combine to make Total Project Productivity— TP = Number of People × Average Skill × Average Productivity = $n/(\log(n) \times \log(n))$, which is shown in Figure 7-1. While the curve is obviously a rough estimate, it illustrates two things that are critically important:

1. As you add people, at some point total productivity goes down.
2. As you add people, eventually total productivity goes up.

The first point, which matches the dip in the curve, I discuss in the next section, Staff Skill Mix. For the moment, notice that total productivity eventually goes up. This is because the number of people contributing adds up faster than the fact that their contribution is getting smaller. So Brooks is right. When you have a large enough project, you need a really large number of people; as you add people, eventually total productivity goes up—as long as you manage them adequately.

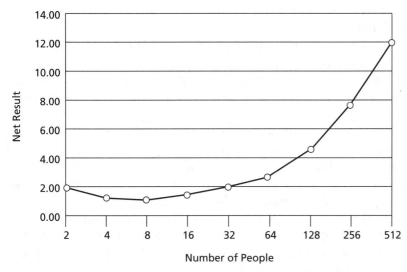

Figure 7-1 *Project result by size—n/(log(n) × log(n))*

The main lesson of Figure 7-1 is that even with radically diminishing productivity per person, a properly functioning large team can get more done than a properly functioning small team. The operational phrase is "properly functioning." Many of us have seen an improperly functioning large team manage to get less done than a decently functioning small team.

Now, let's discuss that dip at the beginning of the curve.

A small team can do an amazing amount, but a properly functioning large team can do more.

Staff Skill Mix

A very good developer may produce functionality at several times the rate of a less skilled developer, who may produce at several times the rate of a beginning or poor developer. Let us use an arbitrary unit for the rate-of-production of functionality, and say that a beginner works at one unit, an average developer works at three units, and a very good developer at nine. These numbers are rough but adequate for the purpose here. Therefore, six very good developers work at a productivity rate of 54 units, which is the same as 18 average developers, not subtracting for communication overhead. It is also the same as 27 trainees and experts mixed, again not taking communication into account. Which would you prefer—a project with 6 very good developers, 18 average developers, or 27 trainees and experts mixed?

This would account for the dip in the curve in Figure 7-1. The model is too rough to be precise about just when the curve goes down and then back up again, but it does indicate that for small and medium projects, skill-dilution alone hurts you more than the extra developers can make up for!

And now for the bad news: You may not be able to get your hands on six very good OO developers; in fact, probably you will be staffing your project with trainees. Project Winifred faced this situation. There were 18 object developers in the expert–novice mix. The project leads estimated the project could have moved 50 percent faster if it consisted of only six experts. However, at the time the project started, they could not find six experts to hire. Also, the project was set up as a training program, so they were required to have at least six novices. The following section looks at a team structure for such a mix of people.

Project Winifred, 88

Try for a few good people.

Team Structure

How you pair people affects their productivity. An expert gets better working with another expert. Managing a trainee drains most of the productivity out of an expert. This is the basis for the Day Care strategy discussed in Appendix A. Let us apply the formula from Day Care to two team structures for a project with four experts and six trainees.

training: day care, 232

Even Mix

According to a common staffing strategy, there are three teams, each with one expert and two trainees, under the lead of the senior expert. Within each team, the expert works at one-third his or her full productivity rate of nine units and the trainees each work at their rate of one unit. The combined productivity rate for the team is $(1/3) \times 9 + 2 \times 1 = 5$ units. The leader may be lucky to do one unit of work while coordinating the teams. The combined productivity rate for the project is 16 units.

Progress Team/Training Team

The Day Care risk-reduction strategy advocates splitting the group into a training team and a progress team. One expert is assigned to all six trainees, while the other five experts produce the system. The training expert produces no functionality, and the six trainees produce at a productivity rate of one each, for a team total of six. The progress team, consisting of three experts, works at a rate of 27. The combined rate for the project is

33, more than double that of the Even Mix strategy. There are other factors to add in, such as that the three experts may produce at higher rates by working together, that there are only two teams to coordinate instead of three, and that the trainees may learn better by getting more, dedicated expert time.

To get an idea about the overall effect of teams on a project, read the Eyewitness Account by Jim Coplien in Chapter 8. He has examined a number of organizations for efficiency characteristics.

Jim Coplien's EWA, 198

Team people for synergy.

Productivity Changes Over Time

Even the best programmers do not develop at a constant rate over the course of a project. They must spend some time learning their way around the problem, and during that time, not much is produced. For a while after this, they can produce at some peak level, until the complexity of the system finally starts to tax their recall, and they slow to a sustainable pace. Figure 7-2 illustrates this changing productivity.

During the learning phase, the production of functionality starts off slowly; it increases as the developer internalizes the material and starts programming. For a while, functionaltiy is produced at a great rate, until the system reaches a size and complexity that saturates the developer's head. At this point, the rate of newly produced function starts to decrease because the developer must continually relearn things about the system. After a while, productivity stabilizes at a value lower than the peak productivity.

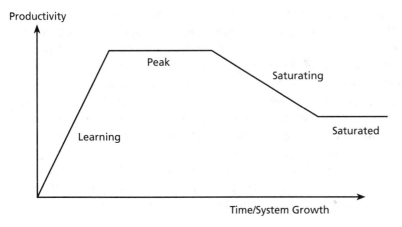

Figure 7-2 *Productivity changes with system growth*

As with all these sorts of curves, there is a great deal of variation from person to person, but we can extract some value from even a rough estimate. I use numbers that match my experience: a two-month learning phase, a four-month peak phase, a two-month saturation phase, and a saturated production rate of one-third to one-half peak production. The time periods roughly correspond to when your first and second increments should be coming out (see Chapter 5)!

increments and iterations, 117

I used this curve to estimate Project Winifred at its start. It indicated that six good developers, operating at just twice an average productivity, could deliver the system in 15 months, instead of the almost two years a team of 12 average programmers would need. At the end of that project, we decided that both the curve and the prediction were right.

The formulae for productivity vary too much from person to person and project to project for us to hope for final numbers here. Nonetheless, they can give you some insight into the effects of time, quantity, and quality of people on your project. They may help you to understand what is happening, or going to happen, on a project.

Lines of Code Per Month

It is a common observation, also mentioned in *The Mythical Man-Month*, that the lines of code produced per person per month are relatively independent of language. I have seen good programmers produce on the order of 3,000 lines per month at their peak and 1,000 lines per month in saturation, whether in PL/AS, FORTRAN, C, Prolog, or Smalltalk. You get the industry standard of 10 to 20 lines of code per workday if you amortize these numbers over a fully staffed project, including nonprogramming staff.

An object-oriented version of this standard is two weeks per class for single-project classes, and four weeks per class for commercially reuseable classes. This is a commonly used figure. The actual result depends on the writing style of the developer. Some developers like to make lots of small classes, while others prefer fewer larger classes. Using published averages, though, an "average" class might be expected to have 15 methods or functions, each with 10 lines of code. At two weeks to develop, that works out to 15 lines of code per day. (For more discussion on these numbers, see Chapter 4.)

estimates, 95

So is there validity to the statements, "count the lines of code" or "count the classes"? I say, yes, but immediately follow with a riddle: You only know how many classes and lines of code there are in the program when you are done! In the middle of the project, they are fluctuating, so it is hard to get them earlier. One expert said he hits his final line count one-third of the way through the project.

The counts serve your purpose at the very beginning of a project, when you are trying to build an order-of-magnitude estimate about the upcoming costs based on the results of a similar project. I used a lines-of-code measure to estimate for Project Winifred. There, I did not care what the actual number of classes were, but used them as a convenient measure of delivered function. Any units could have been used because they vanished in the final result.

Project Winifred, 188

There are two twists to this discussion of lines of code. One I have already mentioned: A good designer will slowly reduce the size of the design over time. It is not that they stop typing; they replace lines as they write. This makes it hard to know which line or class count to use. I suspect their change log would show a steady production of lines of code, even while the total system line count shrinks. The other twist is frameworks.

Be careful about how you use lines of code.

Frameworks

Modern OO design calls for the careful design of frameworks, which contain much functionality and are completed by adding small functions. Non-OO programmers occasionally use such tailoring functions, and one name for them is *user exits*. Object-oriented frameworks are a formalization and extension of user exits. With a framework, that new function can be added in a very short amount of time, proportional to how similar the new function is to the operation of the framework, not proportional to the function delivered.

Frameworks affect productivity measures and productivity itself. The system shows a very slow rate of development while a framework evolves, and then a very rapid rate of development as it is used. This warps the apparent growth-of-function over time, as well as the relationship between lines of code and delivered function.

I wish someone would collect project data so that we would find out more about how the curves shift. In the context of project survival, however, it is sufficient to be aware that frameworks are significantly slower to develop and significantly faster to use than the straight-line code production is.

Productivity Revisited

The discussion about productivity was directed toward choosing between several project strategies, not toward evaluating people. Many people have tried to find a meaningful measure of productivity and success. The trouble is that good design and good reuse both reduce the size of the system. Wayne Stevens, a senior methodologist at IBM, had a working postulate: "Productivity cannot be measured." Another senior development manager told me this: "I have tried measuring everything. I finally concluded that the only acceptable measure is final user happiness, which doesn't help much while you are busy developing."

Two or three factors will drive a large project's productivity.

MIGRATING THE ORGANIZATION

Do you really need to migrate the whole company at once? Probably not. Here are four hypothetical case studies to help work through the numbers. Each suggests only moving 10 to 20 people a year. That is a manageable task and should serve your purpose. If you decide to move several hundred people at one time, reread Glenn House's Eyewitness Account earlier in the chapter.

Glenn House's EWA, 172

Exercise 1. Suppose you are organization Fausto. You do mostly mainframe work, with a few C programmers, but primarily COBOL programmers and application generators. You have decided to start using workstations. How many people do you need to move?

This requires a cultural leap. Learning workstations, client/server, and networks is going to keep your staff mentally taxed. Try to use application generators on the workstations whenever possible. Smalltalk is the simplest and safest language to learn. You should avoid C++ unless there are compelling reasons not yet evident. Move four to six people every six months, using courses and a part-time mentor on a pilot project.

Exercise 2. Suppose you are organization Fern. You make workstation applications in C. Your C programmers are the industry average. You have decided your workstation applications need to be written using object technology. How many people do you move?

Fern lives by getting applications out the door, so you want the most programming power for the money. Try for Delphi, Enfin, VisualAge, or Smalltalk with some purchased class libraries. Wait on Java until an extensive set of class libraries reaches the market. Avoid creating infrastructure subsystems if you can. Move 10 people each year. That represents two new OO projects per year, which is a fair rate of growth.

Exercise 3. Suppose you are organization Finch. You write systems software in C. You have decided that your future lies with C++. Move 10 people per year to OO C++, while the others use the C subset of C++ for the time being. Send the 10 people to training as outlined in this book. Some of them will become the team leaders for the next 20 people who are moved over the next year. Ten to twenty people is a group you can move safely, keeping quality up while not losing too much in productivity over the year.

training, 67

Exercise 4. Suppose you are organization Fontana. You create customer-specific C software. You have not yet decided whether to use C++, Java, or Smalltalk, but you have decided that object technology is critical to your future. You choose to move 20 people per year, in two shifts of 10. You plan to hire a full-time mentor/expert to guide the two shifts. You will run up to five OO projects over the course of the year.

Try migrating 10 people per year.

Chapter 8

Rechecking: A Case Study

Technology is only part of the story.

What else is there to say after going through all the issues? Here, I high-light the following from the other chapters:

- *Objects are here to stay.* They satisfy certain fundamental decades-old needs of the industry. They provide the encapsulation and diversity that data-handling multimedia and networked applications require. The next wave of programming will "ride on top" of object technology, not displace it. Learning to design and work with objects is simply a necessity.
- *You can use an imperfect tool if you know what you want.* Knowing that every tool is imperfect means the burden is on you to decide what you want it for. Decide what you want, determine whether the tool can support you in getting that, and use just the needed subset of the tool's capabilities. Do that and you can substitute a simpler, more generic tool for a specialized one that you cannot afford or is not yet available.
- *Develop your big-M methodology.* Whichever published methodology you start with, it is not *your* methodology until you have used it and adjusted it to fit your organization. At the end of each increment and at the end of the project, spend some time reviewing your priorities, decide what you liked and didn't like, and what you want to keep and what you want to change.
- *Develop a habit of delivering.* Make delivering software part of your organization's identity.

- *Be flexible and stay focused*. Adapt as you need to in order to satisfy time-to-market.
- *Use* what you learned in the preceding 10 or 20 years.

To help you review the topics in this book, here I discuss Project Winifred, introduced in Chapter 2, more closely using the vocabulary and issues established over the course of the other chapters. This chapter concludes with an Eyewitness Account by Jim Coplien, who discusses organizational issues and technology in a more general context.

Jim Coplien's EWA, 198

WINIFRED REVISITED

Project Winifred, 21

This Project Winifred review is given in four parts: summary, history, analysis, and relation to this book's topics. You may find this format useful for re-examining your own project.

Summary

System Type: Business system, OO client to relational server

Project Duration: 1.5 years

Staffing: Peak staff 45; approximately 20 OO developers, 16 novices, 4 experts

Result: Delivered system on time; learned object technology

Quality: Never high, but always sufficient

Success Factors: Increments, determination, a few key players

In Brief: Successful, but delayed by overconfidence and a lack of attentiveness

History

Stage 1: Good Start, with Experience and Support

The organization behind Project Winifred was very supportive. The sponsoring executives allocated ample money for training, consultants, upgraded workstations, and new software tools. They arranged for knowledgeable users to be available up to a full day per week, as needed. The contract company providing the OO expertise had an OO-savvy executive, the project technical lead was an experienced OO designer, as was the mainframe technical lead. The department had done client/server systems before, using various non-OO tools. They were comfortable with prototyping and iterative, incremental development.

The sponsors had installed and knew how to use group communication tools; in this case, Lotus Notes. They established a plan with quarterly deliveries. The first delivery was to have only a tiny amount of function, but was to contain the key architecture and most of the infrastructure. Every subsystem was supposed to deliver something each quarter.

Some aspects did not get off to a good start, however. The consultants had poor communication skills. They argued with each other constantly, differing on every point of concern; and they lectured to, instead of listening to, the business experts. The two organizations, the client and the contract company, were both intent on training as many novices as they could. The result was that there were 12 novices to one OO expert. Other OO experts were brought in periodically to comment, but they disagreed with each other, so this resulted in confusion.

Within two months, staff morale was low and poor communication persisted for the first year of the project.

Stage 2: No Architecture, Almost No First Delivery

The first increment did deliver, but just barely. The OO designers and the relational database designers disagreed vehemently as to the basic entities to model, and finally came to an impasse. The OO designers wanted a highly abstract, recursive design; the relational database designers wanted a straightforward design. In a two-day meeting, they resolved to use a straightforward approach, and immediately found that there was almost no difference between the OO and the relational designs at the conceptual level. It became apparent that the differences were due to technology, particularly the use of inheritance and many-to-many relations in the OO design, or to small differences in assumptions, which were easily ironed out.

Although an infrastructure was built, there was no coherency of design; that is, no architecture. Each programmer designed and wrote as he or she saw fit. Because most of the programmers were novices and the rest disagreed with each other, the resulting design and code were inefficient, hard to read, and hard to change. Also, there was no ownership of classes; instead, ownership was by use case. The result was that classes became bloated with arbitrary responsibilities, and no one person could clean up the classes.

On the plus side, two excellent OO programmers were hired, who almost singlehandedly put out the first release as a result of their arduous work. And, the users were deeply involved in the creation and review of the use cases, and reviewed the intermediate results. They were patient and provided good information. The executive sponsors never backed away from their commitment to objects and a working system. The project management, although frustrated at the OO contractors, understood the nature of a first increment in a new technology.

Due to lack of progress, scope was cut on the delivery. The first delivery, promised to be small, was even smaller. The result was what I call a "bubblegum" release. It worked, but its construction was not robust. The release was well received by the user community.

Stage 3: New Increment; Add Teams, Mentors, Architecture

Following the first release, it became apparent that the project needed architecture-level decisions. Throughout the project, no individual was ever assigned as the "system architect" or even the "workstation architect." Instead, the various team leaders banded together to act as architect surrogates. The result was that there were never any mandates about architecture; still, the teams managed to avoid making big mistakes, and a sense of minor architecture evolved through the team leaders.

Standards and reviews were instituted. Reviews were not held regularly, but the use cases and the business classes were published, reviewed, and errors were found. The coding standards were ignored by the programmers.

Although there was no staff turnover among the novices, there was significant staff turnover elsewhere. The project manager, development manager, and OO technical lead positions each changed twice. The OO consultants changed repeatedly, as did the OO experts. In stage 3, a final, relatively stable group of managers and experts was established. There were still only three OO experts: one assigned to business class design, one to Smalltalk programming, and one to the infrastructure.

In response to the chaotic development of the first increment, one of the managers instituted a waterfall, "throw-it-over-the-wall" approach, that included requirements sign-off and handover to a second team for analysis and design, then to a third team for programming. They were able to terminate this process after a short time. It was clear that the programmers were ignoring the designers during this period.

The result was delivery of a second increment, containing the beginnings of an architecture. Again, the release was well received by the user community.

Stage 4: Owner per Deliverable; New Infrastructure

The strategy Ownership per Deliverable was instituted. Each use case, *Appendix A, 201* subsystem, class, and document to be produced was assigned an owner, even though several people might actually edit any one deliverable. This provided accountability and ease of evolution.

The infrastructure expert decided that the infrastructure had to be rebuilt, with a careful and robust design. This process took over six months, but he was able to hire two experienced OO designers and support the two releases that went out during that period.

Morale, although not high, was stable. The team knew they could produce a release per quarter, and they had come to know the users, the technology, and their own weaknesses.

The primary hazard was that the requirements were unstable. The users and executives frequently changed details of use cases and screens, even just before deployment. The development team adopted a three-pass approach to requirements (three "deep" iterations). The first, based on initial requirements, resulted in a first-user viewing of full functionality. The users changed what they wanted based on that viewing and any new thoughts. Upon second-user viewing, they were asked only to name errors on the screen and in the function. After that, no changes were accepted and the system went out.

The result was a project that was delivered regularly to content users. The architecture, design, and code, while never beautiful, were adequate to the task.

Analysis

The preceding history discussion raises two questions pertaining to survival of projects:

WHAT CAUSED THE EARLY PROBLEMS?

- Forgetting lessons of previous decades relevant to project planning, staff stability, responsibilities, and communication channels
- Consultant ego
- Absence of architecture
- Absence of expert staff, in architecture, UI, design, and code

WHY WAS IT ABLE TO SUCCEED AT ALL?

- Key individuals stepped up at key moments.
- Increments were used to fix the process.
- The team developed a habit of delivering.
- The executive sponsors gave unwaivering support.

Relation to Book's Topics

The sections that follow describe how Project Winifred relates to the topics you have just read about in the preceding chapters.

project purpose, 36

CHARTER. The project fit the charter and stayed within it. It was a production project, replacing a legacy application. The charter included training of 12 novices and outsourcing of most of the design and programming.

project suitability, 34

SUITABILITY. The project was not "suited" to object technology in any particular way, which meant that the learning curve was relatively high for the benefits expected. It was too hard a system to build with the application generators available at the time, which is part of the reason why Smalltalk was selected. The project benefited more from the rapid development environment of Smalltalk than from variation on theme. The project sponsor said she could see that the OO team could respond to changes in the requirements faster than her other groups, even though they were largely novices.

people, 42

STAFF. The project used business specialists from the IS department of the company, and object experts were contracted. The staff members were of mixed temperaments; some did well moving to objects, but a few had a difficult time with the abstractness and the iterations. There were few experts for many beginners, and ego problems with the object-oriented consultants.

technology, 47

TECHNOLOGY. Object technology and Smalltalk were selected by the contracted company, not by the client company. Nonetheless, the client felt it was worth exploring. Three-tier architecture had never been tried before. Although they bought the latest CASE tool and spent a lot of money customizing it and arranging for code generation, people used the tool only reluctantly, and only to draw class diagrams.

The Project Winifred team made organizationwide use of Lotus Notes to capture use cases, meeting minutes, issues and decisions, and defect reports. They used Envy/Developer for Smalltalk versioning and configuration control. They bought, but never used, a tool to simulate overall system performance under load. The 21-inch monitors they installed for every programmer were greatly appreciated.

big-M methodology, 78

METHODOLOGY. The methodology was deliberately minimalist, defined on the fly. At each new stage of development, staff first worked through part of the topic, then defined a first-cut standard for current and future use. They revised the standard based on experience when they encountered it on the next increment.

There were six OO-based roles:

1. *Business analyst:* Got requirements, initial business class design, UI design.
2. *Designer–programmer:* Did domain and UI design and programming.
3. *Design mentor:* Taught and coached OO design.
4. *Smalltalk lead:* Designed and programmed business frameworks.
5. *Reuse point:* Programmed utility classes, bought classes for examination.
6. *Infrastructure designer and programmer:* Designed the persistence and communication frameworks.

There were also the standard non-OO roles: manager, tester, administrative assistant, database designer, mainframe programmer, and so on. The lists that follow detail the key techniques, deliverables, and standards, then the overall process is summarized.

KEY TECHNIQUES

- JAD-style joint requirements gathering
- Use cases for capturing functional requirements
- Class diagrams for the business object model; some CRC-card use; some responsibility-based design without CRC cards; a fair amount of standing around the whiteboard drawing instance diagrams and messages or standing around a screen pointing at classes
- E/R diagrams for the data model
- Standard COBOL design
- Black-box testing by an external test group
- Milestone-based project management

KEY DELIVERABLES

- Use cases
- Class diagrams
- Statements of abstraction and responsibility for each domain class
- Matrix, showing class categories used by each use-case cluster
- Screen flow diagrams, screen snapshots
- Commented source code

KEY STANDARDS

- Only the externally visible UI standard was adhered to.
- Coding standards were ignored.

PROCESS

- One increment per quarter, three deep iterations per increment.
- Key reviews and milestones were identified, but no other ordering was required of the developing software.
- Each next stage was started when the deliverable was judged "stable enough to proceed," acknowledging that there would be requirements flux up to the last day.
- The milestones were of the nature: "ready to start design," "show to users," "review design," "ready for DBA."

training and getting advice, 67

TRAINING. The team arranged one week of Smalltalk programming, one week of use-case and OO-design training per developer. They used project mentoring as ongoing training, which was insufficient given the ratio of novices to experts. Although they did not create self-study groups, a few programmers started teaching themselves after a year.

getting advice, 72

CONSULTANTS. A single major contractor and other outside contractors were used for most of the programming and all of the OO expertise. The consultants and contractors turnover rate was high, which resulted in lost communication and breaks in the continuity of design. The in-house staff and the testing staff were stable for the duration of the project, which gave the project coherence.

Even though it was estimated that all the programming could have been done with 6 to 10 expert Smalltalk programmers, management was simply unable to find that many available experts.

legacy issues, 72

MAINFRAME AND RELATIONAL DATABASE. After the initial mismatch, the OO and database designs became similar. Friction between the relational and object designers persisted throughout the project, with each team dominating during different periods. The project spent about 18 expert work months in the "persistence black hole," making a fast-and-stable object persistence mechanism to join the OO programs in the workstation to the relational database.

The database designers and COBOL programmers could not keep up with the rapid change cycles the Smalltalk programmers created, so they followed single-pass design cycles, starting work only after the main design was declared relatively stable.

the domain model, 140

DOMAIN MODELING. A point of debate at the beginning, it became apparent within a few months of modeling that there would always be several legitimate analysis models and that not all of them would work equally well as software designs. The notion of "analysis model" was therefore given up, in favor of "initial design." Each subsequent design was required to be a valid business model.

CUTTING EDGE. The managers were relatively conservative, given the number of new technology elements they were using. Only the object technology elements were new. They had used client/server designs before. They avoided an object database in order to reduce implementing a new, fragile technology. They avoided discussion of distributed objects entirely.

the cutting edge, 66

ESTIMATING. Estimating, initially, was done from use cases, along with guesses as to the number of business classes to be developed. From those, multipliers were used to guess screens, total class count, and framework count. These were divided by the skilled people needed and available. The result was matched against common sense.

estimates, 95

During an increment, a second estimate was made once a reasonable use-case, screen, and class count could be made. The multipliers were rechecked after each increment for the next increment.

PLANNING. One person was dedicated to creating and maintaining the project plan over a four-month period. He initially tried to create a sequential plan: requirements phase triggers analysis phase, which triggers design phase, and so on. He had to give up because requirements were found to be unstable until the very end. He settled for tracking the key milestones of each deliverable, which worked well and simplified his work.

plans, 98

INCREMENTS AND ITERATIONS. Macroincrements and microiterations, as described in the process part of methodology, were used. There were five increments over 18 months. The incremental development was key to the project's success. One shallow iteration, initial screen design, was followed by three deep iterations on the functionality: draft functionality, correct functionality, delivered functionality. The boogeyman was found to be in the changing requirements, the unstable infrastructure design, and a long test-and-fix QA cycle.

increments and iterations, 117

RISK REDUCTION. A twice-a-month risk assessment was taken. Some of the risks found and addressed were: instability in requirements; code quality; a meaningless requirements "sign-off"; users needing to see a

collected risk-reduction strategies, 201

fully functioning version in order to decide what they really wanted; novices getting insufficient attention, training, and control; a long QA cycle; absence of an architect.

collected risk-reduction strategies, 201

The project used common sense plus most of the strategies given in Appendix A to reduce these risks; the Sacrifice One Person and Gold Rush strategies were the most appreciated. The middle tier of the three-tier system was put in partly to reduce the risk that the object team would damage the mainframe's database with the new and possibly radical business model.

project teams, 136

TEAMS. After trying various teaming strategies, Project Winifred used the strategy Holistic Diversity: closely knit specialists who were jointly responsible for delivering the subsystems. Each team was carefully composed to ensure proper skill coverage and a mix of nonconflicting personalities. Team members developed different specialties. The best communication rate was achieved using one requirements analyst with two or three designer–programmers.

PolyBloodyHardReuse, 146

REUSE. One person was assigned half-time to seek, read, evaluate, and order class libraries from industry sources. There was little inclination to use other project members' solutions or purchased solutions, but the project was small enough so that everyone knew everyone else, which enabled team leads to persuade each other or other team members.

project teams, 136

PRODUCTIVITY. A key factor that determined overall productivity was use of novices in an expert–novice mix. The experts were soon reduced to a fraction of their usual productivity. A second key factor was the use of a handoff-based, requirements/design/programming approach early in the project. This slowed productivity significantly. Productivity improved again when function teams organized by Holistic Diversity were employed.

TECHNOLOGY IS ONLY PART OF THE STORY

To put the entire issue of technology into perspective, I include one last Eyewitness Account by Jim Coplien of Lucent Technology (formerly Bell Labs Research).

◆ **Organizations** *Jim Coplien, Lucent Technology*

My colleagues and I study development environments for a living. The Pasteur project at Bell Labs Research extracts empirical structure from highly effective software development organizations, using data-gathering and analysis techniques similar to those used by sociologists and anthropologists. Studying over 50 organizations, we have been able to correlate some of these metrics to rough measures of software quality and productivity. Three of these measures are:

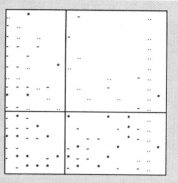

Figure EWA-1   *Project A role–interaction grid*

1. *Coupling per role*—the average number of social contacts of a typical role. Too few means roles are isolated, too many means the roles are overloaded.
2. *Communication intensity ratio*—the ratio of the most connected role's coupling to the least connected role's coupling; a rough measure of the evenness of workload. Lower is better, but because you want some centralized control, usually by those contributing directly to the delivered artifact, numbers much lower than 1.5 are probably contrived.
3. *Graph density*—the internal connectedness of the graph as a percentage of the theoretical maximum.

The table below shows these three metrics for three projects we visited.

Project A showed the best sociometrics of all the projects we visited. It was for a very-successful OO product (see Figure EWA-1). Project B used plain old C and a rather unsophisticated design technique, but showed strong sociometrics and produced a product that took its own world by storm. Project C used object-oriented programming, but was weak both in results and sociometrics. Projects B and C are included to illustrate that object orientation alone does not confer good sociometrics or a successful product.

Project C was about to undergo a 40% downsizing, and morale was low. The organization was the constant focus of project

	Mean (Standard deviation)	Project A— strong group used OO	Project B— strong group non-OO	Project C— weak group used OO
Coupling per role	5.7 (2.45)	9.0	10.4	7.9
Communication intensity ratio	3.0 (1.12)	1.7	2.2	3.4
Graph density	—	72%	29%	13%

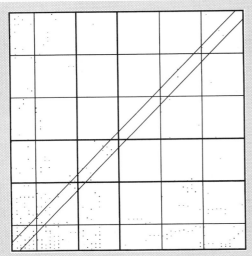

Figure EWA-2   *Project C role–interaction grid*

Note in particular how many fewer job roles there are than in the grid in Figure EWA-2, as well as how much more evenly they interact. The situation of Project A is discussed in more depth in an article by Richard Gabriel.[1]

In the role–interaction grid for Project C (Figure EWA-2) note the large number of roles and low graph density. My colleagues and I think that the points along the upper diagonal in the northeast quadrant reflect the presence of small splinter groups existing in their own comfort zones.

I use these examples to underscore a broader finding: Success, productivity, and quality correlate more closely with good organizational practices than with the use of objects or any other paradigm. Some patterns that show up repeatedly include:

◆ Small project head count
◆ Architectural leadership
◆ Even communication structure (each role carries an equal load)
◆ A strong manager, who avoids technical leadership but helps the organization focus on its task
◆ Roles that contribute directly to the end-deliverable
◆ Lots of coffee

There are other factors, which we did not study, that we are sure are also important, such as getting the best people, providing a good work environment, and understanding your business and your market.

---

[1]Gabriel, R.P., Productivity: Is there a silver bullet? *Journal of Object-Oriented Programming* 7(1): 89–92, March/April 1994.

problems. The high communication intensity ratio (3.4) indicated that work was spread unevenly, and the low graph density (13%) meant that most parts of the graphs were relatively isolated from each other (see Figure EWA-2).

Next is the role–interaction grid. The heavier the mark in the square, the more intense or frequent the interaction. The roles are ordered with those most closely coupled to the organization toward the top and right, those most closely coupled to the project to the bottom left.

Project A, the most productive organization we studied, was an object-oriented project, where even the CEO knew what objects meant and was an OO advocate. The trade press rated the product highly, new features came quickly and easily, and the project produced an astonishing 1,000 lines of C++ code per person per *week*. Its role–interaction grid is shown in Figure EWA-1.

Case material excerpted from Coplien, J.O., A development process generative pattern language, in Coplien J., Schmidt D. (Eds.), *Pattern Languages of Program Design* (Reading, MA: Addison-Wesley), 1995. Used with permission.

Appendix A

Collected Risk-Reduction Strategies

Most of the material in this book is written in an anecdotal style, which is suited to light reading; however, this appendix contains, in a reference format, 12 selected strategies that have been tested on projects.

To reduce project risk, we apply a particular strategy, often a staging strategy: incremental, iterative, spiral, eddy, or fountain. Each gives us new information early, to enable some mid-course adjustment. You can invent your own strategies, creating whatever sequence of development you need, but keep in mind that each action should reduce risk of nondelivery. The following basic risk-reduction strategy is good advice, but it is hard to apply:

- Look carefully all around the project.
- Detect the risks.
- List the risks in order.
- Work on the risks in order of danger.

The risks at the top of your list are those that will keep you from delivering the system you need. Unless they are addressed, the rest of your work will not matter. Be aware that the top risks do not arrive in "waterfall" sequence; they arrive in any sequence, popping up at any time. At some point, the first risk listed may be "absence of good requirements"; at another point it may be "shortage of staff"; then, perhaps, it will be "training," "lack of knowledge about an algorithm," or "questions about a vendor." You will recognize a project based on risk management because it will become increasingly clear over time that the system will ship successfully. Risk reduction would be the favorite strategy among project managers, if only they knew how to describe it.

Every successful project manager has a set of "pet" strategies she or he uses in a pinch. If they could get together to contribute their set, the software industry would have an extensive catalog of project risks and known ways to address them. New project managers then would be able to use it to leverage previous experience.

The following sections are written with such a catalog in mind. The first fragments were published in *IEEE Computer Journal* (October 1996); other fragments were reviewed at the Pattern Languages of Program Design Conference in 1996 and 1997. All of the strategies have been applied on projects and were recommended.

Project management is a balancing act. One strategy remedies several situations, each situation resulting from some force getting out of balance. The strategies in this appendix list the forces they balance; when any one of the forces is excessive, you may need to take the recommended action. Similarly, any situation has several possible remedies, depending on small variations in the situation or your personal management style.

Each entry is written using the metaphor of a medical diagnosis. It starts with subjective information ("indications") that describes how you feel or complaints you may have heard. It continues with the forces that you are trying to balance. Then comes the recommended action (the "prescribed remedy"). This is followed by an overdose note: If you apply the strategy too extensively, you may find yourself with a different "ailment." The "resulting context" is the situation you are likely to find yourself in next, perhaps with a different problem to solve.

I provide a section with each strategy describing the principles involved. The principles are included for future researchers to examine to form more solid theories about project management. Each strategy is illustrated by typical situations you may find yourself in, or that a previous project experienced.

To keep with the medical metaphor format, there should be a "validation procedure," that is, tests that can be run to confirm the diagnosis. Hopefully, we will eventually develop such procedures, but we do not have them yet.

Management strategies and patterns are currently being collected both in the literature and on the Web. The Web-based listings have a tendency to change, of course, but may give you leads and help you to stay current. Here are some books and Web addresses that complement and extend the strategies in this chapter:

http://www.bell-labs.com/cgi-user/OrgPatterns/OrgPatterns

http://www.c2.com/ppr

http://st-www.cs.uinc.edu/users/patterns/patterns.html

Davis, A., *201 Principles of Software Development* (New York: McGraw-Hill), 1995.

Coplien, J., Schmidt, D. (Eds.), *Pattern Languages of Program Design* (Reading, MA: Addison-Wesley), 1995.

Jones, C., *Assessment and Control of Software Risks* (Englewood Cliffs, NJ: Yourdon Press), 1994.

McCarthy, J., *Dynamics of Software Development* (Redmond, WA: Microsoft Press), 1995.

McConnell, S., *Rapid Development* (Redmond, WA: Microsoft Press), 1996.

Vlissides, J., Coplien, J. (Eds.), *Pattern Languages of Program Design 2* (Reading, MA: Addison-Wesley), 1995.

Put your energy to work to eliminate the greatest risks.

Here, first, are thumbnail sketches of the 12 strategies, clustered by major issue.

1. Knowledge: Clear the Fog

You don't know the issues well enough to put together a sound plan, so . . .

- Try to deliver something (almost anything); this tells you what the real issues are.

This is a general strategy with these specializations:

- Early and Regular Delivery (2)
- Prototype (3)
- Microcosm (4)

2. Knowledge: Early and Regular Delivery

You don't know what problems you will encounter during development, so . . .

- Deliver something early; discover what you don't know you don't know.
- Deliver regularly; improve each time.

3. Knowledge: Prototype

You don't know how some design decision will work out, so . . .

- Build an isolated solution; discover how it really works.

4. Knowledge: Microcosm

You have to create a real plan, but have never done this sort of project, so . . .

- Run an 8- to 12-week instrumented pilot to get productivity and throughput data for your plan.

5. Teaming: Holistic Diversity

Development of a subsystem requires many skills, but people specialize, so . . .

- Create a single team from multiple specialties.

6. Productivity: Gold Rush

You don't have time to wait for requirements to settle, so . . .

- Start design and programming immediately; adjust requirements weekly.

This strategy presupposes Holistic Diversity (5).

7. Ownership: Owner per Deliverable

Sometimes many people are working on it, sometimes no one, so . . .

◆ Make sure every deliverable has one and only one owner.

This is a general strategy with these specializations:

◆ Function Owners/Component Owners (8)
◆ Team per Task (10)

8. Ownership: Function Owners/Component Owners

If you organize teams by components, functions suffer, and vice versa, so . . .

◆ Make sure every function has an owner, and every component has an owner.

9. Distractions: Someone Always Makes Progress

Distractions constantly interrupt your team's progress, so . . .

◆ Ensure that someone keeps moving toward your primary goal, no matter what happens.

This is a general strategy with these specializations:

◆ Team per Task (10)
◆ Sacrifice One Person (11)
◆ Training: Day Care (12)

10. Distractions: Team per Task

A major diversion hits your team, so . . .

◆ Let a subteam handle the diversion; keep the main team going.

11. Distractions: Sacrifice One Person

A minor diversion hits your team, so . . .

◆ Assign just one person to handle it.

12. Training: Day Care

Your experts are spending all their time mentoring novices, so . . .

◆ Put one expert in charge of all the novices; let the others develop the system.

1. Knowledge: Clear the Fog

Thumbnail

You don't know the issues well enough to put together a sound plan, so . . .
- Try to deliver something (almost anything); this tells you what the real issues are.

Indications

- You have to write the project plan, but you are missing key information.
- You think you can write it, but you are trying out a new process/technology.
- You just wrote a project plan showing a first deliverable two or more years away.

Forces Being Balanced

- You need more knowledge to proceed.
- You have to move forward into the project.

Factors affecting the balancing of the forces:
- Whether you are missing information about the process or the product.
- Your level of commitment to the project.
- How much you already know.

Recommended Action

Do something (almost anything) that is a best initial attempt to deliver some part of the system in a short period of time.

Resulting Context

As you go through the initial effort, you will discover the issues you need to address, along with their characteristics. Next, you need to create a project plan, fix your first effort, go on to the next part of the system, or repair your process, depending on what you learned.

Overdose Effect

If you only "clear the fog" and "clear the fog" and "clear the fog," you will not make real progress. You will have lots of little experiments and no deliverable results.

Related Strategies

Specializations:
- Knowledge: Early and Regular Delivery (2)—adds knowledge about your development process
- Knowledge: Prototype (3)—adds knowledge about a specific decision or technology
- Knowledge: Microcosm (4)—returns measurable data about process and technology

Principles Involved

The difficulty is that you don't know what it is that you don't know. Only by making some movement will you be able to detect what it is you don't know. After you come to know what it is you don't know, you can pursue that information directly.

Sample Situations

A. This, your first OO project, fills a real production need, but you are unsure how similar to or different from your previous development OO is. First, create a tiny delivery of function in 4 to 6 months. You will see how much is similar and how much is different. See Knowledge: Early and Regular Delivery (2).

B. You are trying out a relational database (or an OO database), and are worried about peak throughput. Create a dummy database and stress it with simulated traffic loads. You will learn how it performs under load early enough to alter your design. See Knowledge: Prototype (3).

C. You are considering a serious project using a totally new language or technology. You don't know whether to proceed or how to size the project. Run a carefully instrumented miniversion of the project. Collect data on staff learning rates, productivity, and technology effects. From this data, you can extrapolate the total effect on your proposed project. See Knowledge: Microcosm (4).

D. You want to gather your own project management strategies, but you are unsure how to do it or how it will be received by the project managers. Gather some of those project managers together for one day, and have them write some of these strategies from their experience. You and they will learn the vocabulary of the strategies; and you will develop a sense of their worth. Odds are, the people will be citing the strategies on their next project.

Suggested Reading

Davis, A., *201 Principles of Software Development* (New York: McGraw-Hill), 1995.
MacGuire, S., *Debugging the Development Process* (Redmond, WA: Microsoft Press), 1994.
McCarthy, J., *Dynamics of Software Development* (Redmond, WA: Microsoft Press), 1995—discusses daily builds.
McConnell, S., *Rapid Development* (Redmond, WA: Microsoft Press), 1996.

2. Knowledge: Early and Regular Delivery

Other Names	Incremental development, Fountain/spiral/tornado development, Staged delivery
Thumbnail	You don't know what problems you will encounter during development, so . . .

- Deliver something early; discover what you don't know you don't know.
- Deliver regularly; improve each time.

Indications

- You are unsure about some part of your development process.
- You just wrote a project plan showing a first deliverable two or more years away.
- You want to improve and optimize your process.

Forces Being Balanced

- You need more knowledge to plan or set up the project.
- You have to move forward into the project.

Factors affecting the balancing of the forces:

- You are missing information related to the process as well as the product.
- You are already committed to producing the system.

Recommended Action

Create a delivery schedule with regular delivery dates of every 2 to 4 months. Determine each release by what can be delivered in that time frame. After each release, hold a small meeting or study group to identify what needs to be fixed or could be improved next time.

Resulting Context

If you get blindsided by an unexpected problem, you have lost no more than the delivery period (2–4 months), and at least you now know about it. If you run into minor obstacles, the period is short enough that your people can push through somehow. Afterward, they can discuss what to do to prevent that problem in the future.

If the release's contents are too small to release to a "true" customer, create an "internal" release. Save up the internal releases until there is enough to release to the actual customer.

You have a chance to reorganize your teams and change your process after each release. You have solid data on the working habits of your team over time. You can improve and tune your process.

Overdose Effect

Each increment takes some setup time and requires regression testing of the new composite system. If the increments are too short, the scheduling, setup, and test times will dominate your effort. Six weeks is usually considered a "short" time, although there are those who recommend daily (internal) releases (see McCarthy 1995).

Related Strategies

- Knowledge: Clear the Fog (1)—the generic version of this strategy
- Knowledge: Prototype (3)—the version of this for improving technical knowledge

Principles Involved

Early Delivery: Most project managers work with new technology, new people, new subject matter, or a new process. They really can't know what to expect, even if they have done something similar before. There is a good chance that there is something they don't know, which will delay them. The team's morale will improve after the first delivery.

Regular Delivery: It takes having information gained from repetitions of a process to improve it. With such information, you have a chance to reduce process variation, improve prediction, and attempt optimization. Because there is so much variation in software design from project to project, high-quality, reliable information is almost impossible to get. Multiple releases of a single project, however, provide the best possible data: The people are largely the same, the subject is the same, and the technology is the same; the process is what you can vary.

Sample Situations

A. Project Ingrid was described briefly in Chapter 2 and again in Chapter 3. Project Winifred was descibed briefly in Chapter 2 and in detail in Chapter 8.

Project Winifred, 188

B. You have been asked to run a project over four years involving 150 people in a company with a strict waterfall culture. You decide to have releases every six months, segmenting the project by architectural component and function.

C. You have been told by your boss that the executives need to see a release only every 10 months. You decide to generate internal releases at months four and seven. This ensures that you have identified and reduced the risks for the 10-month delivery, and keeps the team's morale and confidence up.

Suggested Reading

Boehm, Barry, *Software Risk Management* (Washington, DC: IEEE Computer Society Press), 1989.

Davis, A., *201 Principles of Software Development* (New York: McGraw-Hill), 1995.

MacGuire, S., *Debugging the Development Process* (Redmond, WA: Microsoft Press), 1994.

McCarthy, J., *Dynamics of Software Development* (Redmond, WA: Microsoft Press), 1995.

McConnell, S., *Rapid Development* (Redmond, WA: Microsoft Press), 1996.

3. Knowledge: Prototype

Thumbnail

You don't know how some design decision will work out, so . . .
- Build an isolated solution; discover how it really works.

Indications
- You are designing a user interface.
- You are trying a new database or network technology.
- You are dependent on a new critical algorithm.
- You don't understand your project domain.

Forces Being Balanced
- You need more knowledge to proceed.
- You have to move forward.

Factors affecting the balancing of the forces:
- You are missing information related to the product, not the process.
- You have a "best guess" you can use to move forward.
- You have access to some way to evaluate the result of your best guess.

Recommended Action

Build a small system that isolates that issue, using your best current knowledge. Examine that small system to learn whether your current knowledge is correct and sufficient.

Resulting Context

You will decide that your current knowledge is or is not sufficient. If it is, incorporate that small system's design into your larger system (incorporate it entirely if it was built to production specifications). If not, decide whether you now have enough information to safely proceed or that you need to do another prototype.

Overdose Effect

The process does not converge, the system does not deliver. Continued prototyping without convergence means that the design is constantly shifting and that the team is not learning enough to reach a conclusion. Other teams, depending on the prototyping team, do not get the stable interface they need.

Related Strategies
- Knowledge: Clear the Fog (1)—the generic version of this strategy
- Knowledge: Early and Regular Delivery (2)—adds knowledge about your development process
- Knowledge: Microcosm (4)—returns measurable data about process and technology

Principles Involved

The risk to your project of a small, throwaway effort is a short schedule delay. The risk of making a poor technical choice is a poor product, or perhaps committing to a technology that simply will not work.

Sample Situations

A. You are trying out a relational database (or an OO database), and are worried about peak throughput. Create a dummy database and stress it with simulated traffic loads. You will learn how it performs under load early enough to alter your design.

B. You are designing a user interface. Experience indicates that your developers probably will not get the design correct on the first try, either because the user experts did not know, did not convey information effectively, or the designers did not really hear what was said. Create a paper prototype in a few hours, a screen prototype in a few hours or a day, or a rigged demo using fixed data. Show this to the users to discover missing information.

Suggested Reading

A great deal has been published on prototyping, rapid development, and user-interface prototyping. Consider the following to start.

Boehm, Barry, *Software Risk Management* (Washington, DC: IEEE Computer Society Press), 1989.

Davis, A., *201 Principles of Software Development* (New York: McGraw-Hill), 1995.

MacGuire, S., *Debugging the Development Process* (Redmond, WA: Microsoft Press), 1994.

McCarthy, J., *Dynamics of Software Development* (Redmond, WA: Microsoft Press), 1995.

McConnell, S., *Rapid Development* (Redmond, WA: Microsoft Press), 1996.

4. Knowledge: Microcosm

Thumbnail

You have to create a real plan, but have never done this sort of project, so . . .

- ◆ Run an 8- to 12-week instrumented pilot to get productivity and throughput data for your plan.

Indications

- ◆ You are considering whether a particular technology is for you.
- ◆ You are unsure of how fast your developers will learn it.
- ◆ You are unsure of how well the technology really works.

Forces Being Balanced

- ◆ You need more knowledge to make a decision or a plan.
- ◆ You have to make a decision or a plan.

Factors affecting the balancing of the forces:

- ◆ You may be missing information related to the process as well as the product.
- ◆ You are not yet committed to producing the system.

Recommended Action

Run a carefully instrumented microproject, on the order of 8 to 12 weeks. Use a few of your own people, plus some experts. Make sure that the microproject is meaningfully designed to give you the data you will need. Collect data on staff learning rates, productivity, technology effects, and throughput, as needed.

Resulting Context

Following the implementation of this strategy, you will have some real data. Now you can scale up the results to your original project and decide whether it will work, or how the plan should look.

Overdose Effect

Making the microcosm too short means you will not have time to get sufficient, meaningful results. Doing it too frequently means you will not make your decision or plan.

Related Strategies

- ◆ Knowledge: Clear the Fog (1)—the generic version of this strategy
- ◆ Knowledge: Early and Regular Delivery (2)—adds knowledge about your development process
- ◆ Knowledge: Prototype (3)—adds knowledge about a specific decision or technology

Principle Involved

The principle is that of scaling. As distinct from a "proof of concept," Microcosm is carefully selected so that the key issues are visible and can be measured. The proof of concept demonstrates only that something small and similar can be built—no scaling data is collected in the proof of concept. With Microcosm, you can measure the productivity of the beginners compared to the experts; the fully loaded throughput on a simulated loading of the workstation, database, or network; the memory; and so on. Each of these values can be scaled to give you a prediction for your real project.

I need to caution you that most project teams lack the discipline and care to identify the key issues and to set up the project accordingly, preferring instead to create a "proof of concept." Do not confuse the two.

Sample Situations

A. The project leader ran Microcosm in eight weeks for an untried database application technology. Based on the scaling data, he accepted the technology and created an eight-month project plan. The project finished within a few weeks of the plan and without major technical surprises.

B. You are considering using object technology, but are still unsure of its acceptance, code quality, ease of change, and performance. Run an 8- to 12-week microcosm and get some hard numbers to help you in your decision.

Suggested Reading

Note: I have not seen this technique discussed in software development. Clearly, a system-simulation program addresses part of this strategy, but not all of it.

5. Teaming: Holistic Diversity

Thumbnail

Development of a subsystem requires many skills, but people specialize, so . . .

- Create a single team from multiple specialties.

Indications

- You hear complaints that we are doing "throw-it-over-the-wall" development.
- You hear complaints of a bureaucratic process.
- You notice a breakdown of interteam communication.
- Teams are structured by specialty or phase deliverables.
- People pass work to each other in written format naming required deliverables instead of visiting each other.
- Teams are not able to get their discoveries incorporated into connecting teams' work strategies.
- Team members lack respect for one another.
- Each person is assigned to do everything, and complains about the waste of time from having to change mental gears.

Forces Being Balanced

- You want fast feedback, with fast, rich communications, on decisions.
- You want to be able to hire people with the skill sets you specify.

Factors affecting the balancing of the forces:

- Feedback is fastest within one person's head, but it slows in proportion to the distance between individuals' rooms/floors/buildings/cities, and in relation to the medium of expression (interactive spoken face-to-face/video/written).
- Multiple skills are needed to develop a piece of the system, particularly the user functions; it is hard to hire people with those multiple specialties.
- People specialize.
- People protect their specialties against other specialties.
- People within a team are more likely to help each other.
- People on different teams blame each other.
- You cannot always put an entire team in one room.
- Every activity affects the final design.

Recommended Action

For each function or set of functions to be delivered, create a small team (2–5 people) that is responsible for delivering that function. That team can be assigned or can evolve specialists in requirements gathering, user-interface design, technical design and programming, and databases and testing. Evaluate the team as a single unit, so there is no benefit to hiding within a specialty. Arrange the team size and location so they can communicate directly, instead of by writing.

This team should have no internal documentation requirements, although they will have documentation requirements responsibilities to the rest of the project. They should be allowed to split up their work as they choose.

You will have to coordinate the teams to get the deliverables (requirements document, user-interface design, software architecture, and so on) consistent across teams.

If the team has just one person, that person will have difficulty mastering all the specialties and changing mental focus to perform well in the different specialties (meetings require a different temperament and more concentration than designing OO frameworks).

On the other hand, if the team size is too large, communication will suffer.

Related Strategies

- Ownership: Owner per Deliverable (7)—ensures that somebody owns each function, class, and required deliverable
- Neil Harrison (1995) wrote Diversity of Membership to ensure that requirements gathering teams include users. Jim McCarthy (1995) wrote Feature Teams as a best practice, with much the same intent.
- Michael Hammer (1993) wrote Case Teams in *Reengineering the Organization*. A Case Team may have more authority than is called for in Holistic Diversity, which focuses on the skill mix rather than on the decision-making structure.

Principles Involved

It is hard to find individuals who can master the required specialties and switch work contexts as needed. Creating a small, colocated, mixed-specialty team with no written deliverables between them increases the communication "bandwidth," while letting the individuals develop their strengths. Rewarding them as a team motivates them to help each other deliver rather than hide behind each individual's particular specialty. You are trying to create the impression of one person with several bodies—many ears, legs, and brains with a single sense of ownership.

There is a close connection between specialties. A designer or programmer may discover something that reveals that the requirements are more difficult to fulfill than anticipated. Even though an analyst may have a flawed view of the business, the final code must be a valid business model. The suggested user interface may be impractical to implement, or perhaps the user-interface designer knows best how to implement it. Putting the right people on the same team speeds up feedback, from programming back up the chain to requirements. Separating people and/or putting written deliverables between them, slows up feedback.

Sample Situation

A. Project Winifred was structured by function initially. This caused trouble, because many people would alter the same class at about the same time—see Ownership: Function Owners/Component Owners (8). Next, it was structured by phase deliverables, with requirements analysts separated from designers and programmers. The analysts produced ineffective models, communication between the people became sluggish, the analysts and programmers looked down on each other, and the analysts' designs did not match the final system design (the programmers ended up designing it as necessary to make it work).

There was a very brief period during which "everyone did everything." It did not last long because the mental load was too great and team members soon went back to the specialties they each could handle.

The fourth, and successful arrangement, was Holistic Diversity. Those who could do the requirements gathering and analysis went to meetings, interviewed people, and investigated interfaces and options. They communicated the results quickly, face-to-face, with the people who navigated the class library and designed classes and frameworks. A function team consisted of a combined requirements gatherer–analyst with two to four programmer–designers.

The team used Productivity: Gold Rush (6) to move rapidly through the design. They had no internal deliverables, but created the deliverables as required by the project for interteam communication and maintenance. Most communications within the team were verbal. Team members talked several times a day, either in one-hour mutual-education sessions, or in short interchanges to mention a recent discovery. This volume of communication could not have been handled through formal deliverables.

Suggested Reading

Hammer, M., *Reengineering the Corporation* (New York: Harper Business Press), 1993.

Harrison, N., Organizational patterns for teams, in Vlissides, J. and Coplien, J. (Eds.), *Pattern Languages of Program Design 2*, pp. 345–352 (Reading, MA: Addison-Wesley), 1995.

McCarthy, J., *Dynamics of Software Development* (Redmond, WA: Microsoft Press), 1995.

http://www.bell-labs.com/cgi-user/OrgPatterns/OrgPatterns is a website created by Jim Coplien to hold organizational patterns. Holistic diversity and Diversity of Membership are two of the patterns that can be found there.

6. Productivity: Gold Rush

Thumbnail

You don't have time to wait for requirements to settle, so . . .

◆ Start design and programming immediately; adjust requirements weekly.

This strategy presupposes Teaming: Holistic Diversity (5).

Indications

◆ We applied Holistic Diversity, now what are our designer–programmers going to do while requirements and analysis are going on?
◆ We don't have time to wait for the requirements and analysis to get done!

Forces Being Balanced

◆ You want requirements/analysis/design to be done carefully.
◆ You want people busy.
◆ You want people to avoid redoing work where practical.
◆ You need the system completed as soon as possible.

Factors affecting the balancing of the forces:

◆ The team has a general shape of the requirements or analysis or design.
◆ The team has good communications with their upstream task members, so you can rely on rapid feedback and correction (e.g., Teaming: Holistic Diversity).
◆ The people doing the rework are not the ones limiting the resources of the overall project (i.e., you can afford to have them spend some time redoing their work).
◆ The last piece of rework will take less time to do than the full task would if the necessary inputs were ready.

Recommended Action

Let the downstream people start now. They have some idea of what they are supposed to produce. Rely on the close communication within the team to handle changes.

Resulting Context

The downstream people will start on the obvious parts of their work, and make their best guess as to the rest. The team will have to communicate frequently so that the downstream people know how stable each element of their work is, and to enable them to stay up to date with the latest decisions. They will have to redo some of their work.

Overdose Effect

Overusing this strategy means that the downstream people get ahead of the stability of the upstream decisions, hence have more work to redo. At some point, rework takes too much time.

Related Strategy

◆ Teaming: Holistic Diversity (5) or some equivalent is a prerequisite for fast, effective communication.

Principle Involved

A process that is not constraining the overall system can afford to be done less efficiently and in parallel (see, for example, Goldratt 1986). Often it is the case that the analysts, designers, and programmers can get started right away, without having finalized information. Waiting for finalized information takes longer than doing rework "on the fly."

Sample Situations

A. Project Winifred used Holistic Diversity. Each team had a requirements and analysis person and several designers–programmers. A first cut at the requirements had been done earlier, so a rough set of requirements was available. Much of the system was similar.

The designers–programmers quickly got ahead of the requirements people, who were in meetings trying to nail down details of the requirements. If the designers waited until the requirements were solid, they would not have enough time to do their work. Since they could guess quite accurately what the requirements would be like, they started design and programming right away. The requirements person gave them course corrections after each meeting. The amount of time it took to incorporate those midcourse alterations was short compared to the total design time.

The database group constrained the process. They could not afford to do rework; they had to work in the most efficient way possible. Therefore, they did not start early, but waited until their requirements were stable (per the counterforce). The designers–programmers had enough extra time so that they could afford to prototype some test databases for themselves, which were thrown away when the database designers did their final design.

B. In *The Mythical Man-Month* (1995), Fred Brooks includes a series of suggestions as to what can be done in parallel by various teams, even in the absence of stable upstream information.

Suggested Reading

Brooks, F., *The Mythical Man-Month* (Reading, MA: Addison-Wesley), 1995.
Goldratt, E., Cox, J., *The Goal* (Great Barrington, MA: North River Press), 1986.

7. Ownership: Owner per Deliverable

Thumbnail

Sometimes many people are working on it, sometimes no one, so . . .
- Make sure every deliverable has one and only one owner.

Indications

- You detect a "common area" (an area where multiple people are updating concurrently, without dominant ownership).
- You detect an "orphan area" (an area where no one works or accepts responsibility).
- You hear: "What happens when two people need to program the same function?"
- Classes are getting messy.
- No one is updating the class diagram.
- You have multiple teams working on one task, or one person working on many tasks.

Forces Being Balanced

- You want people to share.
- You want consistency.
- You want every deliverable to have internal integrity, to be consistent and maintained.

Factors affecting the balancing of the forces:

- When people share incompletely, you get a common area.
- If no one is assigned responsibility, you might get de facto ownership, but you might get either a common or orphan area.

Recommended Action

Make someone responsible for each deliverable: project task, project results, overall consistency. Ask, and make sure you can answer, who is responsible for each of the following elements:
- Overall system architecture
- Application software architecture
- User-interface design quality
- OO design quality
- Code quality
- Requirements/domain model/each class/documentation/test cases

Resulting Context

Ownership needs may conflict. You may have to set up a conflict-resolution procedure.

Overdose Effect

The "Swiss accountability" effect: Distinct ownership of every separate element of the project may be perceived by some people as wonderful, and as a nuisance by others.

Conflict management starts to dominate the team's energy (indicates improper ownership boundaries).

Related Strategies

Specializations:

- Ownership: Function Owners/Component Owners (8)—addresses the particular ownership of use cases and classes (more generally, functions and components)
- Distractions: Team per Task (10)—addresses the task as the unit of ownership and conflict
- Training: Day Care (12)—addresses training as a distinct deliverable.

Principles Involved

Sometimes a task is so onerous that only by making it part of a person's job responsibility can you ensure that it gets done. This is the case in updating class diagrams and creating documentation, which are common orphan areas.

People cannot track other people's intentions, which makes a common area hard to clean up. It is also not in any one person's local interests to do so (see Senge 1990).

Sample Situations

A. Object orientation is itself an example of this strategy. A software module owns all of the resources, data, and computation it needs for a particular purpose. This organization of software reduces the trajectory of change for the software (see Tom Morgan's Eyewitness Account in Chapter 2).

B. I was asked on one project visit, "What happens when two people try to program the same function?" That question implies either that the functioning of the system has not been adequately partitioned, or that two people are putting their fingers into the same class. See Ownership: Function Owners/Component Owners (8). It is not surprising to discover multiple groups designing the same functions under those circumstances.

C. In an orphan area, the class diagram often is out of date because it is no one's job to update it. Find out who owns that segment of the class structure, and assign someone to own the diagram as part of his or her job responsibility. In order not to waste too much of that person's time, decide on the fewest occasions at which the class diagram must be current. Note that every piece of final documentation is a deliverable that requires ownership.

D. No one person is responsible for the system architecture or other major element of the system. I often find that no one person answers for the quality and currentness of the class diagram, the quality and consistency of the user interface, the program code, or system performance.

Suggested Reading

Senge, P., *The Fifth Discipline* (New York: Currency Doubleday), 1990—discusses the effects of common areas in the context of feedback loops.

8. Ownership: Function Owners/Component Owners

Thumbnail

If you organize teams by components, delivered functions suffer, and vice versa, so . . .

- Make sure every delivered function has an owner, and that every component has an owner.

Indications

- Your teams are organized by delivered function or use case, with no component ownership.
- Your teams are organized by class or component with no function or use-case ownership.
- You hear the question: "What happens when two people need to program the same function?"

Forces Being Balanced

- You want ownership and consistency in the functions.
- You want ownership and consistency in the components.
- You want components to be shared across teams.

Factors affecting the balancing of the forces:

- Ownership by function turns components into shared areas.
- Ownership by component turns functions into orphan areas.

Recommended Action

Make sure every component and every delivered function has a responsible owner. The component owner answers for the integrity and quality of the component; the function owner ensures that the function gets delivered. If the component owners refuse to incorporate something needed to deliver end functionality, the function owner sees that the missing code is put in a place just for that delivered function.

Resulting Context

No conflict resolution is needed with this strategy because the component owner has right of refusal to any request, and the function owner has recourse to turn to someone else to get the job done. However, the developers will need to communicate with each other more, and friction may arise between component and function owners. There may be a need for the Envy/Developer model of ownership (see D in the following Sample Situations), in which there is a shared part and an application-specific part to each component or class.

Overdose Effect

If the parts being assigned for ownership are too small, the communications overhead and friction between developers could cause difficulties.

Related Strategies

- Ownership: Owner per Deliverable (7)—the general form of this strategy
- Distractions: Team per Task (10)—With this strategy, the unit of ownership and conflict is a task.

Principle Involved

Common area, orphan area—as discussed in Ownership: Owner per Deliverable (7).

Sample Situations

A. Project Reginald started out with teams centered around classes or components. At delivery time, the end function did not work. Each team said, "I thought you were taking care of that. It doesn't belong in my class." Later on in this project, each function had one responsible owner. That person had to negotiate between the teams to see if one team was willing to close the gap, or to create some extra, special code to close the gaps between the classes.

B. Project Winifred started out with teams centered around use cases. They soon found that when no one is responsible for cleaning up a class, it develops into an arbitrary collection of state variables and functions. At that point, nobody *can* clean it up. On another project working the same way, one three-member team sat around a workstation one day to clean up their classes. They all were needed just to be able to understand the code.

C. Brooklyn Union Gas, and eventually Project Winifred, were organized with both class and function owners. A class owner could refuse to put a requested function into a class, saying it was not part of the class's responsibility but rather a special need for an isolated function. The function owner would then have to put the function in the class for the use case.

Fortunately, there are tools, such as Envy/Developer, that allow a method or functions to be attached to a class just for a specific application. They support creating ownership around common parts of a class and application-specific parts of a class.

D. Object Technology International also used this strategy. They developed a tool set to support their way of working: Envy/Developer. Envy/Developer lets the methods of a single class be separately maintained and packaged for different applications. Such a tool changes the economics of the argument that view classes need to be separated from model objects. Even though view classes are still valid, Envy/Developer makes it straightforward for one application team to create function-specific methods for the class.

Suggested Reading

McCarthy, J., *Dynamics of Software Development* (Redmond, WA: Microsoft Press), 1995.

9. Distractions: Someone Always Makes Progress

Thumbnail

Distractions constantly interrupt your team's progress, so . . .

- Ensure that someone keeps moving toward your primary goal, no matter what happens.

Indications

- Nonprimary tasks are dominating the team's time, keeping it from moving forward toward the primary goal.
- Common complaints of distraction.

Forces Being Balanced

- You need to pay attention to every task, including small diverting ones.
- You need to complete the primary task by an important date.

Factors affecting the balancing of the forces:

- The time required for a person to switch between tasks.
- The size of the distractions.

Recommended Action

Whatever you do, ensure that someone on the team is making progress on the primary task.

Resulting Context

Various, depending on the tactic employed. You will, however, be closer to your final goal, which is not always the case when dealing with distractions.

Overdose Effect

Eventually, you may get into trouble for not adequately addressing the distractions. If you have too many distractions, they may be a symptom of another problem.

Related Strategies

Specializations:

- Distractions: Team per Task (10)—separates tasks into sympathetic sets
- Distractions: Sacrifice One Person (11)—assign only one person to deal with the distraction
- Training: Day Care (12)—separates the task of training from that of producing software

Principle Involved

If you do not complete your primary task, nothing else will matter; therefore, complete your primary task at all costs.

Sample Situations

A. In Homer's *Odyssey*, Odysseus had to maneuver his ship past Scylla and Charybdis. Scylla was a six-headed monster who would eat six of Odysseus's crew members at a time. Charybdis was a whirlpool that could destroy the entire ship. In this paradigm of the dilemma, Odysseus chose to sacrifice six people so that the rest could get past Scylla's cave.

B.   Atalanta, the fleet huntress of Greek mythology, was assured by the gods that she would remain the fastest runner as long as she remained a virgin. So she told her father, the king, that she would marry only the man who could beat her in a foot race. The losers would be killed for wasting her time. The successful young man was aided by a god, who gave him three golden apples. Each time Atalanta pulled ahead, he tossed an apple in front of her. When she paused to pick up the golden apple, he raced ahead, and eventually won.

The moral of the story might be that Atalanta should not have stopped to pick up the apples, which also illustrates the point of this strategy. I choose to view it more metaphorically, that Atalanta represents distractions, keeping you from meeting your project's deadline. The apples are your team members, whom you will separate from the main team one at a time to ensure success.

Other examples are given in the specializations (see 10 and 11).

Suggested Reading

Csikszentmihalyi, M., *Flow: The Psychology of Optimal Experience* (New York: Harper Perennial), 1990.

DeMarco, T., Lister, T., *Peopleware* (New York: Dorset House), 1987.

10. Distractions: Team per Task

Thumbnail

A major diversion hits your team, so . . .

- Let a subteam handle the diversion; keep the main team going.

Indications

- You hear: "We have too many tasks, causing us to lose precious design cycles."
- And, "We are getting distracted from our primary purpose."
- The common complaint is that the group gets distracted by marketing requests, management requests, and the like, from the outside.
- Novices needing training overwhelm the experts' ability to make progress.
- Requirements gathering is taking longer than the schedule allows.
- The schedule needs major, immediate attention.
- The version being tested needs attention, but so does the version that is in development.

Forces Being Balanced

- You must pay attention to every task, including small diverting ones.
- You need to complete the primary task by an important date.
- You want team members to be satisfied with their jobs.

Factors affecting the balancing of the forces:

- It takes a significant amount of time for people to switch between tasks.
- There really is such a thing as the "primary" task.

Recommended Action

Split the team, and sort the activities so that each team has a primary task with additional, "sympathetic" (complementary) activities. Sitting in meetings, answering phone calls, and writing reports, for example, are nonsympathetic to designing software. Arrange it so that each team can focus on its primary task, and see that each task has at least one dedicated team member.

Resulting Context

A smaller primary team with a secondary team working on the interrupting task.

Overdose Effect

You eventually have one-person teams. Prior to that, you may discover that it is not worth splitting up the team's task set because losing the working synergy between people is more harmful than gaining dedicated time per task.

Related Strategies

This strategy treats each task as both an activity and a deliverable. Therefore:

- Ownership: Owner per Deliverable (7)—the general form of ownership and accountability
- Ownership: Function/Component Owners (8)—team for each artifact, as well as the task of designing it
- Distractions: Someone Always Makes Progress (9)—the general distraction management strategy

◆ Distractions: Sacrifice One Person (11)—specialization to lose only one person
◆ Training: Day Care (12)—addresses training as a separate deliverable from the software

Principles Involved

Increase flow time and decrease distractions, thus trading personnel parallelism for "time slicing." *Flow* is the quiet time in the brain when the problem flows through the designer (Csikszentmihalyi, 1990; DeMarco, 1976). It is when the design alternatives are weighed and decisions are made in rapid succession as mental doors open. The problem, the alternatives, and the state of the decision process are all kept in the head. It is a not only a highly productive time, it is the only time when the designer feels comfortable making decisions.

It takes about 20 minutes to reach the internal state of flow, but only a minute to lose it. In addition to getting into flow, the designer must have time to make actual progress, which may take another 10 minutes. Any significant interruption within that half hour essentially causes the entire half hour to be lost. Because it takes energy to get into the flow, a distraction costs energy as well as time.

To increase flow time, distractions have to be reduced. Certain activities are more distracting than others. Fixing a bug requires flow in the old system, hence distracts from flow in the new system. Sitting in meetings, answering questions, and spending time talking on the telephone are major distractions to design flow. Therefore, group tasks into sympathetic sets. Requirements and analysis involve meetings, reading, and writing. Design and programming require concentrating on the implementation technology and keeping a great number of details in one's head.

Parallelism versus time-slicing: There is a tradeoff to be made between letting the developers do all the tasks in alternation (time-slicing) and splitting the group (parallelism). Which you should choose depends on the personal interests of the developers and the time needed to switch between tasks. If the group is split, some of the team members may adopt the new task as their profession. For examples, see Distractions: Sacrifice One Person (11), Training: Day Care (12), and Coplien's *Firewalls*.

Sample Situations

A. On Project Winifred we tried assigning each person to do requirements, analysis, design, and programming. We thought the developers would enjoy the variation in activity and also that this would reduce the meetings and bureaucratic documentation.

What happened was that the first two activities were so different from the latter two that people were unable to switch easily between them. After having attended and documented meetings for much of the day, it was difficult for them to start working on design and programming. As with bug-fixing and new development, every time a designer was pulled away from her or his work, it cost an additional hour to recover the train of thought.

We applied this strategy (Team per Task), and split the teams along task lines; each team selected some people to gather and analyze requirements, and other people to design and program. The result was that the requirements/analysis people sat in meetings, read and wrote specs, examined interfaces, and the like, then communicated their findings to the designers–programmers. They communicated orally, for the most part, because they were closely linked on the same team—Holistic Diversity (5). The designers–programmers stayed within their train of thought, while getting fresh input from their requirements colleagues. Some of the team members who were assigned to the requirements task really wanted to program, so this was quite a sacrifice for them. See Distractions: Sacrifice One Person (11).

Two things we did not do. We did not put the requirements analysis people into a separate team (Holistic Diversity again). A team was jointly responsible for a section of the system, from requirements to delivery. Splitting was done within each team. We also did not expect the requirements group to document their decisions for the designers' benefit (they did document for the project's benefit). The requirements and design people were in close contact at all times, and most information was passed along orally. There was, therefore, no "throw-it-over-the-wall" effect. These were both important teaming decisions made earlier, which we were intent on preserving.

B. Training is distracting to the experts; see Training: Day Care, (12).

C. Refer to other examples discussed in Distractions: Sacrifice One Person (11).

Suggested Reading

Coplien, J., A development process generation pattern language. In Coplien, J., Schmidt, D. (Eds.), *Pattern Languages of Program Design* (Reading, MA: Addison-Wesley), 1994.

Csikszentmihalyi, M., *Flow: The Psychology of Optimal Experience* (New York: Harper Perennial), 1990.

DeMarco, T., Lister, T., *Peopleware* (New York: Dorset House), 1987.

http://www.bell-labs.com/cgi-user/OrgPatterns/OrgPatterns contains many patterns and strategies dealing with team partitioning.

11. Distractions: Sacrifice One Person

Other Name	Sacrificial Lamb
Thumbnail	A minor diversion hits your team, so . . .

- Assign just one person to handle it.

Indication

- Same as for Distractions: Team per Task (10), except the distraction is less significant; probably it could be handled by one half-time to full-time person.

Forces Being Balanced

- You must pay attention to every task, including small diverting ones.
- You need to complete the primary task by an important date.
- You want team members to be satisfied with their jobs.

Factors affecting the balancing of the forces:

- It takes a significant amount of time for people to switch between tasks.
- There is such a thing as the "primary" task.
- The diverting task seems to be minor, but is very important.

Recommended Action

Assign one person to the distraction full-time rather than several people part-time. With luck you may find someone both amenable and suited to the task, so they feel less "sacrificed."

Resulting Context

The rest of the team moves forward distraction-free. The person assigned to the distracting task may be unhappy, so try to get him or her back on the team again as soon as possible. If you feel that one person is too much to sacrifice to this task and want to make it part-time work, compute the loss of flow time that will result from someone trying to work on the distraction *and* some other task.

Overdose Effect

If this keeps happening, you will have no one performing the primary task, and you should examine why you have so many distractions in the first place.

Related Strategies

- Ownership: Owner per Deliverable (7)—the general form of ownership
- Distractions: Someone Always Makes Progress (9)—the general distraction management strategy
- Distractions: Team per Task (10)—the general form of this strategy
- Training: Day Care (12)—addresses training as a separate deliverable from the software; produces mentor as a profession
- *Firewall* is Coplien's (1994) pattern, in which the distraction comes from a series of requests from outside the team, and one of the developers is sacrificed to act as project manager. This strategy produces project manager as a profession.
- *Mercenary Analyst* is Coplien's (1994) pattern, in which documentation is the distraction. This strategy produces technical writer as a profession.
- *Gatekeeper* is Coplien's (1994) pattern, in which the constant inflow of technical information is the distraction, and one person is assigned to manage that information as a distinct, part-time task.

Principles Involved

Same as for Distractions: Team per Task (10). The fact that handling the distraction looks like less than a full-time job illustrates the significance of the amount of time spent getting into a productive mental flow.

Maximum parallelism, profession, or sacrifice? If people do not like the task, they will consider it a sacrifice. If they like the task, it will become their profession. Thus, Firewall gives rise to the profession of project management, and Training: Day Care gives rise to the profession of mentor.

Sample Situations

A. Updating the project schedule: On Project Winifred, the schedule was out of date. We thought it would be fair to let everyone on each team evaluate their own work in order to distribute the experience, discomfort, and load. What really happened was that progress came to a complete halt. When the design team got back to designing, a month had gone by.

One of the teams used this strategy (Distractions: Sacrifice One Person). They drew straws to see who would do the whole team's estimation while the others got on with the main task. At the end of several weeks of estimation, that team had moved forward while the other teams were at a standstill. Thereafter, the other teams applied the same strategy. Of course, the person working on the schedule felt sacrificed, which is why this strategy was originally called "Scylla"— see story about Scylla and Charybdis in Distractions: Someone Always Makes Progress (9).

B. Simultaneous release to QA and development of the next release: Project Winifred had one increment entering test at the same time design was starting on the next. We thought that defect fixes would take a relatively short amount of time, so assigned the whole team to both fixing defects and doing new design.

Each fix broke a designer's train of thought for approximately an hour beyond just the fix. Three or four of these caused the designer to lose most of the day. Eventually, the designers gave up on the new release, because they knew the next defect report would arrive before they would had recovered their thoughts and progressed on the new design.

We applied Sacrifice One Person (this strategy), and assigned one person to detect fixes. We originally planned it as a half-time job, but found there was not enough time left over for the person to do any useful design work. The person rejoined the new design team as soon as the release went through test.

Suggested Reading

Coplien, J., A development process generative pattern language, in Coplien, J., Schmidt, D. (Eds.), *Pattern Languages of Program Design* (Reading, MA: Addison-Wesley), 1994.

This pattern language is also among those on http://www.bel-labs.com/cgi-user/OrgPatterns/OrgPatterns.

12. Training: Day Care

Other Names	Progress Team, Training Team
Thumbnail	Your experts are spending all their time mentoring novices, so . . .
	◆ Put one expert in charge of all the novices; let the others develop the system.

Indications
- You hear, "We are wasting our experts."
- And, "A few experts could do the whole project faster."
- The experts are not proceeding at the rate you or they expect.
- Training is draining people's energy, time, and concentration.
- You have to add new people to an existing project.

Forces Being Balanced
- You need people trained.
- You need the system built.

Factors affecting the balancing of the forces:
- Trained people and a delivered system are both required results of your project.
- You want the newcomers working near an expert to learn good habits.
- Novices distract and drain the energy of experts.

Recommended Action

Separate an experts-only "progress" team from a training team that is under the tutelage of one or more mentors. Select the mentors for their ability to teach OO design and programming to novices. Let the progress team design 85 to 95 percent of the system; have the training team focus on quality training, delivering only 5 to 15 percent of the system. Transfer people to the progress team as soon as they can meaningfully contribute.

The training team does not simply conduct training exercises, but actually contributes to the final system in an ever-increasing way.

Resulting Context

The progress team gets to move at the speed of the experts; the novices get dedicated training.

If those on the training team are the ones who know the domain, you will have to make some further adjustment to transfer knowledge of the domain.

Overdose Effect

Eventually, you may have too few people to constitute a progress team. How many people can one mentor train? I would suggest 5 to 10, although I have heard of one person mentoring 15 people on five concurrent mini-projects.

Related Strategies

This strategy is a cross-specialization of several in this appendix:
- Ownership: Owner per Deliverable (7)
- Distractions: Someone Always Makes Progress (9)
- Distractions: Team per Task (10)
- Distractions: Sacrifice One Person (11)

Principles Involved

The principles are synergy versus distraction—the synergy of having a novice learn directly from an expert versus the distraction to the expert. Experts who must answer novices' questions will have their productivity reduced to a fraction of the norm, often without particularly raising the productivity of newcomers. Just one novice paired with an expert may cut the expert's productivity in half; adding two may cut it to a third; adding three may stall productivity altogether.

Assume there are **X** experts who work at productivity 1 each, a larger number of **N** novices who each work at **n** productivity, with **n** much smaller than 1, on the order of 1/10. If the experts could work together, they would have, in this simple model, a total productivity of (**X**) for the experts working together. The expert sacrificed to train the novices has 0 productivity other than training novices, so the group's total productivity for Training: Day Care (the upper curve in Figure A.1) is

$$\text{Day Care: } (\boldsymbol{X} - 1) + \boldsymbol{N}*\boldsymbol{n}$$

Call it "Even Mix" if they are all mixed together with **N/X** novices per expert. Assume each expert's productivity falls from 1 to something like **1/((N/X) + 1)**. The group's total productivity is now

$$\text{Even Mix: } (\boldsymbol{X}*\boldsymbol{X}/(\boldsymbol{N} + \boldsymbol{X})) + \boldsymbol{N}*\boldsymbol{n}$$

Figure A-1 shows Day Care versus Even Mix, assuming novices work at one-tenth the productivity of the experts.

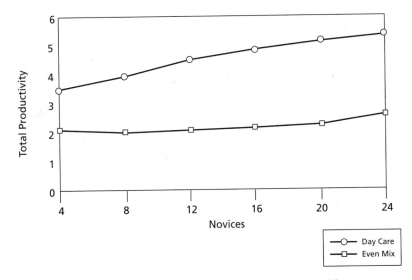

Figure A-1 *Day Care vs. Even Mix as a function of novices with 4 experts, 10 times the productivity difference (n = 1/10)*

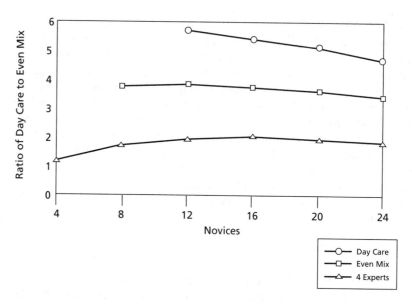

Figure A-2 *Relative Productivity of Day Care vs. Even Mix as a function of varying number of experts (n = 1/10)*

The results are similar over a wide range of staff size and productivity differences. Figure A.2 shows how quickly the difference between the strategies takes effect as more novices are added.

The true behavior of Day Care should actually be better than this simple model predicts. Experts feed off each other in a positive way. This is the "corn field" factor (corn produces better yield when grown close together than when serarated). Let the cornfield factor be $c > 1.0$. Each Day Care expert produces c instead of 1. The novices produce more under the mentor's guidance than alone. Let the mentor's contribution to the novices' productivity be $m > 1.0$. The novices also learn faster under guidance, so their performance improves with time, $n'(t) > n$ (where n' is the new time-based productivity, n is the base novice productivity as used before). The improved model gives the still higher productivity (not shown in the graph) for the team as

$$(X - 1)*c + N*m*n'(t)$$

The nature of the training does not matter. Design and teaching are antagonistic tasks, as described in Distractions: Team per Task (10), and are better handled when split into separate teams.

Treating the delivery of trained people as separate from the delivery of running software gives you access to Ownership: Owner per Deliverable (7), and Distractions: Someone Always Makes Progress (9) protects the delivery of running software.

Sample Situations

A. *Mentoring:* The standard recommendation in the industry is to put 1 to 5 novices under each trained expert. The consequence is that the experts spend most of their energy halfheartedly training. Besides being drained of energy for designing the system, the experts typically do not have the personality, background, or inclination to successfully teach novices how to design. They are caught between trying to get the maximum out of their trainees and trying to do the maximum development themselves. Thus, they neither develop the system nor adequately train novices.

Some companies have developed apprenticeship programs, in which novices are put under the tutelage of a dedicated mentor for two weeks out of three for six months.

B. *Adding Staff:* In *The Mythical Man-Month*, Fred Brooks (1995) talks about the training costs of adding people to a project, the new people draining the productivity of the experts. The same suggestion applies: Put the newcomers on a separate team so that they can learn the system. Move them to the progress team as soon as they "get up to speed."

Suggested Reading

Brooks, F., *The Mythical Man-Month* (Reading, MA: Addison-Wesley), 1995.

Lave, J., *Situation Learning: Legitimate Peripheral Participation* (Cambridge, England: Cambridge Press), 1991—describes apprentice situations more generally.

Appendix B

Crib Sheet

This crib sheet is meant to act as a reminder of the keys points in the book; it has seven sections: Critical Success Factors, Prime Failure Indicators, Truths From Myths, Expectations Under Control, Selected Survival Recommendations, Key Actions of Successful Projects, and Hazardous Phrases. Bookmark this section, copy it to post on your wall, and/or refer to the card at the back of the book. Check the points here periodically to see how you are doing. You cannot apply everything on this list all at once, so use a few ideas at a time.

Critical Success Factors

- Incremental scheduling and staging
- Willingness to find and fix failing ideas
- A habit of delivering
- Executive sponsor, project manager, technical leader

Prime Failure Indicators

- Absence of a delivery after eight months.
- Use of C++ in an I/S shop.

Truths From Myths

Truth	Myth
Managing object development is mostly the same.	Object development is completely different.
Any new technology is difficult to learn.	Objects are easy to learn.
Retraining in object-think swamps all other costs.	We should use C++ because we know C.
Iterative development still requires handoffs and milestones.	Iterative development means no "handoffs."
An expert produces the system quickly; a mentor communicates well.	Any expert programmer is a good mentor.
Smalltalk is large.	Smalltalk is small.
Object COBOL is OO, or else just COBOL.	Object COBOL is like COBOL.
C++ is much harder to learn than C.	C++ is like C.
Methodology is learning what to use, when, and how to communicate the result.	The project will succeed if we use XYZ methodology.
Every job involves design, and everyone is responsible for finding defects.	Requirements analysts only gather, designers only design what analysts tell them, and programmers only program what designers design.
Specialties develop; different tasks use different mind-sets.	The OO programmer should do everything: interview users, model the business, design, and program.

Expectations Under Control

Chapter 2, 11
- First, understand where your organization is in need.

Chapter 3, 44
- Objects change the project manager's life relatively little, while changing the developers' lives significantly.

Chapter 2, 25
- Requirements gathering, requirements analysis, system test, rollout, installation, and training times are roughly the same as for non-OO projects.

Chapter 2,25
- Programming time will be reduced only if you are using experienced OO programmers.

Chapter 2, 27
- Object development requires more, rather than less, communication.

Chapter 5, 129
- In normal life the boogeyman is apocryphal; on a software development project he is real—he is "What You Don't Know You Don't Know."

- Plan on 9 months for a novice to fully earn her or his salary. *Chapter 2, 30*
- Although most of the staff will enjoy the move to OO, some will not. *Chapter 2, 26*
- Whichever deliverables notation you choose, you must still decide who does what to produce it, who reads it, how people interact. *Chapter 4, 78*
- Late-breaking design issues will be found during programming and will change the model. *Chapter 5, 142*
- Your first project will show what you *really* need in the methodology. *Chapter 4, 82*
- Your time-to-market benefit will vary depending on the amount of internal and external similarity you can exploit. *Chapter 2, 24*

Selected Survival Recommendations

- Choose a technology that minimizes time-to-delivery, minimize the constraints on that choice. *Chapter 3, 51*
- Assume that knowing the current language and tool set does not reduce training time. *Chapter 3, 51*
- Plan and measure by delivery milestones. *Chapter 4, 102*
- Use your previous experience to avoid the most common traps. *Chapter 2, 32*
- Put a business specialist on the development team. *Chapter 3, 38*
- If it is not your specialty, buy it; until you can buy it, assume it can't be built. *Chapter 3, 67*
- Find someone who has worked on a project this big. *Chapter 7, 165*
- Run 2 weeks of language training, 1 week of training on OO design thinking, a half-day internal class on coding conventions, and internal training on the contribution of each role. Continuously add training as you encounter the need. *Chapter 3, 68*
- Have access to versioning and configuration management, team communication, and performance monitoring tools. *Chapter 3, 61*
- Exercise extreme sobriety when judging CASE tools. *Chapter 3, 62*
- Set standards for system design, language-based design, and coding. Encourage and enforce them. *Chapter 2, 13*
- Allow one person to have the time and task of finding and importing class libraries. To improve reuse, change people's attitude toward its economic feasibility. *Chapter 5, 150*
- Manage precision and accuracy to keep discussions on target and produce needed information. Dive briefly into high precision to evaluate a risk or get needed information. *Chapter 5, 112*
- Analyze just enough to build and ship the next increment. (Note: this, of all the recommendations, is tuned to surviving and delivering; a small project with expert staff may work differently). *Chapter 5, 142*
- Design and program properly from the start. *Chapter 4, 104*

Chapter 3, 69	◆ Provide developers with the time and encouragement to write truly object-oriented C++/COBOL/Ada.
Chapter 4, 89	◆ Assign an owner to each deliverable, including use cases and classes.
Appendix A, 214	◆ Let specialties flourish; let each team contain different specialties.
Chapter 3, 40	◆ Separate a training team from the progress team.
Appendix A, 224	◆ Make sure that someone always makes progress.
Chapter 7, 184	◆ "Seed" the organization: Migrate perhaps only 10 people at a time to expert level; use them to seed the next team.
Chapter 5, 127	◆ Rebuild the project schedule only after each increment is delivered.
Chapter 7, 165	◆ Change techniques, drop deliverables, drop function, improve staff skills, in preference to adding staff.
Chapter 5, 129	◆ Find the boogeyman as early as possible.
Chapter 5, 112	◆ Be willing to change anything to deliver.
Chapter 4, 99	◆ Show working results every 3 to 4 months.
Chapter 5, 132	◆ Pause and learn after each increment.
Chapter 3, 37	◆ Terminate the current project if its charter changes, then create a new project with a new charter.

Key Actions of Successful Projects

Chapter 2, 22	◆ Their upper management gave unwavering support, which provided constant encouragement and the freedom to maneuver during periods of low morale.
Chapter 2, 12	◆ They built the running domain model first, prior to any user interface.
Chapter 2, 13	◆ They selected and followed simple, conservative standards.
Chapter 2, 13	◆ They allowed for several revisions of key, risky, important areas.
Chapter 2, 20	◆ They started over, with a small team.
Chapter 2, 20	◆ The small team worked to create an architecture.
Chapter 2, 14	◆ They used variations on themes to take advantage of the internal similarities.
Chapter 2, 14	◆ They instituted an internal self-tutoring process.
Chapter 2, 17	◆ They hired good people and gave them good tools to help them get their work done.
Chapter 2, 22	◆ They got real users involved.
Appendix A, 214	◆ They arranged for total-ownership teams, responsible for everything from requirements to code, testing, and documentation.
Chapter 5, 111	◆ They established weekly self-teaching meetings.

Hazardous Phrases

In this section I present 31 indications of project hazards that have been mentioned in this book. The first 15 are sentences someone might say to you. The next 16 are things you might observe on your project. Give yourself or your group a risk point for each one you believe is a safe recommendation or that applies to your OO project. If you are not comfortable with your resulting score, reread those sections in the book that apply to the phrases to see how to lower project risk. Because I don't want you to mistake these phrases for the constructive advice in this book, I have put each line in parentheses.

- ("Object technology fixes your software process.")   *Chapter 2, 27*
- ("Object technology gives you reuse.")   *Chapter 5, 146*
- ("Never mind previous experience, OO is completely different.")   *Chapter 2, 31*
- ("Define the entire business model at one time.")   *Chapter 5, 141*
- ("Prototypes replace design.")   *Chapter 6, 157*
- ("Prototypes become production software.")   *Chapter 6, 157*
- ("Iterations control themselves.")   *Chapter 6, 157*
- ("An 'accurate' business model makes a 'good' software design.")   *Chapter 2, 30*
- ("Requirements, analysis, design, and implementation are easily separated.")   *Chapter 4, 83*
- ("We should use C++ because we already know C.")   *Chapter 3, 48*
- ("We have someone who knows part of C++ already.")   *Chapter 3, 49*
- ("We should use this CASE tool because we already have it in house.")   *Chapter 3, 48*
- ("Moving an entire company to object orientation is as simple as issuing a decree and selecting a compiler.")   *Chapter 2, 17*
- ("Use a technical architect only 2 to 3 days per week, or one who appears to be a really bright person but has poor communication skills.")   *Chapter 3, 74*
- ("A successful smaller project ensures a successful big project.")   *Chapter 5, 111*
- (Inventing productivity gains that object technology will bring, in an effort to gain executive sponsorship.)   *Chapter 3, 43*
- (Separate analysts, designers, programmers.)   *Chapter 4, 83*
- (Using new technology for a time-critical project.)   *Chapter 2, 19*
- (Contractors learning the technology on your project.)   *Chapter 3, 67*
- (A deliverables-heavy methodology.)   *Chapter 2, 18*
- (Changing project scope.)   *Chapter 2, 18*
- (Continually shifting user group.)   *Chapter 2, 19*
- (The experienced users do not find time to come to the meetings.)   *Chapter 2, 20*
- (Experts teaching and programming concurrently.)   *Appendix A, 232*

◆ (No, or shared, ownership of the classes' design.)

◆ (Mastery of language syntax, but not OO thinking.)

◆ (Trusting that the tools will somehow guide your people in their thinking; working through all the diagrams it supports, hoping that the software will pop out.)

◆ (Budgeting 1 week of language training for novice OO developers who are about to build a $2,000,000 system.)

◆ (Producing huge amounts of code per day using copy–paste techniques.)

◆ (Relying on indirect links to the users.)

◆ (Community alteration of classes—no ownership.)

Index

Abstract thinking, 46
Accuracy 58, 112, 114–117, 128, 239
   pitfalls related to, 127–128
Activities, in methodology, 80, 92–93
Advice, getting, 72
Aggressiveness of project, 42
Analysis model, 27, 142, 156, 195, 239
   interaction with design, 83–84, 107, 142, 195, 239
Analysts, 161, 241
Application generators, 175
Architect, 85, 89
   communication skills of, 74
Architecture
   framework as, 9
   importance of, 20, 106, 172–173, 189–190
   mainframe vs. workstation, 72
   teams, 89, 111, 129–130
   timing, 129, 131–133
Atalanta, 225
Auditing, code vs. model, 141, 142
Automatic code generation, 27, 30, 64–65

Beck, K., *Smalltalk Best Practices Patterns,* 53
Bellin, D., Simone, S., *CRC Card Book, The,* 94
Benefits of object technology, 23–27, 153
   automatic coded generation, as non-, 27, 30
   communications, improved, 2, 24, 94, 153
   encapsulation of design decisions, 2, 7, 23, 28, 153
   maintainability, 24, 28
   morale, 26, 153
   productivity, 25
   responsiveness to change, 9, 23, 153
   reuse, 25, 153
   software process, as non-, 27
   time-to-market, 24, 153
   window-based user interfaces, 26, 153

Big-house methodology, 81
"Big-M" methodology, 77–81, 187
Boehm, B., *Software Risk Management,* 209, 211
Bongo GUI toolkit, 63
Booch, G., *Object-Oriented Analysis and Design,* xvi, 118
Booch, G., *Object Solutions,* xvi
Booch methodology, 78
Boogeyman, 129–132, 191, 239, 240
Brooks, F., *Mythical Man-Month, The,* 97, 167, 177, 182, 219, 235
"Bubblegum" release, 132, 190
Burnt-pancakes, 114, 128
Business analyst–designer, 79, 87–88, 90, 193
Business design team, 79
Business expert, 38, 84, 142
Business model, 12
   vs. software design, 29–30, 241
Business process reengineering, 140

C programmers, need for, 175
C++
   benefits, 36
   design and coding standards, 55–58
   eyewitness account about, 58
   hazards, 29, 53–54, 237
   Java, vs., 62
   managing, 55–57
   portability, 51
   Smalltalk, vs., 55
   teaching, 49
   used in, 14, 16, 18, 109, 172
   when to consider using, 55
C@+, 29, 55
Cafe development environment, 63
Case studies
   Alfred, **12**, 39

Note: Italics indicate the names or risk-reduction strategies and book titles; boldface type denotes pages where case studies are described and strategies are defined.